An Introduction to British Arthurian Narrative

New Perspectives on Medieval Literature: Authors and Traditions

UNIVERSITY PRESS OF FLORIDA

Florida A&M University, Tallahassee
Florida Atlantic University, Boca Raton
Florida Gulf Coast University, Ft. Myers
Florida International University, Miami
Florida State University, Tallahassee
New College of Florida, Sarasota
University of Central Florida, Orlando
University of Florida, Gainesville
University of North Florida, Jacksonville
University of South Florida, Tampa
University of West Florida, Pensacola

An Introduction to
British Arthurian Narrative

Susan Aronstein

Foreword by R. Barton Palmer and Tison Pugh

University Press of Florida
Gainesville/Tallahassee/Tampa/Boca Raton
Pensacola/Orlando/Miami/Jacksonville/Ft. Myers/Sarasota

Library of Congress Cataloging-in-Publication Data
Aronstein, Susan Lynn.
An introduction to British Arthurian narrative / Susan Aronstein ; foreword by R.
Barton Palmer and Tison Pugh.
p. cm.
Includes bibliographical references and index.
ISBN 978-0-8130-4189-6 (cloth: alk. paper)
ISBN 978-0-8130-6032-3 (pbk.)
1. Arthurian romances—History and criticism. 2. English literature—Middle English,
1100–1500—History and criticism. 3. Great Britain—History—Henry II, 1154–1189. I.
Palmer, R. Barton, 1946- II. Pugh, Tison. III. Title.
PR328.A76 2012
820.9'351—dc23
2012009806

The University Press of Florida is the scholarly publishing agency for the State University
System of Florida, comprising Florida A&M University, Florida Atlantic University,
Florida Gulf Coast University, Florida International University, Florida State University,
New College of Florida, University of Central Florida, University of Florida, University
of North Florida, University of South Florida, and University of West Florida.

University Press of Florida
15 Northwest 15th Street
Gainesville, FL 32611-2079
http://www.upf.com

Contents

Foreword

As part of the University Press of Florida's New Perspectives on Medieval Literature: Authors and Traditions series, Susan Aronstein's *Introduction to Medieval British Arthurian Narrative* provides a strong introductory text for undergraduate students and general readers interested in the Arthurian tradition. Her analysis provides persuasive readings of individual Arthurian narratives, such as Geoffrey of Monmouth's *History of the Kings of Britain* and Malory's *Morte D'Arthur*, coupled with a judicious explanation of how these texts reflect their historical context. This combined approach of textual explication with sociohistorical exploration provides an intriguing perspective for readers new to the field, in line with our series emphasis on the Scholarship of Teaching and Learning, a critical discipline that emphasizes the mutual harmonies between research and teaching.

An internationally recognized scholar of medieval and Arthurian literature, Professor Aronstein is dedicated to exploring the ways in which Arthurian literature continues to intrigue modern readers, notably in her fascinating monograph *Hollywood Knights: Arthurian Cinema and the Politics of Nostalgia* and her forthcoming coedited collection of essays, *Disney's Middle Ages*. Beyond her credentials as a scholar, Professor Aronstein's career truly models the importance of teaching excellence to scholarship, as she has won, at last count, fourteen teaching awards at her home institution, the University of Wyoming.

The books of the New Perspectives in Medieval Literature: Authors and Traditions series will help readers grasp the continuing relevance and appeal of the masterpieces of medieval literature, a body of work that ages and yet never dies. Professor Aronstein's work ensures that this will continue to be so.

R. Barton Palmer
Tison Pugh
Series Editors

Preface

This book is an introduction to the medieval Arthurian narratives composed within what Arthurian tales often call "the whole island of Britain": now England, Wales, Cornwall, and Scotland. It covers more than four hundred years and discusses texts written in Latin, Welsh, French, Middle English, and Middle Scots. Some of these works claim to be histories, others are romances, still others parodies. It does not—indeed an introduction cannot—include every tale about King Arthur written in Britain during the medieval period. Instead I have chosen those tales that I think will most interest readers new to the Arthurian tradition. All of these tales stand on their own merits (even if those merits are not always recognized by the academy); many of them influenced the later Anglo-American Arthurian literature that gave rise to our popular conceptions of Arthur and his Round Table.

In addition to choosing from among the many available narratives, I have also focused my examination on selected key issues, since the scope of this study precludes a comprehensive analysis of each tale. This book concentrates on the medieval British Arthurian narratives in their historical context, examining the ways in which these tales functioned to legitimize (or question) regimes, shore up (or parody) class identities, and soothe (or stir up) cultural anxieties. As it does so, it does not argue that the Arthurian tales were explicitly written with these goals in mind. However, the very nature of the legend, with its chronicle of the rise and fall of a great king, its vision of a united and imperial Britain, and its portrayal of the brave men and beautiful women who lived and feasted in Camelot, lends itself to examining the issues of rulership, warfare, privilege, and power that were prevalent throughout the medieval period.

An Introduction to British Arthurian Narrative traces the ways in which

Arthurian tales participated in the cultural and political dialogues of medieval Britain, beginning with Arthur's first, brief appearances in ninth- and tenth-century chronicles and continuing through his early incarnation as a Welsh warrior-king in the eleventh-century tale *Culhwch and Olwen*. It then turns to his introduction to the Anglo-Norman conquerors in Geoffrey of Monmouth's twelfth-century chronicle *The History of the Kings of Britain*, his transformation into an English king in Wace's and Layamon's adaptations of Geoffrey, and his vexed role both in later Welsh romances and in Middle English and Middle Scots popular tales. It concludes with a brief examination of Caxton's edition of Sir Thomas Malory's *Morte Darthur*, finished in the month before Henry VII took the throne of England, ushering in the Tudor dynasty. Each discussion focuses on the legend in its historical context: Norman incursions into Wales and Scotland; the war between Stephen and Matilda for the English throne; the Hundred Years War; plague, famine, and economic crises, class conflict, the Wars of the Roses.

This volume provides readers with an avenue into the medieval British Arthurian tradition, giving them an overview of the historical context in which these texts were written, a survey of the major medieval Arthurian genres, and a brief discussion of individual chronicles and romances. It builds on the long history of Arthurian scholarship and contributes to this body of work by synthesizing varying accounts of Arthur's rule; also, in keeping with the mission of the New Perspectives on Medieval Literature: Authors and Traditions series to make the literary traditions of the Middle Ages easily accessible to students and general audiences, I focus on the texts themselves, rather than on academic discussions concerning them, and keep the critical apparatus to a minimum. However, it is my hope that readers of this book will use its bibliography to expand their knowledge of both Arthurian texts and the critical discussion of them. To encourage further reading and study of the Arthurian legends, I cite editions that may not be the standard scholarly ones, but that are all readily available and relatively inexpensive. Whenever possible, I have used the online texts of the TEAMS Middle English Texts site www.lib.rochester.edu/camelot/teams/tmsmenu. htm; these versions are both scholarly and easily accessible. In addition, the translations that I supply here strive for a balance between readability and strict accuracy. Following this preface you will find a chronology of texts and history. At the end of the book is a glossary of Arthurian names and places, medieval concepts, and key historical events, and a bibliography with reference information for the primary and secondary texts discussed in this volume as well as suggestions for further reading.

Arthurian narrative, from the earliest medieval texts through Starz television's *Camelot* (2011), provides us with fascinating stories, grand spectacles, and historical insight. It has also provided me with both a subject of study that I never tire of and a community of colleagues and friends. I would like to thank that community here: my conference companions, who helped me focus this discussion and offered their advice; my colleagues at the University of Wyoming, who read my drafts and kept me writing; my editors at University Press of Florida, Barton Palmer, Tison Pugh, and Amy Gorelick, who have all provided invaluable feedback; and Jason Kirkmeyer and Ann Marlowe who helped me prepare the manuscript for publication. I am also deeply indebted to my family, my husband, Kent, and my sons, Robin and Taran, who keep my world in balance.

Chronology

late 5th c.: Anglo-Saxon invasion of Britain.

516: Arthur's victory against the Saxons at Mount Badon (date in
   ***Cambrian Annals*).**

537: Arthur falls at the Battle of Camlann (date in *Cambrian Annals*).

6th c.: Gildas's *Concerning the Ruin of Britain*.

ca. 731: Bede's *Ecclesiastical History of the English People*.

829–30: Nennius's *History of the Britons*.

9th/10th c.: *Y Gododdin*.

mid-10th c.: *Cambrian Annals*.

978–1016: Aethelred of England battles Cnut's invasions.

1016: Aethelred's heir, Edmund, divides kingdom with Cnut; Edmund dies;
   Cnut claims England.

1042: Aethelred's son Edward the Confessor reclaims his father's kingdom.

1066: Edward dies without an heir; William of Normandy takes the throne
   (Norman Conquest).

1087: William divides his kingdoms between his two oldest sons, with
   Normandy going to Robert and England to William Rufus.

1093: William Rufus defeats and kills both Rhys ap Tewdwr of Wales and
   King Malcolm of Scotland.

1094–98: Series of Welsh revolts.

early 12th c.: *Culhwch and Olwen*.

1100: William Rufus dies; his brother Henry I takes the throne.

1106: Henry I invades Normandy, captures and imprisons Robert, and
   claims Normandy.

1135: Henry I dies, leaving only a daughter, Matilda, as heir to throne; civil
   war breaks out between Matilda and Henry's nephew Stephen of Blois.

1136–38: Geoffrey of Monmouth's *History of the Kings of Britain*.

1139: Matilda, backed by the forces of her husband Geoffrey Plantagenet,
   Count of Anjou, arrives in England.

mid-12th c.(?): Short version of *Peredur*.

1153: Treaty of Winchester; war ends with Stephen adopting Matilda's son Henry as his heir.

1154: Henry II takes control of Angevin Empire (England, Normandy, Anjou, and Aquitaine).

ca. 1155: Wace's *Roman de Brut*.

ca. 1160–90: Romances of Chrétien de Troyes; lais of Marie de France.

1173–74: Rebellion against Henry II.

1175: Henry II ceremonially reasserts control over Wales, Scotland, and Ireland.

1189: Death of Henry II; accession of Richard I.

1199: Richard's brother John ascends the throne.

late 12th/early 13th c.: Layamon's *Brut*.

ca. 1200–1282: Princes of Gwynedd, beginning with Llewelyn ap Iowerth, consolidate power in Wales and both conciliate and clash with English rulers.

early 13th c.(?): Long version of *Peredur*; *Gereint*; *Owein*; French *Quest of the Holy Grail*.

early 13th c.: French *Prose Lancelot* and verse continuations of Chrétien's *Perceval*.

1204: John loses Normandy.

1209–12: John's successful campaigns in Wales and Scotland.

1215: Magna Carta.

1216: John dies; Henry III takes the throne.

1230: Henry III unsuccessfully attempts to regain Angevin lands in France.

1259: Treaty of Paris; England loses all lands in France except Gascony, now a fief from the French king.

1264–65: Civil war between Henry III and rebel barons led by Simon de Montfort, ended when the future Edward I kills Montfort.

1266: Military campaign against Llewelyn ap Gruffydd in Wales.

1272: Edward I ascends the throne.

1277: More military campaigns in Wales; Gwynedd no longer independent of England.

1278: Edward demands homage from Alexander III of Scotland.

1282: Wales renews struggle against England.

1284: Statute of Wales annexes Wales to England.

1286: Edward establishes John Balliol on throne of Scotland as client subject to the English throne.

1295: John Balliol allies himself with France; Edward retaliates.

1299: Performance of a version of the Gawain and Ragnelle story at a Round Table for Edward I.

1301: Edward bestows the title Prince of Wales on his heir, the future Edward II.

1305: Death of William Wallace, leader of the Scottish independence movement.

1306: Robert Bruce proclaims himself king of Scotland.

1307: Death of Edward I; Edward II takes the throne.

1312: Civil war against Edward II.

1325: Edward II cedes Scotland to Bruce and exiles his queen, Isabella, to France.

1327: Isabella and Roger Mortimer invade England and depose Edward II.

1328: Mortimer brokers a treaty that confirms Bruce as king of an independent Scotland.

1330: Edward III seizes power from his mother and Mortimer.

1331: Military campaign to Ireland.

1335: Edward III advances into Scotland and forces King David II to flee to France.

1337: Beginning of the Hundred Years War between England and France.

1340: Agricultural crisis and famine in England.

1346–47: English victories at Crécy and Calais.

1348: Black Death arrives in England.

1349: Ordinance of Laborers.

ca. 1350: Boccaccio's *Decameron*.

1351–1430: Repeated legislation to regulate labor and retain serfs.

1356: English capture John II of France.

1360: Treaty of Brétigny: England gains French territories and a ransom, returns John II to France.

1363–1483: Series of sumptuary laws aimed at regulating consumption and preserving class distinctions.

1375: Charles V of France regains most of England's French territories.

mid-to-late 14th c.(?): *Ywain and Gawain*; *Lybeaus Desconus*; *Sir Perceval*.

1376: Death of Edward III's heir, Edward the Black Prince.

1377: Death of Edward III; ten-year-old Richard II ascends the throne.

1381: Peasants' Revolt.

1387: Civil war against Richard II.

late 14th c.: *Sir Gawain and the Green Knight*; Chaucer's *Canterbury Tales*; *The Avowyng of Arthur*; *Sir Launfal*.

1396: Twenty-eight-year treaty with France.

1399: Bolingbroke deposes Richard II and ascends the throne as Henry IV.

1402–6: Welsh uprising led by Owain Glendower.

1408–9: Henry IV regains his Welsh territories.

1413: Henry V ascends the throne.

1414: Lollard uprising.

1415: Southhampton Plot to assassinate Henry V.

1415–20: Henry V's successful campaigns in France, from victory at Agincourt to Treaty of Troyes, establishing him as heir to French throne.

1422: Death of Henry V; nine-month-old Henry VI ascends the throne.

1435–53: French under Charles VI push back, regaining all English territories in France except Calais.

second half of 15th c.: *The Jeaste of Sir Gawain.*

1453: First of Henry VI's attacks of insanity; birth of his heir.

1455: Battle of St. Albans, beginning Wars of the Roses.

1461: Edward IV claims the crown after defeating the Lancastrian forces.

1470: Rebellion against Edward IV.

1471: Restoration of Edward IV; death of Henry VI.

1471–83(?): Winchester Manuscript of Malory's Arthurian tales.

1483: Death of Edward IV; ascension of Richard III.

late 15th c.: *Lancelot of the Laik; The Adventures of Arthur; The Knightly Tale of Gologras and Gawain* **(printed 1508);** *Sir Corneus.*

1485: Battle of Bosworth Field; ascension of Henry VII, beginning Tudor dynasty.

1485: Caxton's edition of Malory's *Morte Darthur.*

Introduction

The Once and Future King

We all know—or think we know—the story of Arthur and his knights: the sword in the stone, Camelot, the Round Table, might for right, Guinevere and Lancelot, Mordred, the day of doom, the promise of a "once and future king." In most cases we are not sure how we know it. We just do. But take a look around you. Las Vegas's Excalibur Hotel, the Round Table Pizza chain, Bugs Bunny in *A Connecticut Rabbit in King Arthur's Court*, the *Camelot 3000* comic books, the King Arthur video game, the Broadway musical *Spamalot*—the Arthurian legend permeates modern culture. It sells us pizzas (Guinevere's Garden Delight) and adventures ("Build Camelot," the King Arthur game invites you. "Lead hundreds of brave warriors on the magnificent battlefields of Britannia!"), shapes the narrative framework for hundreds of fantasy and science-fiction books and films, and provides the inspiration for countless takes on the tale, both epic (*The Mists of Avalon*) and parodic (*Monty Python and the Holy Grail*).

The Arthurian story's persistent popularity is remarkable. From early medieval Welsh folk tales, through twelfth-century French romances and Victorian verse, to modern American films, this legend has crossed oceans and genres. It has done so because the tales of King Arthur and his knights were, and are, less about the past than about the present. C. S. Lewis, who wrote about the Middle Ages before he discovered Narnia, is reputed to have observed that "the age of chivalry is dead. It always was." Arthurian legend, however, allows its tellers, whatever period they live in, to return to the days of chivalry: a return that enables them to go "back to the future," as these narratives of a lost political and social ideal both critique today and argue for tomorrow.

Think about some of the best-known Hollywood versions of the story: Disney's *The Sword in the Stone* (1963), Lerner and Loewe's *Camelot* (1967), and John Boorman's *Excalibur* (1981). Each of these films uses the Arthurian tale to juxtapose a barbaric "mid-evil" past and a "modern" Arthurian order. A Disneyfied Merlin mutters about the "medieval muddle" of Sir Kay's England while preparing a boy with wit and imagination to institute a democratic "Tomorrowland"; a whimsical king discovers the slogan "might for right" and unites his divided realm, banishing the bad old days; the promised king remembers that "the king and the land are one," forging utopia from chaos. Even *Monty Python and the Holy Grail* (1974) presents a rather clueless Arthur desperately attempting to rise above the mud and muck of medieval Britain.

Yet, while chivalry may indeed be always-already dead, Arthur's story tells of chivalry's birth as well. The tale of the rise and fall of Camelot counters loss with promise to promote ideas about national identity, political authority, gender roles, spirituality, honor, war, and conquest. As it does so, the Arthurian legend participates in the larger discourse of medievalism: postmedieval re-creations of the past. It may seem odd to identify a tale that comes into its own in the twelfth century, the very period we most strongly identify with the Middle Ages, as an example of medievalism, but even the medieval texts present the tale of King Arthur as a story of the "good old days," a nostalgic re-narrating of the past. If the twenty-first-century teen playing an Arthurian video game fantasizes about returning to a time when men were men and monsters abounded, so, it has been argued, did Chrétien de Troyes's twelfth-century audience in France. A nostalgic return to a lost golden age, however, is a tricky thing, even when it presents itself as fantasy—and the Arthurian story is not always presented as such. In his groundbreaking essay on the persistence of "medievalism," the Italian novelist and critic Umberto Eco warns us that we know not the Middle Ages of "history" but an appropriated and re-created Middle Ages; thus it is imperative that we recognize exactly what ideas and values ride in with its knights in shining armor.

We must also be aware that no version of the medieval past or of the Arthurian narrative can entirely break free from all the versions that have come before it. Everyone comes to the Middle Ages with a concept of what they "were really like," even if those concepts are often in direct competition: a Monty Pythonesque scenario of dirt, violence, and superstition, or a Lerner and Loewe vision of a shimmering castle on a hill, or both. Any new "Middle Ages," say one about a rising middle class and bustling commerce, will be haunted by these previous conceptions. Some Arthurian tales, as we have seen, actually employ this dichotomy between the barbaric and the utopic, pre-Arthur and post-Arthur. However, these tales are haunted by their own generic past; each new version of the story finds itself in competition with all those that have preceded it. The musical *Camelot* may desperately try to present Arthur as a philosopher-king, but Malory's violent and bloody warrior lurks behind him; the 2004 film *King Arthur* gives us a warrior-Guinevere in a leather bikini but cannot erase the faithless and disruptive queen of hundreds of other tales. Contemporary tales of King Arthur carry within them a long history of other Arthurs and other Camelots. Given the prevalence of the narrative in our own culture—the number of people playing Arthurian-themed video games, the bookshelves full of Camelots and pseudo-Camelots, the marketers piling onto the Arthurian bandwagon—an awareness of the legend's past and how it functioned in that past, what dreams and desires it invoked and to what purpose, is a very useful thing.

Arthurian tales generally focus on four subject matters: Arthur's "history," chivalric adventures, the Arthur-Guinevere-Lancelot love triangle, and the Grail quest. These matters can be treated either separately or in any combination, with each exploring different desires and anxieties. Histories relate the consolidation of Arthur's chaotic kingdom, the rise of Camelot, and its ultimate demise; these tales focus on political concerns. As they present the rise and fall of the ideal kingdom, they inscribe their own vision of political utopia, the behavior and values necessary to achieve that utopia, and the misbehaviors that will ultimately doom a realm. Chivalric adventures follow a knight who seeks fame and fortune for both himself and his court; these narratives center around the aristocratic individual, asserting that such individuals are key to the ideal political order as they explore class identity and privilege and both illustrate and enforce proper gender roles. The Lancelot-Guinevere-Arthur love triangle examines the violation of gender roles, which upsets the balance between the political and the personal. Finally, the Grail quest introduces the spiritual into the political and, with it, questions about the religious subject, the competition between church and state, and visions of crusades and conquests. Taken together, these four narratives explore how individuals both contribute to the realization of a utopic dream of order and precipitate its fall into a chaotic nightmare.

The modern Anglo-American version of the Arthurian tale stems from Sir Thomas Malory's fifteenth-century compendium *Le Morte Darthur*. But Malory himself writes at the end of the tale's first period of widespread popularity, a period that begins in Britain with Geoffrey of Monmouth's Latin chronicle *The History of the Kings of Britain*, written somewhere between 1136 and 1138, and continues through more than three hundred years of chronicles based on Geoffrey and romances originating in French texts and Celtic traditions. This volume, which begins with the "historical" records and ends with Malory, introduces readers to British Arthurian texts in their historical and cultural context. As will become clear in the following chapters, the very definition of "British" in this period is both complex and contested. It can function as a geographical designation (of the island of Britain) or as an ethnic identification (of the Britons, generally referring to the pre-Roman inhabitants of the island). Furthermore, when the Anglo-Normans began to identify themselves as "English," they appropriated, as we shall see, the British past, blurring the distinction between English and British. The medieval British Arthurian texts discussed here reflect this history. Written in the various languages of medieval Britain, from Latin to Welsh, they are all "British" by virtue of being composed in Britain. However, as Arthur's transformation from a "leader of battles" in early histories to a powerful chieftain in Welsh tales and, finally, into England's legendary Once and Future King shows, they are also British in their subject matter: the ongoing contest for sovereignty over the island of Britain.

Desperately Seeking Arthur: Legend and History

In July 1998 a group of students from Glasgow University excavating at Tintagel in Cornwall—where, according to legend, Uther, magically disguised as the Duke of Cornwall, fathered Arthur on the duke's unsuspecting wife—unearthed a purportedly sixth-century stone inscribed PATER COLIAVIFICIT ARTOGNOV (Artognou, father of a descendant of Coll, has had this constructed). The conservation group English Heritage immediately jumped on it, explaining that Artognou would almost certainly have been pronounced "Arthnou" and opining that the stone added "a new dimension to the possibility of there having been a real Arthur on whom the mythical figure was based" (news.bbc.co.uk/2/hi/uk_news/146511. stm). This new piece of "evidence" is the most recent of many archaeological finds that purportedly support the theory of a "real king Arthur." In fact, such discoveries date back to 1190 or 1191, when the monks of Glastonbury Abbey announced they had exhumed the bodies of Arthur and Guinevere from a grave marked by a cross inscribed, according to Gerald of Wales's late-twelfth-century account, with the words "Here lies entombed King Arthur, with Guenevere his second wife, on the Isle of Avalon" (www.lib.rochester.edu/camelot/gerald.htm).

The Glastonbury Cross and the Arthnou Stone play into a popular and, to a lesser extent, academic desire for a real Arthur. While Arthur's literary career began, most critics agree, with Geoffrey of Monmouth's *History of the Kings of Britain*, many people also want to believe that, even if Geoffrey's claim to authentic sources is exaggerated, a historical Arthur stands behind his fictionalized king. If one conducts an Internet search on "King Arthur," several theories about this original king will arise. The most common derives from Geoffrey's narrative and is generally presented as simple fact; it identifies "Arthur" as a sixth-century general who led the native Britons in their battles to protect the island from the invading Saxons. This Arthur finds his origin in two medieval texts, *Historia Brittonum* (*History of the Britons*), written in A.D. 829–30 and traditionally attributed to Nennius, although this attribution is now mostly regarded as fictitious, and *Annales Cambriae* (*Cambrian Annals*, or *Annals of Wales*), compiled in the mid-tenth century. The *Historia* describes the Briton's heroic defense against the Saxons in twelve battles, culminating in the battle on Badon Hill: "in it nine hundred and sixty men fell in one day, from a single charge of Arthur's, and no one laid them low save he alone; and he was victorious in all his campaigns" (www.lib.rochester.edu/camelot/Badon/nennius.htm). The *Annales* also offers an account of Arthur's victory at Badon in the entry for 516 and adds, in the entry for 537, a record of the fall of Arthur and Medraut (Mordred) at the Battle of Camlann. Both the *Historia* and the *Annales*, however, are extremely suspect historical records. First of all, they date from at least three hundred years after the events they purportedly recount. Furthermore, the text closest to these events, Gildas's sixth-century *De Excidio Britanniae* (*Concerning the Ruin of Britain*), attributes the Britons' victory at Badon to Ambrosius Aurelianus rather than Arthur.

These problems do not deter those who, working from the premise that Geoffrey's narrative has some basis in history, hold to the Arthur-as-sixth-century-general theory. They insist that careful examination of the historical record, mostly limited in this period to archaeological evidence as opposed to written documents, will help historians to reconstruct Geoffrey's lost original; from the connection between Arthur and the battle with the Saxons presented in the early "historical" records, they turn to the excavations at Tintagel and Glastonbury, both associated with Arthur in Geoffrey, for further evidence. They argue that archaeological work at Tintagel, including the discovery of the Arthnou Stone mentioned above, confirms that the site was occupied in the late fifth and sixth century, and the presence of pottery imported from the Mediterranean indicates that the occupants were wealthy, as a leader's household would have been. Excavations at Glastonbury, they continue, suggest that Glastonbury Tor, which began as a center of pagan religion, housed a group of British monks by the time of the Saxon invasion and thus would have been an appropriate place to receive the wounded Arthur.

The fact that this archaeological evidence merely suggests that these sites housed aristocratic, religious, and military settlements during the sixth century hampers many scholars' Arthur-as-general argument. Thus, advocates for a historical Arthur seek to bolster their archaeological claims by turning to other types of evidence. For instance, they argue that the early Welsh *Y Gododdin*—an account of a late-sixth-century battle, responsibly dated to the ninth or tenth century, in which the poet observes that a warlord who slaughtered three hundred men, glutting "black ravens on the rampart of the stronghold," "was no Arthur"—clearly situates Arthur as a historical figure (Jackson, 112). They also point to a handful of actual Arthurs in sixth- and seventh-century records, although the fact that there is a mere handful would seem to undermine, rather than bolster, their claim. Finally, they look to topography and folk traditions, pointing to the natural formations associated with the legend, Arthur's Seat, Arthur's Cave, Mote of Mark, St. Govan's Head, that pepper the landscape of Britain in support of their assertion that the legends of Arthur mythologize a man situated in history and geography.

Arthurian scholar and enthusiast Geoffrey Ashe has built a career out of developing the idea that the mythological Arthur grew from a historical figure; his studies identify the "originals" of several literary locales, proposing, for instance, that South Cadbury Castle became Camelot and that the Round Table may derive from outdoor amphitheaters or a variety of raised, circular performance spaces. Ashe's concern with historical prototypes—not Camelot and the Round Table themselves, but the space that gave rise to the tales—extends to his speculations about the real Arthur. Rather than seeking a historical Arthur, he searches for the historical figure who inspired the mythological/literary character, finding him in a fifth-century British king, Riotamus, whose military campaigns on the Continent, Ashe argues, provided the early Arthurian chroniclers with their narrative materials. Others writers have taken Ashe's premise that the historical Arthur may not have been Geoffrey's sixth-century general at all and advanced an earlier candidate, one Lucius Artorius Castus, a second-century Roman general whose many military duties may have included a stint in Britain. Originally his candidacy was based on his name alone, but later writers have added a "Sarmatian theory," which argues that Castus led Scythian recruits from Sarmatia in Britain—and that the folklore of these recruits, including versions of the Grail and the Sword in the Stone, provides the basis for the later Arthurian stories. One of Hollywood's most recent Arthurian offerings, Jerry Bruckheimer's 2004 film *King Arthur*, which promoted itself by promising to reveal "the truth behind the myth," adopted Castus as Arthur and presented its audience with a group of Sarmatian prototypes for both his knights and the Round Table, although the film situated this story more traditionally in the fifth century and retained Arthur's role in the battle to repel the invading Saxons.

King Arthur's promotional claim to Arthurian "truth" would, its studio hoped, sell tickets. After all, a piece of the "real" Arthur has proved to be a profitable commodity. Both the modern and medieval archaeological finds discussed earlier had tourist dollars at stake (English Heritage relies on Tintagel's admission fee to fund its operation, and scholars have speculated that the Glastonbury monks' "find" followed suspiciously close on the heels of a fire that had destroyed the Old Church). "Arthuricity" sells—rooms and tours, meals and beers, posters and souvenirs. And Tintagel, Glastonbury, Mont-Saint-Michel, Brittany, the Forest of Brocéliande, and all the other places that a well-traveled mythological Arthur visited in the course of his fictional career still make a living out of our continuing desire for an Arthur who emerges from the mists of legend to become part of history.

The Battle for King Arthur: Legend and Literature

This desire for "Arthuricity," an attachment to historical origin, affects even those who technically "know better," as evidenced by a recent business meeting of an international society of Arthurian scholars who, if presented with the Arthnou Stone, the Glastonbury Cross, or the Sarmatian theory, would most certainly dismiss all three. Yet, when it came time to vote on the location for the next conference—France or Australia—many argued that Australia was out of the question. "King Arthur," they proclaimed, "was never in Australia": no Arthur, no Arthurian sites, no conference. On the one hand, this exchange made no sense. Certainly these scholars knew that King Arthur, a fictional character, was never anywhere. On the other, it revealed that a long-standing, apparently dormant, competition for "ownership" of the Arthurian legend has not entirely run its course; these scholars asserted France's superior claim to the conference based on the nation's "Arthuricity," its stake in the "real" tradition.

As they argued for their site's roots in Arthurian tradition, the France contingent, however unconsciously, perpetuated the scholarly equivalent of the quest for the original Arthur. While the writers and enthusiasts discussed above looked to history to find Arthurian origins, generations of literary scholars have looked to literature. Indeed, from the early twentieth century and into the 1960s, the question of origins permeated Arthurian scholarship. Where, these writers asked, did the story come from? If proponents of the historical Arthur, using Geoffrey and the chronicle tradition as their starting point, sought their evidence in the dating and interpretation of partial texts, archaeology and speculation, so did these literary critics, using the romance tradition. The result was a heated debate, with the participants divided into warring camps and, often, ignoring the actual texts as they argued about origins.

The debate began in the nineteenth century with the first scholarly editions of many of the major medieval Arthurian texts, particularly the works of the late-twelfth-century poet Chrétien de Troyes, whom many critics dub the Father of Arthurian Romance, and the Welsh narratives collected by Owen Jones, Iolo Williams, and William Owen Pugh (translated by Lady Charlotte Guest as *The Mabinogion* in 1838). The marked similarities among three of Chrétien's romances, *Erec and Enide*, *Yvain*, and *Perceval*, and three of the Welsh tales, *Gereint*, *Owein*, and *Peredur*, sparked the controversy, and the critics engaged in a battle over Arthur's literary origins. The battle lines formed around questions of dates, "literariness," transmission, and lost texts. While Chrétien's dates can be reliably narrowed to the last half of the twelfth century (1160–90), the Welsh texts are not so easily dated. Indeed, the actual manuscripts they appear in were compiled considerably later than the late twelfth century—proof, the French camp concluded, that the Welsh narratives adapt Chrétien's romances. Not so fast, argued the Welsh camp: The fact that the manuscript evidence for the three Welsh romances is post-Chrétien does not necessarily mean that the tales are. In fact, linguistic evidence—spelling, word endings, sentence structure—indicates that the surviving written texts derive from originals that predate Chrétien's romances. The Welsh camp asserted that Arthur's association, from Geoffrey onward, with not France but Britain, combined with pre-Chrétien mentions of Arthur in early Welsh texts such as *Y Gododdin*, increased the probability that such versions had indeed existed. All well and good, proponents of Arthur's literary French roots conceded, but these earlier Welsh Arthurs are not *the* Arthur, the famous leader of the Round Table and its legendary knights. *That* Arthur is clearly French, created by Chrétien as he translated an oral Celtic tradition into the French literary tradition. The later Welsh authors got it from him.

The question of "how" permeates both of these scenarios. The French camp did not argue that the figure of Arthur originated in France—Geoffrey stood in the way of that—but merely that the literary legend did. How, then, did Chrétien come by the oral traditions on which he based his tales? And how did those tales reach the Welsh authors who adapted them into their native language? They found the answer to these questions in hypothetical Breton storytellers, Celts who had, in the face of the Saxon invasion of the island, fled across the channel to settle in Brittany. The scenario for the Chrétien-first, Welsh-second version of the development of the Arthurian legends speculated that these storytellers provided Chrétien with his raw materials, which he recast into his French romances. Meanwhile, the original Celtic tales were somehow lost or forgotten in their native Wales, but were then reimported in their French form by bilingual bards in the train of Norman nobles. The Welsh camp responded that this explanation, which depended upon the argument that the Welsh had somehow managed to completely lose their own literary tradition, was ludicrous and that the theory that Chrétien merely translated and adapted Welsh/Celtic stories, which continued to thrive in Wales, was a much more reasonable explanation. Thus, these scholars argued, both Chrétien and the later Welsh writers/scribes must have been working from a lost common source, an original Welsh version of the romances that could, perhaps, be re-created by looking at the various surviving manuscripts.

As even this brief outline of decades of scholarly debate indicates, the battle over Arthur's literary origins required ingenious "archaeological" work; instead of digging into geographical sites, unearthing fragments of pottery and weapons, and re-creating cultures, these critics dug into manuscripts and linguistics, unearthed fragments of texts and history, and re-created tales. Their tools were philology, the examination of linguistic evidence, and source studies, the quest to identify where particular motifs and scenes originated. This prevailing approach to Arthurian literature, focused completely on history and origins and the texts themselves, became a starting point for looking backwards.

Why were Arthurian scholars so obsessed with origins? Many factors contributed to this pursuit. As literary studies developed out of philology in the late nineteenth century, they proceeded from the assumption that "older is better." Later texts were almost always seen as a corruption of an earlier, pure tale; the task of the scholar, then, was to re-create, as accurately as possible, that tale. The earlier a text or manuscript could be dated, the purer it was likely to be: a twelfth-century text was good, a ninth-century text better, and a sixth-century one even better. But what other assumptions fed into this romance of origins? Again, the roots of literary scholarship in the nineteenth century provide a possible answer. A growing sense of nationalism among European countries fed a search for a national literature, the older and purer the better. German, French, English, Welsh, and Scottish scholars, among others, embarked on a quest to claim their national traditions—to keep up with the Joneses in early epics and poems. Such antique traditions, in turn, asserted the nation's or language's claim to greatness, proving that the native languages could compete with the classical traditions of Greece and Rome. Much was at stake, and the claims to literary tradition and ownership became, in retrospect, somewhat silly. For instance, Kenneth Jackson, editing *Y Gododdin* (written in Welsh), subtitled it "The Earliest Scottish Poem," arguing that the action took place in the vicinity of Edinburgh. Needless to say, the Welsh were not amused. Another example is a series of Welsh poems known as *The Songs of Llywarch Hen*, a compendium of a father's laments for his fallen sons. This text was subjected to what might be termed "saga envy." The Irish tradition includes prose-verse sagas, but the Welsh tradition does not. Welsh scholars responded to this lack by identifying Llywarch's songs as the verse portion of such a saga, and even set about re-creating the lost prose.

This desire for origins becomes even more contentious when it concerns Arthur. The Matter of Britain, as medieval writers called the Arthurian materials, was one of the three recognized "matters" of medieval literature (the other two were the Matter of France, or tales of Charlemagne, and the Matter of Rome, or the story of Troy and its survivors). Stories about King Arthur and his knights were the hot literary commodity of the medieval period. Versions of them appeared not only in France and the British Isles but also in Germany, Italy, Spain, and the Netherlands. Ownership of this tradition, therefore, confers considerable cultural status, identifying one's national literary tradition as the source of, arguably, the most influential literature of the period. Furthermore, to claim Arthur and insert him and his legends into a national tradition authorizes political and cultural identities and imperial ambitions. Thus the quest for the "real" Arthur and the competition for Arthurian ownership have historically merged, as illustrated by the two examples with which the Welsh historian R. R. Davies begins his book *The First English Empire*. The first, a mid-thirteenth-century chronicle, *The Flowers of History*, places Arthur in a succession of historical English kings that traces the royal line from Arthur through Edward the Confessor to John. The second, a fifteenth-century stained glass window, also depicts Arthur as part of England's royal lineage, making no generic distinction between him and Henry V. As they do so, they bring all of Arthur's literary capital, his miraculous election, military might, imperial prowess, and utopian court, out of narrative and into history.

1

Arthurian History

The History of Arthur's Britain

Arthur's unlikely insertion into the genealogy of English kings demonstrates both the blurring of the line between history and legend in medieval Britain and the role Arthurian legend played in the political and cultural debates of the period. The island seldom enjoyed the political and social order that marks the high point of Arthur's rule; political unrest at home and military action abroad were much more common than prosperity and peace. In this context, the stories of Arthur's succession to the crown, his consolidation of his kingdom and restoration of political order, his spectacularly successful Continental military campaigns, and the tragic dissolution of this utopian historical moment provide a space for the exploration of issues of sovereignty, colonization, conquest, proper rule, the role of king and nobles, and the distribution of land and power. To the increasingly subjected Welsh, Arthur's court confirmed their glorious past and promised their return to power and independence. To the Norman/English rulers, Arthur's history provided what Patricia Ingham identifies as a "fantasy of insular union," legitimizing their claim to sovereignty over the island and their imperial ambitions.

Given this context, it is not surprising that many of the medieval British Arthurian texts come from periods when questions of succession, colonization (or independence), and conquest (or invasion) were most fraught. *Culhwch and Olwen,* the earliest of the Welsh Arthurian texts, dates from the period of Welsh revolts following William Rufus's invasion of Wales in 1093; the first Arthurian chronicle, Geoffrey of Monmouth's *History of the Kings of Britain,* was written in the years 1136–38 as civil war waged over the succession; Sir Thomas Malory composed his Arthurian tales during the Wars of the Roses, another bloody conflict over the crown. Since Arthurian legend so often addresses its historical moment, a survey of the historical conditions that gave rise to the medieval British Arthurian traditions will help us situate the narratives we will discuss. This chapter provides such a survey, one focused on the circumstances that made the legend particularly appealing to writers and their audiences: invasions from the Continent, the competition between Saxons, Welsh, Scots, and Normans for control of the island, civil war both for the crown and between the king and his disaffected nobles, and the imperial ambitions of England's kings.

Although the "island of Britain" presents historians and chroniclers with a clear geographical unit upon which to base their narratives, the truth of the matter is that the island itself has rarely been unified and was never less so than in the period that gave birth to both the putative historical Arthur and his literary legend. The first recorded invaders were the Romans, who, after some difficulty, subdued and theoretically assimilated the Britons before withdrawing their troops in the fifth century to defend Rome, leaving the Roman Britons to fend for themselves against the invading Saxons. This second invasion, which split the land between the Germanic invaders and the Britons, gave birth, as we saw in our discussion of the "real King Arthur," to a "historical" Arthur who led the Britons as they defended the island. These stories about Arthur's battles to ward off the invaders reflect the fact that the Saxons never successfully controlled "the whole island"; they shared it with the displaced Britons, who occupied the outer territories: Wales, Scotland, and Cornwall. In addition to this ethnic and geographic fragmentation, neither the invaders nor the "native" inhabitants were themselves a unified entity. Many of the years between the Anglo-Saxon invasions and the Norman Conquest saw both struggles for power between the Germanic kingdoms in Briton and threats of invasion from those abroad. In fact, the situation that led to William of Normandy's famous conquest in 1066 began two generations earlier, as Aethelred (978–1016) battled to stave off the Danish invasions led by Cnut, king of Denmark. In 1017 Aethelred's heir, Edmund, achieved peace by dividing the kingdom with Cnut; when Edmund died that same year, Cnut simply laid claim to both halves, only to be displaced by another of Aethelred's sons, who returned from exile in Normandy in 1042 to reclaim his father's kingdom and rule as Edward the Confessor.

Edward died without an heir in 1066, and the battle for the succession began immediately when Harold Godwin infamously had himself consecrated king on the day of Edward's death. He held no clear claim on the crown, although neither did William of Normandy. However, after his successful military invasion, William quickly established his right to the throne by re-creating the past, both through chronicles that recounted his designation as heir by Edward, followed by stories of Harold's homage to William, and through the version of events presented in the Doomsday Book, a land survey and census commissioned by William in 1086 with an eye to raising taxes. This description of the state of the kingdom essentially writes Harold out of history, presenting William's accession not as conquest but as orderly succession. In these accounts, William acts as the restorer of proper order. He returns the kingdom to the day of Edward's death, and the texts represent his reign as an unbroken continuation of the past.

The story of William and his chroniclers exemplifies the history of medieval Britain: crises of legitimacy led to warfare and then gave way to an appropriation of the past to shore up the victor's often shaky claims. This pattern, combined with insular fragmentation, challenges from Wales and Scotland, and the ruling dynasty's Continental ambitions, resulted in almost constant war and a continual redrawing of the political map. William sowed the seeds of the crises that would give rise to England's ongoing conflicts in France, which culminated in the fourteenth and fifteenth centuries in the Hundred Years War. Distinguishing between Normandy, which he claimed as his by inheritance, and England, which he claimed by acquisition, he divided the two kingdoms in 1087. Normandy went to his eldest son, Robert, on the basis of primogeniture, and England was deeded as chattel to his second surviving son, William Rufus, for whom William—from his deathbed—arranged a coronation. Conceding Normandy to Robert for the time being, William Rufus, and after him his brother Henry I, spent the next two decades consolidating their power over their own barons and extending that power into Wales and Scotland.

William Rufus's forays into Wales and Scotland bore fruit in 1093, a year that historians identify as virtually apocalyptic for both countries. Rhys ap Tewdwr, king of Deheubarth in South Wales, was killed in battle, as were Scotland's King Malcolm and his eldest son. This was the beginning of a systematic campaign of conquest and colonization, furthered by the building of castles and importation of settlers in Wales, and the attempt to establish Scotland as an English territory, held by a king (Malcolm's son Edgar) who owed homage to the English crown. While the Scots, at least temporarily, seemed to accept their client status, the Welsh resisted, setting the tone for their relations with the Anglo-Normans with a series of revolts between 1094 and 1098. These revolts, however, did not succeed in reversing William Rufus's gains in Wales, nor did matters change when Henry I claimed the throne three days after Rufus's death in 1100. We will return to this period of Welsh history in our discussion of two of the earliest Arthurian texts, *Culhwch and Olwen* and the short version of *Peredur*, both of which respond to the Norman incursions into Wales.

When he ascended the throne, Henry I, like his father before him, bolstered his claim to the crown through an appeal to the past, promising in his Coronation Charter to restore the kingdom's laws to those of Edward the Confessor. He also represented himself as the people's choice, arguing that he was crowned by barons of the land. As both designated and proclaimed heir, Henry sought to return the kingdom to the time of William the Conqueror—by acquiring Normandy from his older brother. In 1106 he invaded Normandy and captured Robert, imprisoning him for life. When Henry died in 1135, he exercised at least partial control over an extended version of his father's kingdom: England, Wales, Scotland, and Normandy. On his death, however, Anglo-Norman insular ambitions suffered a serious setback.

Although Henry had attempted to secure the succession for his daughter, Matilda, after his son and heir died in 1120, civil war ensued when Henry's nephew Stephen of Blois, not coincidentally the wealthiest baron in England, rushed home from Normandy and had himself anointed king. Matilda, calling on baronial fealty and backed by the military forces of her husband Geoffrey Plantagenet, Count of Anjou, pressed her claim with some success. She arrived in England in 1139 and, two years later, briefly held Stephen prisoner. However, Stephen's forces also had their successes, and from 1139 the nation suffered. The writer of the *Anglo-Saxon Chronicle* observed:

> I neither can, nor may I tell all the wounds and all the pains which they inflicted on wretched men in this land. . . . they plundered and burned all the towns; that well thou mightest go a whole day's journey and never shouldest thou find a man sitting in a town, nor the land tilled. Then was corn dear, and flesh, and cheese, and butter; for none was there in the land. Wretched men starved of hunger. . . . Never yet was there more wretchedness in the land; nor ever did heathen men worse than they did: for, after a time, they spared neither church nor churchyard, but took all the goods that were therein, and then burned the church and all together. . . . To till the ground was to plough the sea: the earth bare no corn, for the land was all laid waste by such deeds; and they said openly, that Christ slept, and his saints. (Entry for a.d. 1137, omacl.org/Anglo/part7.html)

During this period of devastation and despair, Geoffrey of Monmouth penned his *History of the Kings of Britain*. In this chronicle Geoffrey, as we shall see, uses the island's past, particularly the tale of the rise and fall of Arthur, to address a kingdom at war with itself.

The war finally ended in 1153 with the Treaty of Winchester, whereby Stephen agreed to disinherit his own son and adopt Matilda's son Henry as his heir. Miraculously, in 1154 Henry II acceded without incident to the throne and to control of the Angevin Empire: England, Normandy, Anjou, and Aquitaine. The years of civil war, however, had disrupted the kingdom and cast doubt upon the legitimate line of succession, a problem Henry II addressed in the same way as had his great-grandfather: he turned back the clock, striking Stephen from the legitimate line and putatively restoring the kingdom to its state on the date of Henry I's death, theoretically returning to their original owners all the lands that had been grabbed by various barons during the chaos.

After subduing a Continental rebellion in 1175, Henry II turned his attention to the Celtic borders. In the years of civil war, these lands had managed to break partially free from Anglo-Norman control as Stephen and Matilda directed their dynastic ambitions primarily toward securing England and northern France. On his triumphant return from France, Henry II summoned the leaders of Wales, Scotland, and Ireland to a series of ceremonial occasions in which he received public reaffirmation of their fealty, thus restoring the kingdom essentially to the days of Henry I. Henry II's assertion of English control over the island provides the backdrop for Wace's *Roman de Brut* (ca. 1155), an adaptation of Geoffrey's *History* that, as we shall see, figures Arthur's consolidated insular kingdom and Continental conquests as the precursors of Henry's own Angevin Empire.

In spite of Henry's issues with his wife and sons (dramatized in the play and film *The Lion in Winter*), the crown passed in a reasonably well-ordered manner to his son Richard the Lion-Hearted—perhaps best known for his capture on the way home from the Crusades, an event that provided the setting for the Robin Hood legends. The Angevin Empire that had been reconsolidated by Henry II, however, was fractured after Richard's brother John ascended the throne in 1199. Not only did John lose Normandy to the French king in 1204, but his reign was plagued by his continuing struggle with his barons, who despised him and sought to increase their own power at his expense. They argued that the kingdom was an abstract "commonwealth" rather than the personal property of the king; this established the idea of the "commune," the community of all free men, and asserted that even the king was subject to its judgment. Not surprisingly, John resisted the barons' attempts to curtail royal authority, but after years of civil unrest he was forced to acquiesce to their demands. In 1215 he signed the document we now know as the Magna Carta, which defined and guaranteed the rights of England's freemen. To sign, however, was one thing; to abide by it was another. John secured a papal annulment, arguing that his signature had been gained by coercion. His barons, unamused, solicited the aid of the king of France, and when John died in 1216, he was still fighting to quell the rebellion.

John's troubles with his barons, coupled with his loss of Normandy, have contributed to the popular readings of him as bad king, exemplified by his role as the evil usurper in the Robin Hood tales. Yet John's contemporaries did not necessarily identify him with his defeats; instead they wrote about his successes in Wales and Scotland. His military campaigns between 1209 and 1212 cemented English authority in the Celtic borders. These campaigns provide the context for the Welsh Arthurian romances, composed as Llewelyn ap Iowerth sought to forge a native identity capable of resisting John's attempts to conquer and colonize his people. Llewelyn's successes, however, were tenuous at best; in the end, as Brother Walter of Coventry wrote, "There is now no one in Ireland, Scotland and Wales who does not obey the command of the king of England" (qtd. in Davies 2000, 17). Thus, while John may have left his heir, Henry III, without Normandy and somewhat subject to baronial control, he also left him with the hope of achieving control over the island of Britain.

The first Arthurian chronicle written in English, Layamon's *Brut*, is commonly dated to the time of either Henry II or his sons. As a text that recasts Arthur as an English hero and places him—and, with him, Welsh hopes of a return to power—firmly in the grave, Layamon's narrative definitely endorses Henry's and John's reconsolidation of insular power. Furthermore, its author's clear sense of himself and his countrymen as *English* rather than Norman particularly plays to England's vexed relationship with its Continental territories, culminating in John's loss of Normandy, during this period.

After John's tumultuous tenure, the first years of the reign of his son Henry III were relatively uneventful. Only nine when he was crowned, Henry III waited until 1230 before unsuccessfully attempting to regain his Angevin lands in France. However, his minority was marked by baronial objection to the influence his Continental relatives waged at court. The struggle between Henry and his barons came to a head in 1258 when Henry, in debt to the pope and under threat of excommunication, attempted to impose taxes. This pushed the barons to reassert their authority and draft a document, the Provisions of Oxford, that transferred a significant amount of royal power to a newly created council of fifteen men. Not surprisingly, Henry resisted. His situation worsened in 1259 when England lost most of its French territories in the Treaty of Paris, retaining only Gascony, to be held as a fief from the French king. This loss increased the nobles' animosity toward both Henry and his French relatives, contributing to a growing sense of us (English) versus them (French). Civil war broke out in 1264, but royal power was restored in 1265 when Henry's heir, the future Edward I, defeated and killed Henry's brother-in-law Simon de Montfort, leader of the rebel barons.

This military victory provided a taste of what was to come. When Edward I inherited the throne in 1272, he immediately set about consolidating and expanding his power. While, until recently, most historians have regarded Edward I's agenda with approval, dubbing him Edward the Great and Edward the Conqueror, his contemporaries called him *le roy covetous*, the covetous king. Edward I coveted a great deal of land—Wales, Scotland, the lost French territories. With respect to Wales and Scotland, he was spectacularly successful. When Llewelyn ap Gruffydd, whom Henry III had recognized as "Prince of Wales" in 1267, refused to pay homage to Edward, the new king retaliated with a series of military campaigns that ultimately forced Llewelyn to sign the Treaty of Aberconwy, buying peace at the price of his and Gwynedd's independence. When Llewelyn and his brother Dafydd renewed their struggle against England's domination in 1282, Edward offered no quarter. Llewelyn died in battle, Dafydd was executed as a traitor, and in 1284 Edward I instituted the Statute of Wales, declaring "the whole land of Wales shall be entirely annexed and united to the crown of our kingdom . . . to be a dominion of our ownership . . . part and parcel of the body of our crown and kingdom" (qtd. in Saul, 109). Having subdued and claimed Wales, Edward launched a campaign to make sure it stayed that way. He appropriated sites associated with Welsh sovereignty, such as Llewelyn ap Gruffydd's hall, which became the site of Harlech Castle, and Caernarvon, the alleged resting place of Emperor Constantine's father, Magnus Maximus, where Edward built Caernarvon Castle, modeling it on the walls of Constantinople. In addition, he transferred to his seat at Westminster the royal regalia and relics of Wales, including, some speculate, King Arthur's crown. In 1301 he proclaimed his heir, Edward II—born at Caernarvon—the first English Prince of Wales, an act that linguistically and symbolically appropriated Welsh sovereignty.

Scotland fared little better. In 1278 Edward demanded homage from Alexander III and then mostly ignored the country while he concentrated on Wales, but when Alexander and his seven-year-old heir, Margaret, both died, Edward I seized the opportunity. In 1291 he ordered an archival search that would support his right to be the *dominus superior* (overlord) of Scotland, and in 1292, acting as Scotland's feudal lord, he supervised the selection of the next king, establishing John Balliol on the throne and requiring the new king to perform military service in England and to allow Scottish petitions to be heard in English courts. King John of Scotland, however, was not as complaisant as Edward had hoped, and in 1295 he allied himself with France. Edward responded swiftly, marching on Scotland, deposing John, and removing the Stone of Destiny, the traditional coronation seat of the Scottish kings, from Scone to Westminster. This was only the first of nine Scottish military expeditions over the next decade. The Scots, led by William Wallace, hero of Mel Gibson's *Braveheart*, and Andrew Moray, fought against England's rule. The English captured and killed Wallace in 1305, but in 1306 Robert Bruce proclaimed himself king. When Edward died in 1307, war over Scotland was ongoing. Still, Edward I had at least temporarily achieved dominion over the British Isles, and in the year of his death the *Annals of Connacht* observed: "Edward Mor [the Great], King of England, Wales and Scotland, Duke of Burgundy and lord of Ireland, rested in Christ. . . . The crown of the King of England, Wales, Ireland and Scotland was afterwards given to Edward son of Edward" (www.ucc.ie/celt/published/T100011/index.html).

Edward II proved a poor guardian of the crown. When his father died, he aborted the Scottish campaign, a decision that ultimately allowed Robert Bruce to secure more than twenty-three years of Scottish independence. Bruce captured and destroyed English castles in Scotland and then proceeded to raid in England, acquiring the Isle of Man in 1317 and pieces of northern England including Berwick in 1318; in 1325 Edward conceded Scotland to Bruce on the condition that Bruce leave England alone. Not only did Edward II fail to hold Scotland, in the end he also lost England. His insistence on backing the greedy sycophants who surrounded him at court finally boiled over into civil war in 1312. Edward won, but in his vicious triumph he continued to alienate both his barons and his queen, Isabella, whom he exiled to France in 1325. Isabella aligned herself romantically and politically with Roger Mortimer, and in 1327 the queen and her lover returned to England with a small army and deposed the unpopular king. This coup and Edward II's subsequent murder had very little effect on English-

Scottish relations. In 1328 Mortimer brokered a treaty, disdained by many English barons, that confirmed Bruce's position as king of an independent Scotland, in essence dividing the British Isles into two parts: Scotland with Man and the Western Isles, and England with Wales and Ireland.

When Edward III seized power in 1330, executing Mortimer and relegating his mother to a convent, he turned his attention not only to tightening his hold on the British Isles by regaining Scotland and Ireland but also to "his" lost lands on the Continent. He began his rule with a military expedition to Ireland in 1331, recaptured Berwick in 1333, and by 1335 had advanced far enough into Scotland to force King David II to flee to France. David's flight offered an excuse for a renewal of hostilities between France and England, beginning with a dispute over Gascony, which Philip VI refused to settle unless Scotland was also on the table. Philip confiscated Gascony, and Edward promptly responded by laying claim (through his mother) to the throne of France, providing a rallying point for Philip's discontented nobles and ushering in the Hundred Years War. While the first years of this war were expensive and ineffective in terms of Edward's ambitions in both France and Scotland, the English had the upper hand by 1346, when they captured David in battle and won a decisive victory at Crécy. In 1347 they took Calais. After a lull in hostilities during the Black Death—the bubonic plague that raged through Europe and then England between 1348 and 1350—the war continued, culminating in the 1356 capture of John II of France, which led to the Treaty of Brétigny in 1360. Edward III regained Gascony and added Calais, Ponthieu, and various northern holdings to his Continental properties. The French paid a ransom of half a million pounds in addition to the lands, and John II was returned to France.

The Treaty of Brétigny held for nine years, but when Charles V ascended the throne of France, he successfully challenged England's control of French territories. By 1375 he regained most of what Philip VI had lost. His victory marked the beginning of a decline in power for the English monarchy. Edward III's promising heir, the Black Prince, died in 1376, the same year that Edward's senility became increasingly worrisome. When Edward died in 1377, he was succeeded by his ten-year-old grandson, Richard II, who, along with the throne, inherited both the ongoing war with France and a raft of domestic problems—excessive taxation, rivalry at court, social and religious tensions. From the Peasants' Revolt in 1381, in which the leaders of a popular uprising succeeded in occupying London for three days, through the threat of French invasion in 1386 and a civil war in 1387 in which the royalists were defeated, the first decade of Richard II's reign was fraught with conflict. A truce with France in 1389 allowed Richard to begin recouping his financial and political losses, including exacting revenge on those who had curbed him following his 1387 defeat. He banished two of the leaders of the resistance, Henry Bolingbroke and Thomas Mowbray, and confiscated their inheritance. This, as anyone who has read Shakespeare's *Henry* plays knows, proved to be a fatal error: Bolingbroke, himself of royal blood, took advantage of Richard's absence on campaign in Ireland, returned with an army, and deposed Richard, who, like his great-grandfather Edward II, was subsequently murdered.

Bolingbroke's victory marked the beginning of a new Lancastrian dynasty. The transition was not an easy one. Domestically, the first years of the new king Henry IV's reign were marked by royal bankruptcy, hostile parliaments, and internal rebellions. On the margins of Edward I's empire, Scotland and Ireland had already slipped from English control, and Wales, under the leadership of Owen Glendower, mounted the first serious challenge to English control in more than a century. Between 1402 and 1406 Glendower, who was allied with France by 1405, fought under the Red Dragon standard as the Prince of Wales and undermined English sovereignty in Wales, capturing key castles at Harlech and Aberystwyth. His success, however, was short-lived; in a campaign waged between 1408 and 1409, Henry IV regained his lost territory. Glendower disappeared, never to be heard from again.

When Henry V succeeded his father in 1413, he inherited a still-unruly kingdom that faced an uprising led by a group of religious dissenters known as the Lollards in 1414 and an attempt to assassinate the king in the Southampton Plot of 1415. Partly as a ploy to unite his barons in a common cause, Henry V turned their eyes to France, where the combination of a civil war and Charles VI's chronic insanity provided an opportunity for Henry V to press his claim to the French throne; the Hundred Years War resumed. Beginning with his famous victory at Agincourt in 1415 and continuing through his conquest and colonization of Normandy to the Treaty of Troyes in 1420, Henry V waged a stunningly successful campaign. At the end of it, he was married to the French princess and, disinheriting Charles VI's son, was recognized as the heir to the French throne. Henry did not long enjoy his triumph; he died in 1422, leaving the kingdoms of England and France to the nine-month-old Henry VI.

Henry VI's reign was disastrous, both for England's Continental ambitions and for its domestic tranquility. At its beginning, England occupied Normandy, Maine, and Paris, but in 1429, pushing south toward Orleans, the English army confronted the armies of the displaced French heir Charles VII and Joan of Arc. After 1435 the re-allied French pushed the English steadily back. By 1453 they had regained all of the territory won by Henry V, leaving only Calais in English hands. The English left France in defeat, and the Hundred Years War ended.

Defeated in France, plagued by debt, and threatened by unrest among the nobility, Henry VI suffered the first of many attacks of insanity. Even the much-awaited birth of a son and heir could not avert the civil war that broke out two years later. The Wars of the Roses, the red rose of Lancaster (Henry VI) versus the white rose of York (the future Edward IV), eventually pitched the entire nation into chaos. Edward's father, emboldened by another bout of royal madness, claimed the throne in 1460. The resulting compromise left Henry VI as king but disinherited his young son in favor of York. Henry VI's French queen, Margaret, fought for her son's rights, and York himself was killed in battle two months later, but in 1461 his son Edward defeated the Lancastrian army and declared himself Edward IV. He routed Margaret in 1464 and captured her son in 1465. Edward IV failed, however, to reckon with Margaret's determination and his brother George's ambition. In 1470 the two allied and invaded from France, forcing Edward IV to deal with rebellion. The deaths the next year of the Lancastrians Henry VI and his heir helped to secure the throne. For the remainder of his reign, Edward IV successfully avoided further warfare and tended to his treasury. He died in 1483, solvent—the first English king since Edward II to achieve such a feat.

Edward IV also died without an adult heir; his sons were aged twelve and nine at the time. What happened next remains one of the mysteries of history: his brother Richard was crowned Richard III, and the young princes disappeared. Two years later, the Wars of the Roses recommenced with the claims of a new Lancastrian heir, Henry Tudor. Henry was descended from John of Gaunt and his third wife, Katherine Swinford, which cast some doubt on his legitimacy, since the children of that union had been born well before the marriage, and Richard II's affirmation of their legitimacy had specifically barred them from inheriting the throne. Strictly legitimate or not, Henry triumphed at Bosworth; Richard III fell on the field, and Henry took the throne as Henry VII.

Henry VII's ascension marks the end of a period of Continental conquest and civil conflict that stretched from the Hundred Years War (1337–1453) through the Wars of the Roses (1455–71) and concluded with the Battle of Bosworth Field (1485). These years, particularly rich ones for British Arthurian legend, produced a variety of tales about Arthur and his knights. Some, such as *The Adventures of Arthur, Lancelot of the Laik,* and the *Alliterative Morte Arthure,* addressed the issues raised by constant warfare both at home and on the Continent; some, including both the *Alliterative Morte Arthure* and the *Stanzaic Morte Arthur,* reflected the anxieties produced by the political and economic crises that followed the Black Death; some, like *The Wedding of Sir Gawain and Dame Ragnelle* and *Sir Gawain and the Carle of Carlisle,* grappled with changes in class identity and social structures. These tales culminated in Sir Thomas Malory's Arthurian compendium, written during the Wars of the Roses and published by William Caxton just before Henry VII's victory at Bosworth Field.

Malory's text caps a long medieval British Arthurian tradition, beginning with Geoffrey of Monmouth's *History of the Kings of Britain,* written during the civil war between Stephen and Matilda, continuing through a competition between the Welsh and the Norman invaders for possession of the island, as evidenced by Wace, Layamon, *Culhwch and Olwen,* and the Welsh Arthurian romances, and concluding with the both the Death of Arthur tales and the popular romances. In this tradition, Arthur and his knights functioned both therapeutically and politically. Tales of Arthur returned their audiences to a glorious past; they also used that past to advance class interests, shore up dynastic legitimacy, and justify imperial ambitions. It is not surprising that Henry VII turned to legend and named his firstborn son Arthur, thus figuring the coming of the Tudor dynasty as the promised return to England's golden past.

Writing Arthur into History: The English Chronicle Tradition

If we look back at the stretch of history from Aethelred to Henry VII presented in the previous section, we can extrapolate several recurring conflicts and anxieties that shaped the Arthurian materials as various chroniclers translated a mytho-heroic Welsh leader into a historical king. First, royal legitimacy and the peaceful transmission of power were by no means to be assumed during this period. Of the nineteen monarchal transitions we have examined, four were the result of invasion (Edward the Confessor, William the Conquerer, Henry IV, and Henry VII), one led to a civil war (Stephen and Matilda), two others were decided by civil war (Henry II and Edward IV), and two (Edward III and Henry IV) stemmed from the deposition of the anointed monarch. Second, war itself was an almost constant fact of life. The period is littered both with civil wars over the possession of crown and the extent of royal power and with military expeditions to gain territory, retain territory, or regain territory. Third, England struggled consistently to maintain control over the Celtic borders, Wales, Scotland, and Ireland, which struggled just as consistently to throw off that control. Fourth, England's Continental ambitions—rooted in William I's initial division of England and Normandy between his two sons—were never fully realized nor fully abandoned. Fifth, one of the most powerful tools employed by each new regime was the pen, sketching out a fictitious past that could justify the present.

In this historical context, the Arthur of the chronicles provides "historians" with a narrative that validates both Norman/English control over the "whole island of Britain" and its Continental ambitions at the same time that it addresses anxieties about orderly succession, royal power, and civil war. Beginning in the twelfth century, with Geoffrey of Monmouth's *History of the Kings of Britain*, and continuing well into the fifteenth century, the chronicle tradition evolved to address the concerns of the time, and Arthur transformed to meet the needs of individual writers, their audience, and their patrons. While a discussion of Britain's chronicles in their considerable breadth and complexity is beyond our scope, we shall look at three of them: Geoffrey's *History*, Wace's translation of that history a generation later into French verse, and Layamon's English alliterative verse adaptation, written around the beginning of the thirteenth century. These three tales provide a strong overview of the ways in which the history of Arthur became central to arguments about Britain's past and future.

Geoffrey of Monmouth was the first to remove Arthur from the mythic past and carefully place him in the historical record. As he did so, Geoffrey, in spite of his own association with Monmouth in southeast Wales, "hijacked"—to use R. R. Davies's term (2000, 48)—the Arthurian myth both to create an insular history and to support Norman ambitions. Critics generally agree that Geoffrey completed the *History* sometime between 1136 and 1138, right on the heels of Stephen's dethroning of Matilda in 1135, an act that, as we have seen, plunged the country into nearly two decades of civil war. Geoffrey's multiple dedications to key players in the conflict, including Robert of Gloucester (Matilda's half brother, who switched his support from Stephen to his sister in June 1138), Waleran, Earl of Worcester, one of Stephen's most important military leaders, and Stephen himself, clearly place the account to follow in a political context, reaching into the past to confront the present and shape the future. In each of these dedications, Geoffrey reminds his patrons of both their place in the line of British kings, whose origins he is about to chronicle, and their importance to the realm as its "pillars" and, in Stephen's case, its king. As leaders of the realm, Geoffrey implies, these men should be aware of its history, and he begins his joint dedication to Robert and Waleran by musing on an absence of information about "the kings who lived here before the Incarnation of Christ, or indeed about Arthur and all the others who followed on after the Incarnation" (51). Notice that, while Arthur is indeed given pride of place in Geoffrey's musings, Geoffrey's concern here is not only to present an Arthurian history but, more important, to construct a unified history of the island, one that ultimately supports both Henry I and his descendants and the continuation of a long and prosperous Norman rule.

Geoffrey's first concern in this history is to claim continuity—a direct line from the past to the present. He declares that, in spite of the apparent absence of a written account, the island's history has been "handed joyfully down in oral tradition, just as if [it] had been committed in writing"; furthermore, it actually had been committed to writing, and—thanks to one Walter, archdeacon of Oxford—Geoffrey himself has had access to "a certain very ancient book, written in the British language . . . attractively composed to form a consecutive and orderly narrative" (51). This book, Geoffrey asserts, he has translated into Latin, eschewing flowery rhetoric to present a fast-moving story that traces British history from the island's first king, Brutus, through Cadwallader, last of the British rulers. We will probably never know whether Geoffrey really worked from an ancient book rather than orally transmitted narrative traditions; it seems unlikely. However, by claiming that he is working from such a text, Geoffrey lends to his work an authority his medieval readers would respect, regardless of whether or not that authority can be verified.

Geoffrey begins his history—as did Gildas, Bede, and Nennius, authors of three of the most influential British histories before him—with a description of the island: its geographical features, climate, and natural resources. This description presents Britain as "the best of islands," emphasizing its plenitude: "It provides . . . everything that is suited to the use of human beings. It abounds in every kind of mineral. It has broad fields and hillsides . . . in which, because of the richness of the soil, all kinds of crops are grown. . . . Pasture lands . . . provide the various feeding-stuffs needed by cattle. . . . It is watered by lakes and rivers full of fish" (53). However, he immediately contrasts this initial plenitude with a recognition of the transience and degeneration that permeates his history. "In earlier times," he writes, "Britain was graced by twenty-eight cities. Some of these, in the depopulated areas, are now mouldering away, with their walls broken. Others remain whole and have in them the shrines of saints" (54). This odd juxtaposition of transformed and moldering cities represents the history of the island in microcosm—conquest and devastation. Geoffrey continues this theme in the final paragraph of his description, which cuts straight to the heart of the matter: "Lastly, Britain is inhabited by five races of people, the Norman-French, the Britons, the Saxons, the Picts and the Scots. Of these the Britons once occupied the land from sea to sea, before the others came. Then the vengeance of God overtook them because of their arrogance" (54). Here Geoffrey states his "thesis," positing an initial unity, disrupted by a series of invasions and, finally, lost by divine vengeance. By presenting the island as a coherent entity, from sea to sea, Geoffrey argues that, in spite of its five inhabiting races, ideally it should be ruled by one of them. Furthermore, as he introduces the notion that the Britons' loss of the island comes about as a result of divine retribution for their degeneracy and their penchant for civil war, Geoffrey both clears the way for the new regime and warns that regime about the possible consequences of its behavior. In this thesis, he provides his audience with an interpretive framework that invites us to be alert for the arrogant behaviors that will doom the Britons' sovereignty.

After divulging his history's conclusion, Geoffrey returns to origins. Beginning with the fall of Troy, he follows the journey of a group of survivors, led by one Brutus, as they seek a new land in which to establish a New Troy. As Geoffrey chronicles their adventures, he introduces many of the themes that will structure his history: divine mandate, conquest and colonization, the "civilizing" of the wilderness. Brutus, guided by Diana, leads the dispossessed Trojans to "an island in the sea, once occupied by giants. Now it is empty and ready for your folk" (65). There, she promises, Brutus will found a "second Troy" and produce "a race of kings . . . and the round circle of the whole earth will be subject to them" (65). Geoffrey presents the Trojans' establishment of this second Troy as a civilizing process: they drive out the giants, divide up the land, cultivate fields, and build houses. "In a short time," Geoffrey concludes, "you would have thought the land had always been inhabited" (72). By defining the island's native population as monstrous and the land as uninhabited, Geoffrey writes the pre-British inhabitants of the island out of history; furthermore, by identifying Britain with Brutus, Geoffrey also writes the original Celtic people out of their own history. Britain is not Celtic but Trojan; its timeline begins with Brutus, who names the land and the language after himself and divides up the kingdom, builds its capital city, and establishes laws. In this sequence, history and conquest are written on the very landscape: Britain (after Brutus), Cornwall (after Brutus's comrade Corineus), Gogmagog's Leap (the hill in Devon where Corineus slew one of the last of the giants), and Troia Nova (New Troy), which in later years will be named Kaer Lud, or Lud's City: London.

From Brutus's successful founding of Britain, Geoffrey segues into a series of pre-Roman kings, beginning with Brutus's three sons and the division of the island into Logres (central Britain), Cambria (Wales), and Albany (Scotland), which are named after these sons. As the history of the island unfolds, Geoffrey adds to his central themes. Civil war between brothers lusting for power, tyrannical and vicious kings, and unsuitable marriages to pagan women disrupt orderly succession and prosperous rule. Occasional forays into Gaul and Italy fill the coffers; unwise alliances invite invasion. In his account of the kings who ruled before the Roman Conquest, Geoffrey concentrates on the brothers Belinus and Brennius, a narrative that sets the stage for the Arthurian section of the chronicle. Their tale begins with the usual brotherly struggle for the crown and continues through a negotiated peace, broken by a foreign alliance in which the younger brother, Brennius, recruits the king of Norway to launch an invasion. Belinus not only repels the invasion but also consolidates his power, acquiring Denmark, ruling the "entire kingdom sea to sea," and establishing the laws that will later be translated from Welsh into Latin by Gildas and then into English by King Alfred. Meanwhile Brennius flees to France, gathers his forces, and invades England, interrupting the peace and prosperity Belinus has established. The brothers' mother manages to forestall civil war by convincing Brennius and Belinus to turn their attention to the conquest of Gaul. After annexing Gaul, the royal pair move on to add Italy and Germany to their budding empire.

This account delineates the conditions under which imperial ambitions are both necessary and possible. As the brothers' mother realized, Continental conquest was essential to the continued peace of Britain because Brennius needed territories to satisfy his own royal ambitions; without them, he would continue to battle his brother for the British crown. Yet in order to hold both Britain and the Continent, two royal figures are necessary. Belinus establishes Brennius on the Continent, where the text tells us "he treated the local people with unheard-of savagery" (99), and returns home, having rid his own kingdom of both civil war and the threat of a vicious king. Once back in Britain, Belinus rules over one of the *History*'s many golden ages. He "governed his homeland in peace, . . . restored existing cities wherever they had fallen into decay, . . . founded many new ones"—including Caer Leon at Usk, later associated with Arthur—"ratified his father's laws, . . . administered his own justice . . . [and produced] such an abundance of wealth as no previous era had ever witnessed and no subsequent era was ever to acquire" (99–100).

Geoffrey presents Belinus's reign as the acme of the pre-Roman era. The series of kings who follow him alternate between the good and the bad, and the realm veers from peaceful prosperity to civil war as cities are built and destroyed. The pre-Roman account ends with a long line of wise and good kings including Lud, "famous," Geoffrey tells us, "for his town-planning activities" (106). When Lud dies, his brother, Cassivelaunus, is "preferred" over Lud's two sons. The new king grants duchies to his nephews and rules "in authority over both of them and over the princes of the entire island, for he was the overlord by virtue of his crown" (106). Cassivelaunus's peaceful reign as overlord represents an ideal that runs throughout Geoffrey's text. He avoids disputes over the succession, and the resulting civil chaos and military devastation. This vision of an orderly transmission of power must have resonated, however wistfully, in the midst of the civil war over the succession devastating England as Geoffrey wrote.

This peaceful and orderly transmission of the crown to the person most suited to wear it, even if that person is not in the direct line of descent, ultimately protects Britain from Rome's imperial ambitions. Julius Caesar, fresh from conquering Gaul, spies the island in the distance and, assuming that the British are a backward people cut off from the modern world and advanced military technology, decides that "it will be a simple matter to force them to pay tribute and to swear perpetual obedience to the majesty of Rome" (107). The Britons, however, united under Cassivelaunus, defeat Caesar not once but twice. And the text implies that they would have remained free of Roman rule had it not been for an internal feud that led, ultimately, to the betrayal of the kingdom by one of its own. Geoffrey concludes: "How remarkable the British race was at that time! Twice it had put to flight the man who had subjected to his will the entire world. . . . They were ready to die for their fatherland and for their liberty" (117).

It is a glorious moment, but it marks the beginning of the end for the Britons, and in the years following the alliance with Rome, bad kings and troubled successions outnumber good rulers and the peaceful transmission of power. The Christianization of the kingdom under Coelius seems less important than his heirless death and the resulting battle between the Roman and British choices for king. The dust finally clears, five regime changes later, with Constantine, a good king who fosters peace, punishes thieves, and controls tyrants. Constantine's campaigns on the Continent, however, leave the island vulnerable to another regime change. One of the dukes he left behind, Octavius, usurps the throne, and civil conflict ensues. Although Octavius eventually triumphs, after his death he leaves only a daughter to inherit the throne, and yet another civil war breaks out over the matter of her marriage and, ultimately, the kingship. The victor, Maximianus, must deal with the royal nephew he defeated, and he comes up with the same solution that the mother of Belinus and Brennius hit upon: Continental conquest. Together they march into Gaul. This conquest, however, differs from the excursion of Belinus and Brennius. Maximianus strips his country of its soldiers, leaving it vulnerable to usurpation and invasion; chaos ensues, and Rome, tired of rescuing the country from its own folly, refuses to help. "What more can I say," Geoffrey laments. "Cities were abandoned. . . . For the inhabitants banishments, dispersions which were even more desperate than usual, pursuits by the enemy, and more and more bloody slaughters" (147).

This lament sets the stage for the last phase of Geoffrey's history: the house of Constantine and Arthur's reign, the Britons' final moment of glory. The dispirited and desperate Britons make an appeal to the king of Little Britain (Brittany), who dismisses the island as of little worth; however, he offers it to his brother Constantine. Constantine successfully drives off the barbarians, marries a noble bride, sires three sons, Constans, Ambrosius Aurelius, and Uther Pendragon, and settles down to rule. Unfortunately, the events that follow this promising start read like a catalogue of the things that, in Geoffrey's cautionary text, will doom a kingdom: betrayal, usurpation, unwise alliances, marriages to pagan women. Constantine's reign is cut short when he is treacherously murdered by a member of his own household, which provides another council member, Vortigern, with the opportunity to stage a coup. He sneaks off to the monastery where Constantine's oldest son, Constans, is now a monk and persuades Constans to accept the crown. In return for his rise to power, Constans hands the reins of government to Vortigern. As time passes, Vortigern decides to become king in name as well as in fact and incites a group of Picts, native tribesmen from the North, to murder Constans. Once he is king, Vortigern makes an alliance with two exiled Saxons, Hengist and Horsa, marries Hengist's beautiful (but pagan and treacherous) daughter, Renwein, and fills the country with Saxons. The British revolt and crown Vortigern's son, Vortimer, in his place. This coup is short-lived; Renwein poisons Vortimer, and Vortigern regains his throne. Hengist and Horsa, who have been at war with Vortimer, invite Vortigern and his men to a peace parlay and then treacherously murder the unarmed Britons.

Geoffrey's account of Constantine, Vortigern, Hengist, and Horsa pretty much follows the events presented in earlier chronicles such as Bede's *Ecclesiastical History of the English People*. After recounting the massacre at the peace parlay, however, Geoffrey begins to embellish the traditional narrative, introducing the Arthurian materials. Vortigern flees to Wales, where he attempts to build a tower fortress. His tower will not stand, and he summons magicians to explain the phenomenon. This is the first mention of magic in a text that, aside from a few giants and some prophecies, has been rather realistic by medieval standards. The magicians claim that, if it is to stand, the tower's mortar must be mixed with the blood of a boy without a father; such a boy is found: Merlin, the son of a king's daughter and an incubus. In this, his first appearance in the Arthurian narrative, Merlin disdainfully dismisses the magicians' interpretation of events and orders the men to drain a pool beneath the tower, where they discover two sleeping dragons. Realizing that "there was something supernatural about him" (169), Vortigern asks Merlin to reveal "his own end," and Merlin launches into the saga of the "fiery vengeance of the sons of Constantine," Ambrosius and Uther (186). The events proceed as Merlin prophesies: Vortigern is burnt in his own tower; both Ambrosius and Uther die, betrayed, by poison; and Uther's son—the promised one—inherits the throne.

This prelude to Arthur sets him apart—even as Geoffrey's dedication does—at the same time that he is presented in the context of the larger history of Britain. In many ways, the Arthurian portion of Geoffrey's chronicle forms the heart of the text: a microcosm of all the themes that have come before that both glorifies a lost British past and lays to rest any possibility of a British future. In the years since Brutus first landed on an "uninhabited" island, his descendants have constantly fought to protect its borders and repel rapacious pagan invaders; they have dealt with civil war and betrayal; they have rebuilt and destroyed; they have satisfied imperial ambitions and lost domestic territory. (In short, they have behaved much as the real historical kings we examined in the last section.) In this saga, Geoffrey clearly formulates the requirements for successful rule and national prosperity: the orderly transmission of power from one king to the next, united military might, proper disposition of power and land, cities and buildings, piety, generosity, loyalty, and judicious conquest. In complementary contrast, he outlines what must be avoided: wars over succession, civil or military discord, alliances with pagans, tyranny and concupiscence, lust for power, and Continental conquests based on raw desire. Arthur's story encapsulates the *History* by moving from reconsolidation and restoration to expansion and, later, to civil war and destruction. However, Arthur as king remains untainted, and Britain's slide into loss and chaos is caused by another's treachery.

Arthur's reign begins in crises. The treacherous Saxons, having poisoned Uther and much of his military, invite their countrymen from Germany to aid in the extermination of the Britons and "over-run all the section of the island which stretches from the River Humber to the sea named Caithness" (212). The archbishop Dubricius, lamenting "the sad state of his country," organizes a desperate coronation, and Geoffrey's readers receive their first glimpse of the island's great hope:

> Arthur was a young man only fifteen years old; but he was of out-standing courage and generosity, and his inborn goodness gave him such grace that he was loved by almost all the people. . . . In Arthur courage was closely linked with generosity, and he made up his mind to harry the Saxons, so that with their wealth he might reward the retainers who served his own household. The justness of his cause encouraged him, for he had a claim by rightful inheritance to the kingship of the whole island. (212)

This long description of Arthur sets him apart from the other kings in Geoffrey's chronicle. Although young, he epitomizes all virtues, and, when Dubricius bestows the crown of Britain on him, he heralds the possibility of a break with the past and a reestablishment of Britain's former glory, as promised by Merlin's repeated prophecies. Arthur begins his reign with a sustained campaign against the Saxons in which, by displaying personal courage, listening to judicious advice, making prudent alliances, and relying on the Britons' identity as a Christian people, he eventually prevails. Geoffrey expands on Nennius's and the *Annales Cambriae*'s accounts of Arthur's battle prowess: "He drew his sword Caliburn, called upon the name of the Blessed Virgin, and rushed forward . . . into the thickest ranks of the enemy. Every man whom he struck, calling upon God . . . , he killed in a single blow. He did not slacken his onslaught until he had dispatched four-hundred and seventy men with his sword Caliburn" (217). Arthur's inspired killing spree turns the tide of battle; the Saxons flee and the new king focuses his attention on the Scots, Picts, and Irish. He ends his successful insular campaign with several acts of rebuilding and restoration, reestablishing churches and religious communities and returning lands and honors to those who formerly held them. "Finally, when he had restored the whole country to its earlier dignity, he himself married a woman called Guinevere . . . descended from a noble Roman family" (221). This statement both connects Arthur to Britain's glorious past and looks to the future, as his marriage promises British heirs born to the island's rightful king and his noble Roman wife.

Not content with the whole island, however, "as soon as the next summer came round," Arthur sets out to expand his territories, conquering first Ireland and then Iceland, acts that encourage all of the other island kings to submit to him without a fight (221). Geoffrey then records another moment of rest in which Arthur establishes "the whole of his kingdom in a state of lasting peace and then remained there for the next twelve years" (222). Each of these two conclusions—the restoration of the island to its former dignities and the peaceful establishment of a "United Kingdom"—could serve as an ending to Arthur's successful reign; here, as the rhythm of the text has gone, he should secure the succession to the throne and the line of kings should move on. However, Arthur's cultural imperialism leads to territorial ambitions and gives us our first glimpse of what will become Camelot and the Knights of the Round Table, where "distinguished men from far-distant kingdoms" join Arthur's court and follow "a code of courtliness" that inspires "people living far away to imitate" it (222). The fact that all men both admire and fear Arthur encourages him "to conceive the idea of conquering the whole of Europe" (222).

While it might be tempting to look at Arthur's military campaigns in the next section of the *History* as evidence of a fatal addiction to power that eventually dooms the Britons, it is important to realize that Geoffrey does not altogether condemn conquest, which, after all, is necessary to increase economic and military resources. Imperial ambitions are a problem only when foreign campaigns leave the fatherland vulnerable to treachery and invasion, as Maximianus's Gaulish campaigns did. Arthur's invasion of Gaul, on the other hand, shores up Britain's security in several ways: it enhances his military reputation, adds men to his forces and gold to his coffers, and provides land that he can award to his followers, thus reducing the chance of civil unrest. After dividing up the territory, Arthur returns to Britain and announces a festival to celebrate his victories.

Geoffrey's description of this "plenary court" marks the beginning of the Arthurian festival that frames the narrative of the later Arthurian romances. In Geoffrey's version, the courtly games and amusements take second place to the acknowledged function of this court: Arthur's display of power, bolstered by gestures of submission from his vassals (similar to the festivals that Henry II will later hold to reaffirm his authority over the Celtic borders). At it, Arthur places "the crown of the kingdom on his head" and summons "the leaders who owed him homage" and "renew(s) . . . pacts of peace" (226). The regalia, the services, the games, and the feasting all serve to exhibit Arthur's economic, cultural, and military resources. Thus the Roman emperor Lucius's request for tribute and his insistence that Arthur is a criminal tyrant who has failed to pay homage to his rightful overlord is particularly ill-timed, as it challenges the very foundation of the feast. The council that follows Rome's outrageous demand reimagines the history of the island as the court mulls over Lucius's claim to sovereignty. Yes, Arthur admits, Rome did conquer "our fatherland by force," but that was only because "it was weakened by civil dissensions" and they "had been encouraged to come here by the disunity of our ancestors." Besides, he concludes—rather disingenuously, considering his own recent military career—"nothing that is acquired by force and violence can ever be held legally by anyone" (232). The king then proceeds to turn the tables, arguing that since his ancestors Belinus and Brennius, Constantine, and Maximianus had themselves conquered Rome and worn the imperial crown, Rome should pay *him* tribute. Furthermore, Rome has no right to complain about Arthur's own successful annexation of Gaul and the ocean islands; after all, "when we snatched those lands from their empire they made no effort to defend them" (233). Threats produce threats; force meets force. Arthur and his men vow to conquer Rome in defense of their liberty.

Arthur quickly gathers his troops, drawing a united European army from all the lands he has conquered, and sails to Gaul. Once he lands at Barfleur, however, Geoffrey delays the account of the British army's Continental exploits, focusing instead on Arthur's battles against two giants—a delay in the narrative that returns to a motif that has not been seen since Brutus's early days in Britain and introduces two episodes that will become standard features later on in the Arthurian tradition. This interruption strikes a mythic note in Geoffrey's "historical" materials, much as the dragons at the base of Vortigern's tower and Merlin's prophecies did. Like the giants in the first sections of the *History*, these monsters threaten the very foundation of the civilized realm that Geoffrey valorizes, and Arthur's defeat of them both proves his fitness to rule and "inspire[s] his men" (238). The first giant has imprisoned a noble maiden on top of Mont-Saint-Michel. All attempts to rescue her have been futile, and the would-be rescuers have been eaten "while they were still half-alive" (238). When Arthur climbs to the top of the mountain, the maiden's elderly nurse informs him that the girl died from fright before she could suffer a fate worse than death and that "in the madness of his bestial desire he raped me" (239). The narrative continues to emphasize the giant's bestiality—his atavism. When Arthur first spies the giant, he sees a face "smeared with the clotted blood of a number of pigs" (239); clearly, such a primitive figure, related to the giants who inhabited Britain before the arrival of Brutus and civilization, must be destroyed, and after a fierce battle Arthur triumphs. The narrative then segues to the second giant in a flashback that relates Arthur's battle against Retho, possessor of a "fur cloak [made] from the beards of the kings whom he had slain" (240). Desiring to add Arthur's beard to his infamous garment, Retho challenges Arthur to single combat. Arthur accepts, wins, and takes both Retho's beard and his cloak as trophies, providing material proof that he is stronger than both Retho and all of the kings whose beards Retho had skinned.

   While later versions of this story at least raise the possibility that Arthur's defeat of Retho and inheritance of the cloak somehow equate him with the rapacious giant, in Geoffrey this is not the case. The battles with both Retho and the Giant of Mont-Saint-Michel portray Arthur as a civilizing force: he is the one man who successfully stands against the monsters that ravage the land. These episodes allow Arthur to affirm his status as a "civilizing king" before he marches against the emperor, backed by all the forces of the civilized West. Lucius, on the other hand, has been able to muster only the Kings of the Orient, whom the text equates with the monstrous giants Arthur has just overcome. After various skirmishes and a decisive battle in which Lucius is killed, Arthur sends Lucius's body to the Senate with "the message that no other tribute could be expected from Britain," subdues the countryside, and makes ready to advance on Rome (257). News from Britain, however, puts an end to Arthur's imperial aspirations. His nephew Mordred has made an alliance with the Picts and the Scots, lured Guinevere into an adulterous relationship with him, and "placed the crown upon his own head," returning Britain to the bad old days of tyrant kings and treachery (257). Violent civil war ensues, the traitorous Mordred is killed, and Arthur, mortally wounded, is "carried off to the Isle of Avalon, so that his wounds might be attended to" (261).

   In the description of Arthur's final moments as king—in which he does not die, but hands his crown to his cousin Constantine and disappears to Avalon and from Geoffrey's history—Geoffrey performs a clever sleight-of-hand. The triumphant Arthur, the good, civilizing king who acquired an empire, ruled it wisely, and was on his way to reconquering Rome and becoming emperor of the Christian world, becomes "our renowned king," set apart from the degenerate Britons and claimed for the history of the Norman-English who will inherit the island. Once Arthur is safely sequestered on Avalon, the Britons march inexorably toward their doom, harassed by invaders and ruled either by tyrants or by good men unable to unite the kingdom and defend the borders. They ravage the land in civil war and swear allegiance to multiple kings. Finally, weakened by plague and famine, they flee to live, dispossessed, in the remote hills and forests of the island. British rule comes to an end. Geoffrey concludes his history: "Their own inveterate habit of civil discord had caused these proud people to degenerate so much that they were no longer able to keep their foes at bay. As the foreign element around them became more and more powerful, they were given the name of Welsh instead of Britons: this word deriving from "either their leader Gualo, or from their Queen Galaes, or else from their being so barbarous" (284). Thus the Welsh give up not only the island of Britain but also their status as "British," leaving both available to the island's subsequent rulers. Geoffrey's conclusion, written as "civil discord" raged, could not be more pointed, but in case his audience has missed the point, he also includes a diatribe addressed to his contemporaries, "you foolish people . . . never happy but when you are fighting one another" (264). The history of the Britons thus warns the Norman-French conquerors even as it justifies their conquest. Unless they mend their ways, Geoffrey implies, they also could lose the sovereignty of Britain, and the "best of islands" could pass into other hands.

Geoffrey's *History*—in spite of the relatively few pages he devotes to Arthur—both successfully hijacks the legendary king and gives birth to the Arthurian chronicle: narratives that focus on the history of Arthur's kingdom rather than on the exploits of individual knights. It introduces most of the major characters: Merlin, Guinevere, and Mordred. Although Geoffrey borrows some of these characters from Welsh tradition, he molds them to his narrative purposes. He ties Merlin to the Arthurian court, invents Uther's deceptive coupling with Ygerne, names Arthur's sword, provides Arthur with a history of glorious conquests, and shapes his end at Mordred's hands. The immense popularity of his *History of the Kings of Britain* is attested by both the number of surviving manuscripts—more than two hundred—and the fact that several later authors appropriated Geoffrey's materials, translating and reshaping them to suit their own visions of history and political ends.

The rest of this section briefly examines two early appropriations of Geoffrey that strongly influenced later British Arthurian narratives: Wace's *Roman de Brut*, written around 1155, and Layamon's late-twelfth- or early-thirteenth-century *Brut,* the first text to translate the Arthurian story into the English language. Although both Wace and Layamon present Geoffrey's entire history from Brutus to the triumph of the Saxons, we will focus here on their transformation of the Arthurian materials. Wace translated Geoffrey's Latin prose into French verse, dedicating his retelling of the *History* to Eleanor of Aquitaine, wife of Henry II, who assumed the throne upon Stephen's death in 1154. The *Brut* was clearly meant to advance, or at least appeal to, the interests of the Anglo-Norman monarchy, and indeed many of Wace's revisions edge the Arthurian materials toward the romance genre with its interest in courtly manners and matters of the heart, a genre that literary historians often associate with Eleanor's patronage. At the same time, Wace separates his text from romance and codes it, like Geoffrey's narrative, as history, and the history that he presents serves the larger interests of Henry II in its emphasis on Arthur's empire as a predecessor to both Henry's own Angevin Empire and any other imperial ambitions he might harbor.

The fact that Wace merely nods to the romance genre in his adaptation of Geoffrey's *History* becomes apparent as he introduces the fifteen-year-old Arthur. Wace does add courtly details to Geoffrey's description of a generous warrior-leader capable of the military success required to reward his men. He identifies the young king as "one of Love's lovers" and observes that Arthur "ordained the courtesies of courts and observed high state in a very splendid fashion" (43). Yet, in the midst of his description of this famous court, Wace breaks off and addresses the audience: "I know not if you have heard tell the marvellous gestes and errant deeds related so often of King Arthur. . . . The minstrel has sung his ballad, the storyteller told over his story so frequently, little by little he has decked and painted, till . . . the truth stands hid in the trappings of a tale . . . history goes masking as fable" (56). Thus history trumps romance, relegating the description of Arthur as one of "Love's lovers" to essentially a throwaway line.

Arthur's "high state," on the other hand, is central to Wace's "historical" narrative. Wace greatly expands Geoffrey's "court" episodes to emphasize not courtly manners and fashions characteristic of romance, although they do appear, but power: Arthur's ability to attract and co-opt military might. When Arthur returns, after annexing Ireland, Iceland, and the outer isles, to enjoy twelve years of peace, Wace repeats that he "ordained the courtesies of courts" and then adds: "Arthur never heard speak of a knight in praise, but he caused him to be numbered of his household . . . for help in time of need" (55). Wace makes it clear that Arthur uses his court not as a fashion statement but as a magnet to attract the best available muscle. The Round Table, which Wace introduces into the legend, comes about as a solution to the knights' bickering over who is top dog in the court. By designing a table without head or foot, and one that is large enough to seat all his men, Arthur brings together a disparate group of warriors in such a way that "none was alien at the breaking of Arthur's bread. At this table," Wace continues, "sat Britons, Frenchmen, Normans, Angevins, Flemings, Burgundians, and Loherins" (55). This description of Arthur's famous table not only prefigures Henry II's own Angevin Empire and his more-or-less successful annexation of the Celtic borders, but it also presents readers with a vision of a cultural conquest preceding Arthur's Continental military campaigns. His court is *the* place to be; all knights desire to sport "the garb and usage of those who served Arthur about his court" and "from all the lands there voyaged . . . such knights as were in quest either of gain or worship" (56).

The Round Table and its reputation set the stage for what Wace figures as inevitable military conquest: "Hear then how, because of his valour, the counsel of his barons, and in the strength of that mighty chivalry he had cherished and made splendid, Arthur purposed to cross the sea and conquer the land of France" (56). As in Geoffrey's telling, Arthur stops to acquire Norway and Denmark along the way and then moves on to France—a nation that lacks a legitimate king, Wace reminds us, injecting a narrative about French politics that would particularly appeal to Henry and his descendants. In fact, he tells readers, "the very French began to regard [Arthur] as their king" (59). In the end, the citizens of Paris fling open the gates, "desirous to offer him their fealty" (61). Arthur spends nine years establishing order in his new kingdom and then returns home for another celebration of his power and influence, a sequence that expands Geoffrey's account of the festivities leading up to Rome's demand for tribute while emphasizing Arthur's immense wealth and imperial reach. "Nor did Arthur bid Englishmen alone," Wace assures his audience, "but Frenchmen and Burgundian, Auvergnat and Gascon, Norman and Poitivin, Angevin and Fleming, together with him of Brabant, Hainault, and Lorraine. . . . Frisian and Teuton, Dane and Norwegian, Scot, Irish, and Icelander, him of Cathness and of Gothland, the lords of Galway and of the furthest islands of the Hebrides, Arthur summoned them all" (64). The subsequent festivities confirm Arthur's authority on the eve of Rome's challenge to that authority. When Arthur responds to the challenge, "Let him have the fief and the rent who is mightier in the field," observing that "the Romans should not wish to possess that which they may not maintain" (75), the outcome of the upcoming battle is a foregone conclusion: Arthur has the "might" both to conquer and to maintain.

However, the end of Arthur's narrative is also a foregone conclusion, and

Wace's history concludes, as does Geoffrey's, with Mordred's betrayal and Arthur's fall. While Geoffrey merely removes Arthur to Avalon and then proceeds with his history, Wace refers to the Britons' hope of his return: "they say and deem [Arthur] will return from whence he went and live again. Master Wace . . . cannot add more to this matter of his end than was spoken by Merlin the prophet. Merlin said of Arthur—if I read aright—that his end should be hidden in doubtfulness. . . . Men have ever doubted, and—as I am persuaded—will always doubt whether he liveth or is dead" (114). Note, however, that what Wace gives to the Britons—the hope of Arthur's return—he also takes away, not only emphasizing that men "will always doubt," but also ascribing this hope to Merlin's prophecies and, even then, only if Wace has managed to read them correctly, a task that he has earlier identified as impossible: "for I fear to translate Merlin's Prophecies, when I cannot be sure of the interpretation thereof" (19). Furthermore, Wace ends the Arthurian portion of his chronicle with Arthur's failure to return, declaring that Constantine held the realm "as bidden, but nevertheless Arthur came never again," and then describing the final displacement of the Britons (114).

If Wace undermines the Britons' hope of Arthur's return, Layamon, writing in English a generation later as Henry II and John were reestablishing the crown's control over Wales and Scotland, completely dismisses it. Additionally, his *Brut,* which he presents as a compendium of previous histories translated into English for the English, reflects a growing sense of Englishness occasioned, perhaps, by John's loss of Normandy in 1204 (if the *Brut* dates from the early thirteenth century). Layamon's "Englishing" of the Arthurian legend extends to his portrayal of Arthur. He strips him of Norman, courtly trappings and re-dresses him as a Saxon. The elfish gifts bestowed upon the infant Arthur—"might to be the best of all knights; . . . that he should be a rich king; . . . that he should live long; . . . that he was most generous of all men alive" (177–78)—mark him as an Anglo-Saxon warrior-king in the mold of Beowulf and Hrothgar. So too does Layamon's version of the chronicle's standard description of the young king, which emphasizes Arthur's personal might, the courage of his court, and his generosity:

> When Arthur was king . . . he was liberal to each man alive, knight with the best, wondrously keen! He was . . . with the unwise wonderfully stern; wrong was to him exceeding loathsome, and the right ever dear. Each of his cupbearers, and of his chamber-thanes, and his chamber-knights, bare gold in hand, to back and to bed, clad with

gold web. He had never had any cook, that he was not champion most good; never any knight's swain, that he was not bold thane! The king held all his folk together with great bliss; and with such things he overcame all kings, with fierce strength and with treasure. (184)

This Arthur is the ultimate warrior-king, one able to conquer land, bestow riches and maintain the peace.

As Layamon's introduction of Arthur suggests, his account of Arthur's reign focuses on military success that ensures a peaceful and prosperous kingdom. Arthur rules with a hand of iron, as the narrator notes: "Arthur was winsome where he had his will, and he was exceeding stern with his enemies" (207). The king also manages to keep order among his unruly followers—who more resemble Anglo-Saxon warriors than Continental knights, as exemplified by Layamon's tale of the genesis of the Round Table. What begins as a food fight, with loaves of bread and silver bowls of wine flying, degenerates into a bloodbath and ends with the wholesale execution of the male relations of the man who started it and the systematic mutilation of the female relatives. "So," Arthur concludes, "I will all destroy the race that he came of" (210). This massacre leads to the establishment of the Round Table, almost casually offered to Arthur by a handy carpenter so that the king need "never fear, to the world's end, that ever any moody knight at thy board may make fight, for there shall the high be even with the low" (211).

After this rather unpromising description of the birth of the Round Table, Layamon segues into an odd passage in which he puts Arthur and the Britons firmly in their historical place: "This was the same board that Britons boast of, and say many sorts of leasing [lies], respecting Arthur the king. So doth every man, that another can love; if he is to him too dear, then will he lie, and say of him more honour than he is worth . . . ; but this is the sooth respecting Arthur the king. Was never ere such king, so doughty through all things! . . . But Britons loved him greatly and oft of him lie" (211). Layamon then dismisses the Britons, their poets, and ultimately their prophecies:

And of this king's end will no Briton believe it, except it be the last death, at the great doom, when our Lord judgeth all folk. Else we cannot deem of Arthur's death; for he himself said to his good Britons . . . that he would fare into Avalon . . . to Argante the fair; for she would with balm heal his wounds; and when he were all whole, he would soon come to them. This believed the Britons, that he will thus come, and look ever when he shall come to his land, as he promised them. (212)

Another lie, Layamon implies, as he again turns from poetry (leasings) to truth (sooth): "Arthur was in the world wise king and powerful; good man and peaceful; his men him loved" (212).

At the end of his "historical" account of Arthur's reign—after the conquest of France, the aborted Roman campaign, and the final battle with Mordred—Layamon turns once again to the Britons' foolish hope: "The Britons believe yet that he is alive . . . and . . . ever yet expect when Arthur shall return" (264). Layamon first dismisses and then reassigns this hope: "But whilom was a sage hight Merlin; he said with words—his sayings were sooth—that an Arthur should yet come to help the English" (264). With this deft reassignment—by changing Arthur's return to the coming of "an Arthur," an English equivalent of the great British king who himself has been portrayed throughout *as* English—Layamon places Arthur (and, with him, British/Welsh hopes) firmly in the grave at the same time that he claims him for England and marks out England's glorious future. Geoffrey may have hijacked the Arthurian materials, but it was Layamon who relocated them from the British past to a glorious, *English*, future.

The Death of Arthur

In the early chronicles, the Arthurian materials serve to justify insular conquest and imperial ambitions: from Geoffrey's mid-twelfth-century *History of the Kings of Britain*, written as Stephen and Matilda battled over the kingdom's throne, through Wace's later French verse translation, dedicated to Eleanor of Aquitaine, whose husband Henry II reunited England and Normandy under one ruler and then continually fought to maintain his empire, to Layamon's turn-of-the-thirteenth-century unabashed celebration of the "English." Arthur himself figures both as an object of mourning, symbolic of the Britons' lost sovereignty, and a symbol of hope and renewal, the subject of a return to glory. As Britain's greatest king, conqueror of most of the known world, many factions competed to assign meaning to him: dead, he symbolizes the Britons' banishment from the mainstream of history; alive, he promises their return to history. Hijacked as "our king," he becomes the foundation of a Norman/English future. In these texts, then, Arthur's whole history matters: his rise to power, his consolidation of the kingdom, his many conquests. His life, not his death, serves as the focal point of the narrative.

This focus on Arthurian history, and indeed on the history of the island, was extremely popular with twelfth- and thirteenth-century audiences. In the fourteenth century, however, two poets altered the presentation of Arthur's life, starting not at the beginning, not even in medias res, but at the end, inaugurating what would become a very English genre: the Morte Arthur (death of Arthur). By the time these poets wrote their narratives, the competition between the native Britons and invading Normans over Arthur had been all but settled: with Arthur co-opted for the line of English kings, these poems simply present the assimilated Welsh as Arthurian subjects. Furthermore, the question of imperial ambitions had become much less theoretical: England, in the midst of the Hundred Years War, was all too aware of the bloody price of such ambitions. In this context the Morte Arthur is a melancholy genre suited to a melancholy time. Numerous crises troubled the aristocracy and citizenry of England throughout the fourteenth century: the Hundred Years War (begun in 1337), the death of the Black Prince (1376), the plague (1348–50), famine (1340), civil conflict (1312, 1387), the Peasants' Revolt (1381), the minority of Richard II, the deposition and murder of two kings, Edward II (1327) and Richard II (1400).

In keeping with the mood of this century, the *Alliterative Morte Arthure* and the *Stanzaic Morte Arthur* focus on the fall, not the rise, of the Round Table, which allows their authors both to examine "what went wrong" and to provide their audiences with a space for mourning. Of the two texts, the *Alliterative Morte Arthure* more closely follows the chronicle tradition. Written (scholars presume) from the Anglo-Welsh borderlands in the north, this narrative is a product of the Alliterative Revival, a literary movement that harked back to an Anglo-Saxon poetic style based on stressed alliterative lines rather than the more common octasyllabic rhyming lines adapted from French verse. In addition to its use of "native" verse forms, this movement's subject matter and theme also tended to be more "English," emphasizing military action, heroic deeds, and bloody struggles rather than the more courtly, chivalric, and amorous concerns of French and Italian models adopted by London and the court. As such, the *Alliterative Morte* is a determinedly *English* poem. Its Arthur is far removed from the somewhat rarefied king who presides over the courts of French romance but engages in little action himself; this poem's Arthur is more like Beowulf than a French king, and he fully engages in the narrative's bloody combats. This poem features conquest, not courts; battles, not manners; men, not women. Chivalry and courtly love vanish in favor of heroic boasts and brute strength. In its depiction of Arthur the Conqueror and his military enforcers, the poem takes on an almost strident "national" note. These lands belonged to Arthur's ancestors, they are Arthur's now, and if not, they should be. Concepts such as "right," "ownership," and "sovereignty" are connected to both past and future, to inheritance and might. At the same time, what the narrative gives with one hand, it takes away with the other: in the end, all are subject to the whims of Fortune. History is doomed to the war, devastation, and famine that accompany the rise and fall of kings. This celebration of military conquest, coupled with the poem's depiction of an ultimately arbitrary fate, would certainly have resonated powerfully in the late fourteenth-century.

As all good tragedies should, the narrative begins in the court of a powerful and wealthy hero. The narrator takes twenty-some lines to recap the material in the chronicles that leads up to the poem's opening feast with a review of the lands that Arthur had won "by conquest" (line 26), from his initial campaigns for insular unity in Scotland, Wales, Ireland, and the outer isles to his forays through the Scandinavian countries and into the Continent. Having set the stage, the narrator focuses on Arthur's Christmas festivities—emphasizing the king's power to command both men and resources. Throughout this opening description, the narrator refers to Arthur as "the Conqueror," an epithet that clearly marks him as the alpha king at a table full of kings. When the Roman senator enters with his demands—"I make thee summons in sale to sew for thy landes / That on Lamass Day . . . thou be redy at Rome with all thy Round Table" (91–93) [In this hall I summon you to plead for your lands. On Lammas Day . . . be in Rome, with all the men of your Round Table]—Arthur responds just as one might expect an alpha male to react to such a challenge to his authority: "with cruel lates / Looked as a lion and on his lip bites" (119–20) [with a cruel expression, looking like a lion, he gnaws his lip]. His raw wrath alarms the senator and his entourage, who grovel before the king and remind him that to shoot the messengers (so to speak) would impugn his own honor. Arthur agrees; instead, he treats them to the courtesy of the Round Table, summoning them to a rich feast.

From Geoffrey's description of Arthur's plenary court to cinematic versions of the Arthurian legend, feasts serve as a central motif in tales of the Round Table. Usually associated with the liturgical calendar, feasts mark the passing of the year, and Arthur uses them to consolidate and celebrate his sovereignty. In later traditions, the feast becomes the site of history and memory as returning knights recount their adventures to the court. Later still, all knights renew their vows annually at the Feast of Pentecost. The *Alliterative Morte*'s initial Christmas feast is a statement of sovereignty and a reinforcement of Arthur's authority over his summoned subjects. The feast he holds for the subdued Roman envoys deliberately demonstrates his power and resources. Turkish pastries, rich and rare spices, wines from Alsace, Venice, and Crete, all served to the Romans on plates of silver and gold by richly clad servants, demonstrate Arthur's imperial reach. The abundance of game and meat illustrates the richness of the island's own resources, and the cunningly designed wine taps and the brilliantly presented dishes mark Arthur's court as a place of high civilization. Arthur's self-deprecating apology to the Romans, "We know nought in this countree of curious metes" (223) [We know nothing in this country about fancy food], reinforces his regal position, a fact that is certainly not lost on the envoys, who scurry back to Rome and urge Lucius to guard his borders well.

The council that follows this feast outlines Arthur's claims to imperial rule. As he does in the chronicles of Geoffrey, Wace, and Layamon, Arthur turns to history to reverse the terms: "Rome, actually," he claims, "is mine." The *Alliterative Morte* then adds a series of speeches that augment Arthur's historical claim: the kings of Scotland and Wales, as well as the duke of Britanny, identify Rome as a marauding power, one that devastates the land and abuses the people. After these speeches, Arthur crosses the Channel and begins his Continental conquests armed with both historical precedent and moral right. He begins in his own land, France, which he says has been improperly and unlawfully invaded, and then moves inexorably through Italy and to the gates of Rome itself.

Arthur's first battle on the Continent, his famous encounter with the Giant of Mont-Saint-Michel, reemphasizes his moral right:

Here is a tyraunt beside that tormentes thy pople,
A grete giaunt of Gene, engendered of fendes;
He has freten of folk mo than five hundreth,
And als fele fauntekins of free-born childer.
This has been his sustenaunce all this seven winteres,
And yet is that sot not sad, so well him it likes!
In the countree of Constantine no kind has he leved
Withouten kidd casteles, enclosed with walles,
That he ne has clenly distroyed all the knave childer,
And them carried to the crag and clenly devoured. (842–51)

[Nearby is a tyrant who torments your people: a great giant from Genoa, born of fiends. He has wolfed down more than five hundred people, and as many baptized babies of freemen. This has been his food for seven winters. And this barbarian is not sorry; he likes it very well! In the country of Constantine he has left no family that does not have a strong, walled castle that he has not completely destroyed all of their sons, carrying them off to his crag and utterly devouring them.]

The *Alliterative Morte* explicitly codes this giant as a "tyrant," a usurping ruler who, instead of providing a feast for his people, feasts upon them, denuding the land of its proper heritage and future by killing all the male children and raping all the likely maidens. Interestingly enough, Arthur's first response to this news is not an outraged desire to kill the marauder but a pragmatic decision to work out a truce so that he can hold to his original plans. However, when he views the outrages—and the text spends several grisly lines describing the giant's cannibalistic fare, human haunches and limbs being turned on a spit above a fire, a tub "full crammed" of Christian children (1051)—Arthur's horror obliterates all thoughts of truce. He rages, "The Fend have thy soul! / Here is cury unclene" (1062–63) [The Devil take your soul! This is an unclean meal], charging into a fierce and hotly contested battle in which he destroys the giant, slicing through his genitals.

In this sequence, the narrator of the *Alliterative Morte* intensifies an already gruesome scenario, adding blood, guts, gore, and severed body parts. He also accentuates the giant's monstrosity in violating the borders between the human and the bestial, dwelling on his physical bulk, comparing him to a greyhound, frog, hawk, hound-fish, flounder, bear, dolphin, bull, boar, and pig, and emphasizing his grotesque deformities. In addition, the narrator carefully ties the giant to the Romans, making explicit the connections between giants and tyranny implied in the chronicles. First, rather than hailing from Spain, this giant, like many of Lucius's invading soldiers, comes from Genoa. Second, the *Alliterative Morte* collapses the chronicle's double-giant narrative, in which Arthur's battle with the monster of Mont-Saint-Michel reminds him of an earlier battle with Retho, the possessor of the curious cloak made up of the beards of conquered kings. In this version, Mont-Saint-Michel's giant himself possesses the cloak and, as the old woman who warns Arthur that resistance is futile reminds the king, insists that Arthur "polish his jaw" and add his own tribute to the giant's garment. Thus the giant, with his penchant for raping the land and his desire for Arthur to submit and pay tribute, becomes a figure for Rome, and Arthur's successful stand against him foreshadows the king's Continental conquests.

In case his audience missed it, the narrator makes this connection explicit in the aftermath of Arthur's victory. The people hail him as their king and liberator, "Welcome, our lege lord, to long has thou dwelled! / . . . / Thou has in thy realtee revenged thy pople! / Through help of thy hand thine enmies are stroyed, / . . . / Was never rewm out of array so redyly releved" (1200–1207) [Welcome, liege lord, you have been away too long! . . . In your royalty, you have avenged your people! With your hands, you have destroyed your enemies. . . . Never before has a disordered realm been so efficiently relieved]. Then, hard on the heels of the people's celebration of Arthur's return to rescue and restore their disordered kingdom, comes word of Lucius's vicious invasion of France—burning towns, slaughtering citizens, cutting down forests, and generally bringing death and destruction in his wake. The French people, like the people of Mont-Saint-Michel, clearly need the return of their true king to protect and comfort them.

Arthur sends Gawain to order the emperor to leave his lands or face the consequences, and the narrative turns to the heart of the *Alliterative Morte*, a detailed and bloody description of the battles leading to Rome's forced submission. This account features all of the chronicles' various skirmishes, sieges, and wars, but insistently describes the Romans as pagan and demonic. Lucius's army, in addition to giants and Saracens, contains witches and warlocks, and the poem alliteratively equates senators, Saracens, and sultans. Also, the booty yielded by the Roman camp includes camels, crocodiles, and pachyderms. Arthur's triumph over this army on the fields of France provides him with the demanded tribute, and he sends to Rome the bodies of the fallen commanders and the captive senators, newly shaven (a sign of shame, as we saw in the giant's cloak). Thus the text codes Arthur's victory over Lucius as the final answer to Rome's claim on Britain, recording the triumph of the rightful, just, and Christian king over the usurping, tyrannical, and pagan (or at least heretical) emperor.

However, in the *Alliterative Morte*, Arthur's triumph over Lucius—and eventually over Rome—does not account for all of his Continental pillaging. He first lays claim to Lorraine on the grounds that its duke is a rebel to the Round Table. He then marauds his way through Lombardy, declaring, "In yon likand land lord be I think" (3109) [In that desirable land I intend to be lord], and on to Tuscany and Spoleto before heading toward Viterbo. On this march through Italy, the behavior of the king and his knights is less than ideal: they knock down walls, torment the people, lay waste dwellings, destroy vineyards, and in general inspire fear in all who hear of their exploits. Settling down in a pleasant valley, Arthur and his men prepare a feast of roast venison and plenty of wine, and "riotes himselven, / This roy with his real men of the Round Table, / With mirthes and melody and manykin gamnes" (3172–74) [this king and his noble men of the Round Table throw a wild party, with entertainment and music and many kinds of games].

Since many critics read the *Alliterative Morte* as a tragedy, they identify this pillaging and merriment as evidence of Arthur's overreaching pride and acquisitiveness. They argue that this arrogant greed, coupled with his unwise choice of Mordred for regent, a choice that, in this text, even Mordred himself questions, leads to Arthur's death and the destruction of his kingdom. This reading, however, tries to fit the narrative into the mold of a Greek tragedy and, as it does so, ignores the tale's medieval context. While the text does dwell with realistic detail on the price to be paid both by the people and by the land during war—a price that England in the fourteenth century was well aware of—Arthur's pitiless rampage is also good military practice. (In fact, the Black Prince's scorched-earth strategy achieved the English victory at Crécy.) So is the show of strength set forth in his riotous feast. And this strategy works: a cardinal appears, trailing noble hostages, and offers Arthur the imperial crown, which the king graciously accepts, sealing the pact by seating the cardinal and his hostages at a rich table, once again using the feast as a display of power and sovereignty.

The true cause of the tragedy about to unfold is revealed when Arthur dreams that night. In his dream Arthur finds himself lost in a wood, flees from the wild beasts "lapping" the blood of his "lele [loyal] knightes" (3235), and enters a rich meadow to witness a strange sight: a richly clad woman spinning a large, bejeweled gold wheel, to the rim of which "cleved kinges on row, / With crowns of clere gold that cracked in sonder" (3268–69) [clung a row of kings, their bright gold crowns cracked in two]. Six kings have "full sodenlich [suddenly] fallen" (3270), and Arthur listens to each of their laments. The first king begins with an account of his glory and his damnation:

> That ever I regned on this roo me rewes it ever!
> Was never roy so rich that regned in erthe!
> When I rode in my rout rought I nought elles
> But rivaye and revel and raunson the pople!
> [. . .]
> And therefore derflich I am damned for ever! (3272–77)

> [I will forever regret that I ever reigned on this wheel. There was never a king who reigned on this earth as rich as I was. When I rode with my men, I cared about nothing but hunting and partying and collecting money from the people! . . . And therefore I am direly damned forever!]

While this initial lament may support a reading of the text that focuses on Arthur's tragic flaw as just punishment for an arrogant and careless king, the rest of his dream undermines this interpretation. Only this fallen king alludes to any sin on his part; the other five emphasize a sudden and arbitrary turn from bliss to woe, height to depth, fame to anonymity. The final king summarizes his plight: "I was deemed in my dayes . . . of deedes of armes / One of the doughtiest that dwelled in erthe; / But I was marred on molde in my most strenghes / With this maiden so mild that moves us all" (3320–23) [In my time, I was considered one of the strongest men alive in battle deeds. But I was brought down at the height of my strength by this mild maiden who rules us all]. This "mild maiden" spinning her wheel is a standard medieval allegorical figure: Lady Fortune, whose whim makes and breaks kings, lovers, and fools. Her erratically spinning wheel, which brings men (and it is almost always men) to its top—to the pinnacle of power, fame, wealth, romantic bliss—also brings them as suddenly down, flinging them to the earth in despair. The trope of Fortune and her wheel figures a world ruled by random chance and inexplicable change, expressing much the same sentiments as the modern sayings "That's the way the cookie crumbles" and "Life's a bitch and then you die."

Lady Fortune spies Arthur and greets him enthusiastically as her favorite child, assuring him, "Thou shall the chair escheve, I chese thee myselven, / Before all the cheftaines chosen in this erthe" (3347–48) [You shall achieve the top seat. I choose you above all other chosen chieftains on this earth]. She sets Arthur on high, tenderly combing his hair and offering him crown, orb, sword, fruit, and wine—power and plenitude. Yet at midday, at the height of his glory and ease, "all her mood changed, / . . . / 'King, thou carpes for nought, by Crist that me made! / For thou shall lose this laik and thy life after; / Thou has lived in delite and lordshippes ynow!'" (3382–87) [her mood completely changed. . . ."King, by Christ, you cry in vain, for you shall lose this pleasure and then your life. You have lived long enough in delight and power!"]. She whirls the wheel, flinging Arthur to the ground.

Understandably troubled by this vivid dream, the king calls upon his philosopher for an interpretation. The philosopher, like some critics of the poem, points to Arthur's "sin" as the ruthless slaughtering that the text has hitherto glorified and set forth as an example of justified, righteous conquest. In light of the rest of the narrative, this accusation seems like a throwaway line. The dream emphasizes Fortune's whim, not Arthur's sin. Furthermore, the philosopher's conclusion that Arthur should confess his sins and mend his ways carries little force compared to the subject of his unparalleled fame and his vision of the king's privileged historical future as one of the Nine Worthies—a kind of medieval Mount Rushmore of famous kings and leaders: Hector, Alexander, and Julius Caesar from antiquity, Judas Maccabeus, Joshua, and David from the Old Testament, and Arthur, Charlemagne, and Godfrey of Bouillon from the Christian era.

The philosopher has barely finished speaking when a knight steps forward to identify the wild beasts of Arthur's dream as Mordred, Guinevere, and the heathen allies Mordred has invited into Britain. The narrative moves to an account of Arthur's attempt to reclaim the island, concluding with a greatly altered version of the king's death. Instead of being carried off to Avalon for a magical healing of his wounds, Arthur is carried by his knights to Glastonbury—associated with Avalon, to be sure, but a real place in this world—and a surgeon is called to examine him. The *Alliterative Morte* does not shroud Arthur's death in mystery; it provides him with a deathbed speech and an elaborate funeral. In spite of a later reader's hopeful commentary, which concludes the manuscript with the tag "Hic jacet Arthurus, rex quondam rexque futures" [Here lies Arthur, king once and king to be], this poem truly is about the *death* of Arthur.

Since Arthur's "Englishness" and the elision between the British and the English has already been accomplished, the *Alliterative Morte Arthure* is not concerned with the competition for Arthur and his legacy at the heart of the early chronicle tradition. It presents a much darker vision. On the one hand, in the tradition of the Fall of Kings, a genre best known to modern readers through Chaucer's *Monk's Tale*, it tells of a world in which glory, success, wealth, plenitude, and life itself are fleeting. If even Arthur and his knights are subject to the whims of Fortune, so are we all. On the other hand, in the tradition of the Anglo-Saxon heroic epic, it celebrates those heroes who, for a moment, triumph over the forces of pagan and elemental chaos arrayed against them. Thus this tale, like Layamon's *Brut,* ends with Arthur firmly embedded in English literary tradition: an Anglo-Saxon hero who, like Beowulf before him, lived, died, and was buried and of whom it can be said, as the last line of *Beowulf* says of its hero, "that was a good king."

While the *Alliterative Morte* begins with Arthurian plenitude, chronicling Arthur's fall from the height of authority and power with a turn of Fortune's wheel even as it celebrates his military conquests, the *Stanzaic Morte Arthur* tells a very different tale. This version of Arthur's end draws on French, not Anglo-Saxon, models in both its form (octosyllabic verse) and its content. This Arthur is not a warrior but a courtly king, and he faces not an imperial army but the adultery of his queen and rivalry among his knights. In its turn from the battlefield to the court, this romance addresses a set of concerns equally pertinent to its historical moment, one that saw intrigue, corruption, betrayal, and repeated civil uprisings as well as the downfall of two kings, Edward II (who lost his crown at the hands of his wife Isabella of France and her lover Roger Mortimer) and Richard II. As it does so, it denies its audience the satisfactions of plenitude and power with which the *Alliterative Morte* opens. The *Stanzaic Morte* begins its narrative in a court already fallen from its height, desperately seeking to maintain its reputation and position. Instead of introducing Arthur and his knights with a list of their military triumphs, the narrator places his tale after the quest for the Holy Grail, which brought the court's "aunters ferly fele" (line 6) [many marvelous adventures] to an end. His poem begins with Guinevere's observation that Arthur's "honour beginnes to fall" (25) [reputation is fading] as the "court beginneth to spill / Of doughty knightes all bydene" (23–24) [court begins to empty completely of all the strong knights].

No description of plenitude, no great feasts and festivities, merely the king and queen in bed, wistfully discussing the good old days and sketching out a plan to revive them with a tournament that Arthur calls to regain his reputation and reaffirm his power. After a brief and rather dispirited description of the Round Table's knights' departure to this tournament, the tale turns to the circumstances that ultimately doom Arthur's efforts to return his court to its former glory: "Launcelot left with the queen, / And seke he lay that ilke tide; / For love that was them between, / He made enchesoun for to abide" (53–56) [At that time, Lancelot lay sick; because of their love for each other, he made an excuse to stay with the queen]. The adulterous lovers, and Gawain's brother Agravain's determination to expose them, which the narrator reveals in the next stanza, lie at the base of the Round Table, the rotten core that will bring the whole structure down.

This introduction of Lancelot and the famous love triangle confirms the *Stanzaic Morte*'s French roots. While Lancelot, in French versions of the legend, is *the* Arthurian hero, he is absent from the English chronicle tradition. The *Stanzaic Morte* places Lancelot center stage, and not just because of his affair with the queen. Lancelot, as the best knight of the Round Table, is absolutely crucial to its continued success; without him, the court has no hope of maintaining its position, and much of the plot of this romance revolves around the Round Table's quest for its absent champion. In the first sequence, Guinevere avoids Agravain's trap by sending Lancelot to the tournament where, disguised, he enters the lists and sides against Arthur's men, subjecting them to a bloody humiliation: unhorsing Ewain, knocking Bors to the ground, and hitting Lionel "through the helm into the crown" (286) [through his helmet and into his skull]. In dismay, Arthur's knights ponder who this disguised knight, as strong as the missing Lancelot, could possibly be. Although Ector, not himself unscathed, finally manages to wound the mysterious challenger, blinding him in his own blood, Lancelot carries the day, calling Arthurian supremacy into question. The king announces another tournament, a rematch as it were, but when Ewain reports that the knight who knocked them all to the ground lies in a nearby castle, too wounded to participate, he cancels it and, with it, the court's chance to reassert its position.

Lancelot's absence brings the entire court to a standstill. The Round Table empties as knights set off to search for the missing hero. Bors and Lionel swear not to return "til they wiste where Launcelot were" (435) [know where Lancelot is]. This dynamic, in which the narrative cannot continue until Lancelot is found, structures the first half of the romance; when Lionel and Bors bring the news that they have found Lancelot, king and queen and court all rejoice with "herte free" (528). But when Gawain arrives and reports, erroneously, that Lancelot has fallen in love with his host's daughter, Elaine, the fair maid of Astolat, the queen "wept as she were wode" (662) [wept as if she were mad] and takes to her bed "sore seke" (664) [desperately sick]. Thus Lancelot's homecoming, which Bors and Lionel hoped would heal the stricken court and make it "blithe," only precipitates his second absence. Guinevere, quite nobly, given her behavior in other versions of this tale, meekly asks Lancelot not to forsake arms for the sake of his new love, since hearing about his exploits would give her some small comfort. Lancelot mistakes Guinevere's request for a Dear John letter—"by these words thinketh me / Away ye wolde that I were" (768–69) [from these words I think you wish I were gone]—and flees the court. Arthurian chivalry again comes to a full stop. "The queen was in her bed all naked, / and sore seke in her chamber lay" (812–13); as for Arthur, "So muche mone the king gan make, / There was no knight that lust to play" (814–15) [The king began to complain so bitterly that no knight wanted to play]. At a loss, the knights again depart in search of Lancelot.

In the first segment of the narrative, Lancelot's absence led to the Arthurian court's humiliation at the tournament; in the next segment, it places Guinevere in danger and Arthur in an untenable position. An unnamed squire, seeking to slay Gawain, brings to the queen a tray of fruit with a poisoned apple. Guinevere gives it not to Gawain but to a "Scottish knight." The knight dies, and Guinevere is accused of the murder. The knight's brother, Sir Mador, demands that Guinevere be subjected to trial by combat, in which she must find a knight to fight and win for her or be burnt to death. Guinevere and Arthur need a champion, but no knight accepts the challenge, indicating that the king and queen have lost their moral authority. Over and over again, Arthur's knights refuse to defend Guinevere. Some merely assert that "again the right will I not ride" (1370) [against justice I will not fight]; others, less interested in abstract questions of right and wrong, refuse because of her role in Lancelot's loss. Bors blurts out, "Thou art well worthy to be brent! / The noblest body of flesh and blood, / That ever was yet in erthe lente, / For thy will and wicked mood, / Out of our company is went" (1351–55) [You deserve to be burnt! The noblest man ever born of flesh and blood on this earth is gone from us because of your desire and evil moods]. Lionel adds, "We are glad that thou it abye!" (1387) [We are glad that you will pay for it!]. The fated day arrives. "The king looked on all his knightes; / Was he never yet so wo; / Saw he never on him dight / Against Sir Mador for to go" (1520–23) [The king surveyed all his knights. He had never been so sorrowful, because he did not see even one prepared to fight Sir Mador].

Although Bors eventually appears armed and ready, only to be displaced by Lancelot, again in disguise, the king's lack of authority and the queen's lack of champions indicate how far the Round Table has fallen. No longer the mighty ruler of the world—or even the unquestioned champion of the tournament field—Arthur is left to hope desperately that one of his knights will condescend to defend his queen. Once again his authority and reputation are saved by Lancelot's timely arrival, and "hertes free" return with him. The true culprit is found and executed as "it was bothe law and right" (1665) [it was both legal and just], and for one short, glorious stanza, Arthurian order is restored. The next stanza, however, disrupts that order with the beginning of the events that hurtle Arthur and his Round Table helplessly toward the end of the Arthurian era. The narrative transitions from "Launcelot, that was so hende [courteous], / They honoured him with all their might" (1670–71) to Agravain, in council with his brothers, demanding, "How long shall we hele and laine / The tresoun of Launcelot du Lake?" (1678–79) [How long shall we conceal and hide the treason of Lancelot of the Lake?].

The discussion that follows underlines both Lancelot's position and Arthur's vulnerability. Gawain, as the voice of reason, does not deny the queen's affair with Lancelot; in fact, throughout the *Stanzaic Morte*, it is clear that this affair is an open secret, a medieval version of "don't ask, don't tell." Gawain cuts to the heart of the issue: Lancelot's strength, popularity, and military resources. "Yet," Gawain argues, "were it better to hele and laine / Than war and wrake thus to begin" (1694–95) [it would be better to conceal and hide it than to begin war and devastation], concluding, "he were full wode, / That such a thing beginne wolde" (1710–11) [the person who would begin such a thing is completely mad]. Gawain's assessment of the situation makes explicit the court's dependence upon Lancelot, a dependence that has driven the plot so far. Without Lancelot, or with Lancelot on the other side, Arthur's authority is mere pretense, as the events that follow Agravain's refusal to listen to his brother's wisdom prove.

Despite the attempt by Agravain and his faction to lay a trap for the queen and her lover, Lancelot manages to escape. But he kills many of Arthur's knights along the way, and he takes with him "a hundreth knightes and squiers mo" (1895)—an army of enemies to the court. When Guinevere is brought to the fire for treason and adultery, Lancelot and his men descend and bloody slaughter ensues, leaving Arthur without his queen and bereft of knights. "In erthe," the king cries, "was never man so wo; / Such knightes as there are slain, / In all this world there is no mo. / . . . / But wele-away, the rewful reyne, / That ever Launcelot was my fo!" (1975–81) [There was never a man on earth as woeful as I. There are no more knights in this world like these that are slain. . . . Alas this pitiful realm, that Lancelot ever was my foe!]. Arthur's lament recognizes both his irrecoverable loss and the kingdom's plight without Lancelot: Camelot is no longer a site of plenitude; it has become a pitiful realm. And things go from bad to worse as Gawain, incensed by the death of his two brothers during the queen's rescue, rejects Lancelot's offer to settle the matter with trial by combat, and a devastating war breaks out. Knights fall to the ground; horses wade in blood. "There was dole [grief] and weeping sore; / Among them was no childes play" (2244–45).

With England on the verge of ruin, the pope steps in. This is the first time in the English Arthurian tradition that divine authority and Arthur's secular authority have been presented as in conflict. In earlier versions of the legend, Arthur has always been an instrument of God, the promised ruler who restores the kingdom and rebuilds the churches. Here he endangers the land—"in Yngland was such sorrow strong" (2249)—both physically and spiritually. The pope threatens to place the entire kingdom under interdiction, denying the subjects access to sacraments such as baptism and marriage, unless Arthur reunites with Guinevere and makes peace with Lancelot. Arthur, again goaded by Gawain, refuses, choosing instead to let England "turn to sorrow" (2285), a decision that casts severe doubt upon his fitness to rule. In contrast, Lancelot obeys the pope, adding moral superiority to his already demonstrated military superiority. The queen returns to court, Lancelot and his knights leave the country, and the king, amid tears and lamentation, refuses yet another chance for peace and prepares to take the war to France.

While Arthur's departure for a Continental war, from Geoffrey's chronicle on, provides Mordred with the opportunity to seize crown and queen, the reason for this departure in the *Stanzaic Morte* differs drastically from the one found in the chronicles. Rather than marching out in strength to defend his kingdom against a false claim of sovereignty and to "justly" add lands to his empire, Arthur and his surviving knights pursue their former champion and companions on a desperate quest for vengeance, one that is almost certain to end badly given all evidence from both the opening tournament and the original battle. Instead of eagerly summoning his knights to glorious conquest, Arthur, "his herte . . . sore" (2501) bids his vassals "on Launcelot landes for to ride, / To bren and slee and make all bare" (2506-7) [to ride on Lancelot's lands and burn and slay and lay waste to everything].

Once Arthur and his army arrive in France, the text's juxtaposition of Lancelot's military strength, chivalry, and common sense with the court's weakness, shortsightedness, and recklessness continues. Arthur and his retinue, goaded by Gawain's implacable desire for revenge, continue to refuse all of Lancelot's truce offers, and the siege begins. After more than half a year, in which "Every day men might see there / Men wounded and some slain" (2764-65), Gawain succeeds in luring Lancelot out to fight. Two extended single-combat sequences ensue; in each, Lancelot severely wounds Gawain but refuses to slay him. After the second, Lancelot again urges Arthur to abandon his siege: "Wendeth home and leve your warring, / For here ye shall no worship win" (2932-33) [Go home and leave your warring, for you shall win no honor here]. This sentiment, against an endless and hopeless war in France, must have resonated in a nation continually engaged in an unsuccessful war with France.

Arthur and Gawain, however, refuse to heed Lancelot's advice. They give up their pointless quest for revenge only when they receive the news that Mordred has seduced the kingdom away from the king with lies and insinuations, using feasts, festivals, and gifts to convince the people that "with him was joy and wele, / And in Arthurs time but sorrow and wo" (2964-65) [with Mordred there was joy and well-being, and in Arthur's time nothing but sorrow and woe]. Finally Mordred issues a false report of Arthur's death; the people, observing that "Arthur loved nought but warring" (2975), willingly choose Mordred as their king. Note that in this version of the tale, Mordred requires no pagan allies; Arthur himself is so little regarded by his own people that they split the kingdom in a civil war in which the "stremes ran all on blood" (3081) [streams ran full of blood].

While other versions of this tale position Arthur's final battle at the height of his glory—he is, after all, nearly in possession of Rome—and attribute it solely to Mordred's treachery, brought on in the *Alliterative Morte* by the fickle and inexplicable turning of Fortune's wheel, the *Stanzaic Morte* presents Arthur's final doom as the result of a long process started by corruption, intrigue, and betrayal. Arthur, more in the French than the English tradition, is a weak king, dependent on knights over whom he clearly has little authority. His queen is both adulterous and childless; Lancelot, the best of his knights, spends much of his time in exile from the court. Thus, when Mordred takes advantage of the king's absence, it is not nearly as surprising as it is in the other texts, because readers have seen little of Arthur the Great King and Warrior. And when, for the sake of the kingdom, Arthur agrees to a treaty in which he promises Mordred the crown upon his own death, such an accommodation seems almost natural from the king who, in the earlier texts, defied Rome itself.

When fate, in the form of an adder that stings a knight and causes him to draw his sword, disrupts the treaty talks and plunges the kingdom once again into bloody war, the doom of Arthur's "rewful reyne" (1980) is sealed. After the dust clears, a hundred thousand men, including Mordred, are dead, and Arthur is grievously wounded. Commanding Bedivere to return Excalibur to the lake, he sets off to Avalon. This text, however, is not a "once and future king" narrative; it offers no hope of Arthur's eventual return. The tale next relates Bedivere's discovery of Arthur's tomb, tended by the archbishop of Canterbury. This discovery foreshadows the *Stanzaic Morte*'s final elegiac verses. In this narrative there is no continuation—no heir, no kingdom to put back together, no promised future—only three graves: Lancelot's, Guinevere's, and Arthur's.

This ending, like the elaborate funeral that concludes the *Alliterative Morte*, reflects the mood of a century battered by crisis. Arthurian optimism is a thing of the past, and both texts focus on a world spinning out of control; in the *Stanzaic Morte*, even the good old days weren't so good after all. The inexplicable whims of an ultimately malign Fortune, or an impotent king helpless in the face of the competing desires and jealousies of his own court, doom the kingdom to war and chaos. No longer part of a larger chronicle justifying Anglo-Norman insular claims, the tale of Arthur's death becomes an occasion to examine transience and loss—a site of mourning, a grave.

2

British Arthurian Romance

Arthur's Golden Age

The chronicle tradition actively seeks to place Arthur and his knights in the context of history. It concerns itself with the whole sweep of the Arthurian story, from Arthur's mystical begetting through his tragic end, and focuses on the Arthurian court's participation in "historical" events: battles and treaties, invasions and conquests. In this focus, any knight who stands out from the crowd does so by virtue of his military prowess, and the text loses interest in that knight when he leaves the battlefield. With the exception of Guinevere, whose position as queen implicates her in the narratives' concerns with conquest and sovereignty, women barely figure in these tales at all. The battles, the conquests, the betrayals, and ultimately the failure of a dream of peace, plenitude, and insular unity take center stage. The chronicles rush through the tale to its certain end, hardly pausing in the middle to relish the golden age of Arthurian plenitude.

The romances unfold in this middle, stopping the relentless forward thrust of the chronicle and suspending time. As they do so, they turn their focus from the group to the individual—from the troops marching off to war to the knight seeking his place in the world. The chronicle occupies the world of battle, whereas romance occurs in the world of the court. This switch from battle to banquet does not mean, however, that the romance leaves questions of power and politics behind—far from it. The romances simply explore those questions from the inside, asking: What threatens Arthurian plenitude? How do men and women need to behave in order to ensure its continuity? Or, more cynically: Is Arthurian plenitude all that it is reputed to be? In these tales, chivalric adventures serve as a test for Arthurian values—one that the court does not always pass.

From Welsh Chieftain to French King: The Origins of the British Arthurian Romance

Arthurian romance is rooted in the Celtic past, in tales of a mytho-heroic king. Some of the early Welsh tales seem to preserve at least fragments of this native tradition, suggesting that well before Geoffrey's account of his history, Arthur and his court were part of the Welsh literary landscape. In addition to Arthurian allusions such as those in the Welsh Triads and *Y Gododdin,* in which Arthur functions as the unsurpassable paragon, these early texts include two cryptic poems, *Pa Gwr yw y Porthaur* (*What Man Is the Porter?*) and *Preiddeu Annwn* (*The Spoils of Annuvin*), and the prose narrative *Culhwch and Olwen.* Taken together, these works help us piece together the Welsh Arthurian tradition that gave rise to the later romances. They set the tone for this tradition: not even the best of heroes and kings can ever hope to equal Arthur. The present can only look wistfully back to the Arthurian past, a moment in which "the best men in the world" quested for marvelous treasures and defeated monstrous men and beasts.

Most scholars agree that *Culhwch and Olwen* comes to us from the period of cultural consolidation and resurgence that followed William Rufus's particularly aggressive series of campaigns into Wales. The Arthurian court depicted in *Culhwch and Olwen* presents its recently conquered—and even more recently quasi-independent—audience with both a celebration of its glorious native past and a disquisition on the martial prowess necessary to carve out and protect a kingdom. The tale begins in a world ruled by marvels and violence, in which Culhwch's mother runs mad, gives birth to a son "of gentle lineage . . . first cousin to Arthur" in a pig-run, and then dies, after attempting to secure her son's inheritance by extracting a promise from her husband not to take another wife until he sees a two-headed briar on her grave, an eventuality that she tries to prevent by hiring a man to keep the grave clear (93). Unfortunately, after seven years this man forgets his graveside duties, and Culhwch's father prepares to seek another wife. On the advice of his counselors, he decides on the wife of King Doged. His decision, the text casually tells us, leads to an expedition against Doged in which Doged is slain, his wife abducted, and his lands possessed. This expedition sets the stage for the main narrative, as Culhwch's stepmother, foiled in her attempt to secure her daughter's future by marrying her to her new husband's heir, swears a "destiny" upon Culhwch: "thy side shall never strike against woman until thou win Olwen, daughter of Ysbaddaden Chief Giant" (96). Unfazed, Culhwch's father responds, "It is easy for thee to achieve that. . . . Arthur is thy first cousin. Go then to Arthur" (96).

While readers generally disregard this opening sequence in their haste to get to Arthur, it actually sets the tone and theme for the following narrative, depicting a world in which women and land are obtained by violence and where one's best chance of success lies in access to superior military might, such as that to be found at Arthur's court. And, indeed, this first literary depiction of Arthur's court emphasizes not only its vast economic and military resources but also its exclusivity. When a spectacularly clad and lavishly equipped Culhwch arrives at the gate, a porter guards it, denying entrance to anyone except "the son of a king of a rightful dominion, or a craftsman who brings his craft" (98). Instead he offers Culhwch sumptuous quarters with "men from afar" and "scions of other countries" (98). Unimpressed, Culhwch repeats his demand, threatening to bring dishonor on the court's men and sterility to its women. The porter carries the news of the comely petitioner to Arthur, who recognizes that his power depends upon such petitioners: "We," he asserts, "are noble men so long as we are resorted to" (99).

Culhwch's arrival and reception at Arthur's court emphasizes both Arthur's centrality, as a granter of petitions and dispenser of gifts to citizens and foreigners alike, and his dependence on being "resorted to" in order to maintain this position. Furthermore, both his reputation and his position depend upon the court's ability to fulfill its promises. Culhwch demands that Arthur "get me Olwen daughter of Ysbaddaden Chief Giant" (100). When, after a year's search, Arthur's messengers return without finding Olwen, Culhwch declares, "I will away and take thine honour with me" (107), which prompts Arthur to choose his most impressive knights to renew the search: the handsome Bedwyr, with his magical spear and his ability to hold off three warriors, even while fighting with one hand (108); Cynddylig the Guide; Gwrhyr, who speaks the tongues of men and animals; Gwalchmei, the best walker and rider, who never comes back without fulfilling his quest; and Menw, who has the ability to render Arthur's men invisible. This roll call showcases the court's talent and might, emphasizing the resources at Arthur's disposal.

The hand-picked crew journeys from the court into the barbaric wastelands of the island, finally encountering Ysbaddaden's shepherd, Custennin. Here they receive news of the giant, a barbaric master who has already slain twenty-three of Custennin's twenty-four sons. Culhwch sees Olwen and urges her to come away with him, and Olwen reveals the reason she is so closely guarded: her marriage is her father's death sentence. Nevertheless, the maiden counsels her suitor on how to achieve her hand: promise Ysbaddaden to provide everything he asks for in return for his daughter. "And," Olwen concludes, "me too shalt thou get" (111).

Culhwch's subsequent audiences with his future father-in-law emphasize the giant's barbarity. Three times he tries to slay Arthur's retinue with poisoned spears; three times they are hurled back. Finally, bereft of spears, the giant presents his catalogue of forty-one requests that are to serve as preparations, he claims, for the wedding feast. Beginning with uprooting a forest, plowing and sowing it, and producing meat and drink for the wedding guests in a single day, continuing through acquiring Ysbaddaden's grooming implements (the tusk of Ysgithyrwyn Chief Boar, the blood of the Black Witch, and the shears and comb that are oddly stored between the ears of another boar, Twrch Trwyth) and ending with gaining the sword of Wrnach the Giant, Ysbaddaden lays out a series of impossible tasks, triumphantly concluding, "Wakefulness without sleep at night wilt thou have in seeking these things. And thou wilt not get them, nor wilt thou get my daughter." To which Culhwch calmly replies, "My lord and kinsman Arthur will get me all those things. And I shall win thy daughter, and thou shalt lose thy life" (121).

The rest of the narrative proves Culhwch's boast, highlighting Arthur's court's ability to make good on its promises. This ability stems from a combination of cunning, violence, and mystical talent, including the ability to seek information from animals. This is not the civilized might-for-right court of later legend. Cei, posing as a polisher of swords, murders Wrnach in his own house and then proceeds to trap the sleeping Dillus the Bearded, knocking him unconscious, "twitch[ing] out his beard with the tweezers," and slaying him "outright" (128). Arthur and his retinue violently raid the fort that holds Mabon prisoner, freeing him so that he can be houndsman to Drudwyn, the only dog who can hunt Twrch Trwyth. They proceed to slaughter Ysgithyrwyn Chief Boar, rout the Irish forces, and appropriate the treasures of Ireland before engaging in an epic and far-flung battle with the boar Twrch Trwyth. They defeat Twrch, snatch the comb from between his ears to comb Ysbaddaden's hair for the wedding feast, and then slice the Black Witch down the middle "until she was as two tubs" to dress Ysbaddaden's beard. Finally the tasks have been achieved, and "every one that wished ill to Ysbaddaden" returns to the giant's court to kill him and claim the bride (136). The tale ends with Ysbaddaden's head on a stake, Custennin's twenty-fourth son in possession of the giant's dominions, Culhwch in bed with Olwen, and Arthur's successful retinue settled in their own realms across the island.

In its depiction of the Arthurian past, *Culhwch and Olwen* harks back to the good old days to reaffirm the values of the Welsh warrior nobility. Arthur and his court possess the military prowess and resources necessary to succeed in an economy based on pillage and plunder, and they have the ability to protect their property from others, including giants, magical beasts, neighboring princes—or marauding Normans. Arthur's rich and lavish court provokes both admiration, inspiring others to petition it for assistance, and a healthy fear, discouraging others from attacking it. This depiction, probably the closest we have to a "native" Arthur, establishes the narrative shape, standard episodes, and major themes used by later writers. It presents Arthur's court as a place men "resort to" either to ask a boon or to pose a challenge. (Culhwch actually does both.) The story depicts an untamed wilderness of giants, beasts, and mysterious lords who must be either destroyed or annexed to the Arthurian order beyond that court, and identifies women as both the means by which young men receive identity and possessions and the marker of male prowess.

Chrétien de Troyes appropriated this King Arthur for the French/Norman aristocracy just as surely as Geoffrey of Monmouth hijacked Arthur's life story for English history. As he did so, Chrétien transformed Arthur and his men from a Welsh chieftain and his military band into a Norman king and his aristocratic knights, recasting them in the image of the colonizer. Since Chrétien is the putative "father of Arthurian romance" and his work clearly influenced the Welsh, English, and Scottish Arthurian narratives, a quick overview of these early romances provides a context for the later British texts.

Chrétien wrote in the late twelfth century for an aristocratic audience seeking to reassert their privileged place in the face of both a rising nonnoble class and the king's centralization of power, a move that stripped them of much of their customary influence. He turned the focus of the romance from the king to the knight, picking up on Arthur's assertion that his power depends upon the men he succeeds in attracting. His four Arthurian romances, *Erec and Enide*, *Ywain*, *Lancelot*, and *Perceval* (his fifth tale, *Cliges*, is only tangentially Arthurian), provide the nucleus of the later tradition, introducing its major characters and concerns, its standard plot and episodes. His poems represent the Arthurian romance in its most classic form, which typically begins in Arthurian plenitude: the knights gathered at court, feasting and enjoying their wealth and privilege. A challenge to the court, be it a hostile knight, a damsel in distress, or news of a marvel, propels an individual knight from court and into the uncharted and unsubdued territories beyond Arthur's realm. There he encounters a series of adventures, fights against various enemies, defends the property rights of minor lords and widowed or orphaned ladies, and rescues unfortunate maidens from fates worse than death, before accomplishing his initial quest. When he has done so, the knight is rewarded—a triumphal return to Arthur, a rich marriage, a crown—and the Round Table's glory is affirmed. Many of Chrétien's romances repeat this narrative structure, resulting in what Arthurian scholars call a double-course romance. These double romances usually conclude their first part after the hero has reasserted Arthur's authority and received his marital reward; their second part begins when the hero needs to learn to balance his public life, with its duty to king and comrades, and his private life, with its temptations of love and leisure.

Chrétien's romances were extremely popular in the high Middle Ages. Not only were they adapted into almost every major European language, but also they gave rise to a series of sequels and spin-offs, a sort of medieval fan fiction. Arthur and his knights became the go-to characters for tales of love, battles, and adventure. The court attracted other tales to it, including the famous story of the doomed lovers Tristan and Isolde, and Isolde's hapless husband, King Mark. Writers intent on completing Chrétien's unfinished tale about Perceval, the Welsh knight who stumbles across a mysterious grail and fails to ask what it is or whom it serves, introduced the quest for the Holy Grail into the Arthurian world. Chronicle, romance, and Grail quest merged, culminating in France in a series of prose romances of which the thirteenth-century *Prose* or *Vulgate Lancelot* is the best known. From the *Vulgate Lancelot* through Thomas Malory's *Morte Darthur* to Alfred Tennyson's *Idylls of the King* and the modern Anglo-American Arthurian tradition, it all began with Chrétien's adaptation of the Welsh warrior-king.

Taking Arthur Back: The Welsh Arthurian Romances

When the Welsh Arthurian romances *Peredur vab Efrawc, Owein, and Gereint* were written, the French and the English had already appropriated Arthur, the native hero. In fact, all three of these romances have a strong affinity with the work of Chrétien de Troyes: *Peredur* with *Perceval, Owein* with *Yvain,* and *Gereint* with *Erec and Enide.* Yet, at the time of these romances' composition, the Welsh were themselves strenuously resisting colonization. Thus, on the one hand, Arthur's Welsh court could function as the ideal past to be returned to; on the other hand, his "French" court could represent a newfangled ideal to be avoided at all costs. This contradiction lies at the heart of the most confusing of these Welsh Arthurian romances, *Peredur vab Efrawc*. The tale exists in two distinct versions: a short version that follows Chrétien's *Perceval* at the beginning before spinning off into a series of adventures that owe nothing to a Continental source, and a long version that draws from a variety of French narratives and continues Peredur's seemingly finished tale but provides a completely different conclusion.

The shorter, and earlier, version of *Peredur* participates in the same isolationist discourse as *Culhwch*, asserting a native warrior identity as a bastion against both military and cultural invasion. What is surprising about the assertion is that, in this version, Arthur is on the wrong side of the equation. As its author tells in Welsh prose the story that Chrétien renders in French verse, he cedes the ambivalent Arthur to the Anglo-Normans, presenting an Arthurian tale in which the hero needs to leave the court to find his identity and destiny. The narrative begins, as does Chrétien's, with the hero's mother's decision to leave the world of men. A widow, whose husband and six older sons have been killed in the wars, she finds herself in the same plight as many Welsh families displaced by English invasion. Her flight from the court and into the barren places is a flight to protect "her son and his dominion" (183). In keeping Peredur from all knowledge of knighthood, she seeks to preserve his native identity; Peredur's favorable reaction to the Arthurian knights he encounters in the forest, whom his mother tries to pass off as angels, thwarts her efforts. "I too," he declares, "will follow thee as a knight this very hour" (184).

Peredur's mother's advice to him before he leaves for court encapsulates this romance's assessment of Arthurian knights: take what you want, earn fame through bribery, and force yourself on reluctant women. And, when Peredur arrives at court, this cynical summation of Arthurian manners seems justified. He enters the hall on the heels of a Red Knight, who has grabbed Guinevere's goblet from her hand, flung wine into her face, and then galloped off with the cup, daring the gathered knights to follow him and avenge the insult to their queen. This challenge paralyzes Arthur's court, and when Peredur in all his uncouth glory, wearing homespun robes, riding a bony nag, and carrying a handful of sharp sticks, rides into the feast, its knights and ladies proceed gleefully to "make fun of him and throw sticks at him, and they feeling pleased that such a one as he had come, for the other matter to be forgotten" (187). While the court does not recognize Peredur's potential, a dwarf and dwarfess, who belong to the anti-Arthurian world of his mother, do. They hail him as "chief of warriors and flower of knights" (187), earning a blow from the infuriated Cei, which propels Peredur from court and into the liminal spaces associated with the barbaric Welsh—the desert, wilderness, and desolate forest. In these spaces Peredur meets his maternal uncles, who, unlike their counterparts in Chrétien's *Perceval*, do not attempt to turn Peredur from a Welsh mama's boy into a polished knight. Instead they help Peredur realize his destiny as "the best man that smites with a sword in this Island" (190). Furthermore, Peredur's "Grail adventure," in which Chrétien's mysterious vessel is replaced by "a great salver . . . and a man's head on the salver, and blood in profusion around the head" (192), recalls other Welsh tales in which the severed head of a leader is associated with defeat and conquest and, thus, functions explicitly as a reminder that Wales has lost its sovereignty to others.

Peredur's subsequent adventures reinforce his duty to Welsh sovereignty, emphasizing his role as a protector of territorial rights. He stops identifying himself as Arthur's man and, for the first time, names himself: "Peredur, son of Efrawg, out of the North" (197). When he receives full warrior status, as represented by a horse and arms, it is not from Arthur but, in good Celtic tradition, from a feminine otherworldly power, the Witches of Caer Loyw. However, instead of taking up his place as the guardian of his native lands, he returns to Arthur's court and assumes "just such a garment as was on Gwalchmei" (202), acts that this version of the tale codes as failure.

The narrative immediately propels Peredur away from Arthur's court and back into the waste spaces in a quest for Angharad Llaw Eurwch's love. In this quest, Peredur functions as a traditional Arthurian knight: he forces the native inhabitants of the Round Valley to convert to Arthur's political and cultural order, then returns to the court, where he rejoins his companions and claims his love. If Chrétien had written *Peredur*, this union between Angharad and the hero would have either marked the end of Peredur's story or served as a catalyst for a second set of adventures in which the hero would have learned to balance the private world of love and the public world of the court. In either case, the romance would end with an affirmation of a dynastic marriage within the Arthurian order. *Peredur*, however, immediately rejects this union, sending its hero back into the native waste forests to seek a proper mate. While hunting with Arthur in the wilderness, Peredur loses his way; once separated from the Arthurian court, he is reminded of his duties to Welsh sovereignty, embodied by the empress, with whom he ultimately rules.

The adventures that culminate in this reign leave Chrétien and the narrative logic of Continental romance behind, entering into a fluid and shifting Celtic narrative. Peredur moves through a strange world of giant serpents, dead men revived in magical baths, sheep that change from black to white and back again, trees half green and half fire, and a fair woman on a mound, proffering a magic stone in return for Peredur's vow to love her best of all women. Peredur's acceptance of her offer both nullifies his vow to Angharad and breaks his tie to the Arthurian court. He takes the stone, defeats the serpent, overthrows hostile war bands, arranges a marriage between his retainer and a besieged countess, and accepts homage in his own right from the denizens of the land. From there, he proceeds to a tournament organized by the empress and battles for his right to three goblets—and, with them, the empress. As both goblets and empress signify the sovereignty of Wales, Peredur's victory in this tournament reaffirms his role as a Welsh warrior, dedicated to defend the independence of Wales. He chooses the empress over Angharad, the Welsh forests over the court, and settles down to reign. The short version of the narrative ends here, with a formulaic tag that signals the end of the tale: "and Peredur ruled with the empress fourteen years, as the story tells" (217).

This version of *Peredur* concedes Arthur and his court to the colonizer: the native war-leader of *Culhwch and Olwen* has been replaced by the Normanized king of a foreign court. The long version of the narrative, however, asks its audience to reread Arthur and his court, and Peredur's identity, in light of the information a mysterious blond youth presents at the end of its tale. This rereading reverses the argument: Arthur's court becomes equated, once again, with an idealized native past. The long version of the romance resumes with Peredur mysteriously back at Arthur's court, the empress and her kingdom apparently forgotten. The action begins with the appearance of the Black Maiden who accuses Peredur of failing to recognize the severed head of his uncle at the Castle of the Lame King, and challenges Arthur's court to rescue a besieged maiden. Her speech sends both Peredur and Gwalchmai into the waste forests associated with the native otherworld. Their adventures there reassign the values attached to the court and the otherworld in the short version of the tale, where Arthur's court stands for the culture of the colonizer and the forest for a native realm in which a Welsh hero can find his destiny and his dominion. In this version, the Anglo-Normanized court provides the proper home for Welsh heroes, and the ambiguous and barbaric forests must be assimilated into the Arthurian order: the native warrior must become the civilized chivalric knight.

This reversal begins at the very beginning of Peredur's and Gwalchmai's adventures. In the episodes leading up to Peredur's union with the empress, Arthur's court consistently lacked bravery and manners, and the otherworldly courts served as models of prowess and courtesy. In this final sequence, Arthur and his chivalric knights now possess both manners and valor, while the courts that Peredur and Gwalchmai encounter in the forest are vulgar and cowardly. Both knights begin their quests by resting at a castle while their host hunts; both are vulgarly accused of illicit dalliances; both are denied the due process of single combat and are instead seized and imprisoned by several men. Yet each responds with bravery and impeccable courtesy as he negotiates his release and resumes his interrupted quest.

As Peredur wanders through the forest, defeating various hostile earls, he again encounters an empress. This empress, however, is not the benevolent helper of his earlier experience but a capricious woman who rules a barbaric realm. As he does in his initial encounter with the empress, Peredur battles and defeats three enemies to win her. His efforts to stop the plagues laying waste to her kingdom fail to gain her favor or to restore order to her kingdom. Instead of culminating in union between the hero and the empress, the long version of *Peredur* abruptly abandons the empress in favor of the Arthurian court when a mysterious blond youth reveals that he was both the bearer of the severed head and the Black Maiden who sent Peredur from Arthur's court back into the forest. He urges Peredur to enact vengeance against the Witches of Caer Loyw. Peredur sends for Arthur and his retinue, and the tale ends: "the Witches of Caer Loyw were all slain" (227). The Continental court trumps the native otherworld.

As the long version of *Peredur* revalorizes Arthur's Anglo-Normanized court, it performs a sleight-of-hand, using Arthur's "ideal past" to argue for a change in native practices and identity. *Culhwch and Olwen* idealizes a warrior past and an economy based on pillage and plunder, in which Arthur's court epitomizes this ideal, and the short version of *Peredur* poses Arthur's court as a threat to this native identity; in contrast, the long version of *Peredur* uses the Arthurian past to redefine it. The long version thus supports the hybrid cultural and political agenda advanced by the Princes of Gwynedd, beginning with Llewelyn ap Iowerth. Llewelyn and his heirs held power in Gwynedd in the early thirteenth century, when King John's excursions into Wales precipitated exactly the kind of assimilation that the short version of *Peredur* warns against. To consolidate their power and to prevent Wales from losing its identity and dwindling into merely an English fiefdom, the Princes of Gwynedd both sought to forge a Welsh identity based on law and native tradition and adopted English political and economic narratives.

As part of his appeal to a native past, Llewelyn supervised the production of new manuscripts of the Laws of Hywel Dda, a legendary king who, according to the prologues to his texts, ruled over a unified Wales and codified Welsh law. Llewelyn also, arguably, influenced the composition of the remaining two Welsh Arthurian romances, *Owein* and *Gereint*. In spite of his narrative appeals to a native Welsh past, however, many of Llewelyn's policies actually opposed Welsh law and custom and introduced English practices, most notably a centralized feudal government and Continental-style political marriage, including his marriage to John's illegitimate daughter. At the same time, he turned to the past to justify his agenda: the consolidation of his own power as a way for Wales to survive the pressures of conquest and colonization and to coexist in peace—however uneasily—with its acquisitive neighbor.

The chronicle of the unification of Arthur's realm in *Owein* and *Gereint* mirrors the Princes of Gwynedd's centralizing agenda. These tales transform a standard Arthurian episode, the hero's adventures in an otherworldly forest, to serve new ideological and political ends. In *Culhwch and Olwen*, the otherworld exists to be plundered and pillaged; in the short version of *Peredur*, it represents a native alternative to a foreign court; and in the long version, it is a hostile enemy to be slaughtered. In these romances, however, the otherworld consists of realms outside Arthur's protective custody that must be made to realize that, in order to survive, they will need to ally themselves with the Arthurian court. This necessity, however, is reciprocal: the survival of Arthur's court, of Wales, depends upon the cooperation of these independent domains.

As *Owein* opens, Arthur is indeed king at Caer Llion, but the authority of his realm is unsettled, both threatened by and a threat to a mysterious earldom in the forest. Relaxing over a hearty snack, one of Arthur's knights, Cynon, entertains his fellows with the tale of the first of three encounters between the court and this earldom. Seeking adventure, he says, he followed the advice of a local "wild man" and poured water into a mysterious basin and then waited for the result. A huge storm arose, and after it died down, the ruler of the domain, the Black Knight, protested this violent intrusion: "Knight, what wouldst thou have of me? What harm have I done thee, that thou shouldst do to me and my dominions that which thou hast done to-day? Didst thou not know that to-day's showers have left alive in my dominions neither man nor beast of those it found out of doors?" (161). Like many of the figures Arthur encounters in *Culhwch and Olwen*, the Black Knight has clearly seen the Arthurian court as a destructive force, an initiator of unprovoked hostility, and charged out to protect his domain's borders, soundly defeating Cynon, who ends his story with an overview of the threat the Realm of the Fountain presents:

> And God knows, Cei, no man ever confessed against himself to a story of greater failure than this. And yet, how strange it seems to me that I have never heard tell, before or since, of any one who might know aught concerning this adventure . . . and how the root of this tale is in the dominions of the emperor Arthur without its being hit upon. (161–62)

The remainder of the first part of this romance chronicles the court's quest to eradicate the "root" of the tale by annexing the earldom to Arthur's dominion. Owein slips away "to go and seek to hit upon that place" (162), and the real story begins—a story of annexation not by conquest but by marriage that emphasizes the political imperative behind such marriages, however distasteful they may be. Owein repeats Cynon's actions: the storm arises, and the Black Knight sallies forth to defend his territory. However, this time Arthur's man wins, and the Black Knight escapes only long enough to flee home—with Owein at his heels—and die. Hidden in the castle, Owein meets Luned, a maiden with a practical streak, who seeks at once to assure the security of the earldom by marrying her lady to the late lord's killer. The subsequent scene between Luned and the countess must have resonated at several levels in thirteenth-century Wales in its advocacy of a self-interested compliance with a "conqueror." In opposition to the countess's older, strictly Welsh, values, Luned advocates this new "practicality." Not feud and revenge, or even loyalty to the dead, she argues, but survival:

> I did not think but that thy good sense might be better than it is. It were better for thee to seek and study to make good the loss of that nobleman than something else thou mayest never obtain. . . . Thou knowest that thy dominions cannot be defended save by main strength and arms; and for that reason seek quickly one who may defend them. . . . There is none can defend the fountain save one of Arthur's household. (167–68)

The countess reluctantly agrees, but when Luned returns with Owein, she protests, "Between me and God, no man reft my lord's life from his body save this man." To which Luned, unfazed, replies, "All the better for thee lady. Had he not been doughtier than he, he would not have taken his life" (169). Finally the countess holds a council in which the local men decide that it would be better for her to take a husband from "elsewhere."

The council's decision reinforces a policy of centralization. The resident lords consent to the fact that they need to look to the outside for protection and turn to the central power. Their lady's marriage to Owein symbolizes the first step of their submission to the Arthurian government, and the second half of the narrative proves the wisdom of this decision, graphically illustrating what happens to territories that lie outside Arthur's dominion. These adventures reflect the Welsh tale's characteristic uninterest in matters of the heart, displacing them in favor of an exploration of the perils that beset an unprotected realm. For instance, *Owein* eschews Chrétien's long disquisition on the exchange of two hearts and the maiden's diatribe against the treacherous lover. In the Welsh tale, Owein's deception lies not in abandoning the lady but in abdicating his duty to the Realm of the Fountain. Owein's absence thrusts his domain into internal disorder and casts doubt on his right or ability to rule. However, the consequences of Owein's absence extend beyond internal issues; since Owein is not there, the lady has none to defend her fountain, and the domain is vulnerable to any passing knight.

In the second half of the romance, Owein repeatedly rescues domains that, like his own, suffer from their vulnerability to attack. These adventures all emphasize the fact that unprotected land, here symbolized by unprotected women, can be taken by anyone strong enough to enforce his will on others, and that submission to Arthur's representatives is the only way to assure stability and order. *Owein's* final episodes vividly portray the alternative to Arthur's regime as a world characterized by plunder and chaos, savage rape and inhuman enslavement. Owein rescues a widowed countess from a marauding earl, a maiden and her father from rape and destruction at the hands of a savage monster, and twenty-four maidens from the Black Oppressor, before proceeding to save Luned from the death to which his abandonment of the Realm of the Fountain has condemned her. This series of adventures establishes Owein's right to rule, both in his own realm, through his freeing of Luned, and as a representative of Arthur, through his championship of the various women in the second half of the romance. He proves that he, and through him Arthur, can protect both women and land from the encroaching outside world. Without him, the text clearly shows, they are doomed. Owein returns to his domains, where he collects his wife without any of Chrétien's discussion of love and loyalty—in fact, without any discussion at all—and where, the text tells us, he remained "from that time forth, as captain of the war-band" (182).

Where Chrétien's *Yvain* explores love and the balance between public and private duty, *Owein* explores instead the politics of centralization. It argues that the threat of an external invasion necessitates submission to a centralized government, an argument that both supports Llewelyn's centralizing agenda and vindicates his political decisions with respect to Norman England. *Gereint* transfers this argument to internal issues and, again, both supports and vindicates Llewelyn's policies. This tale begins with Gereint oversleeping and missing Arthur's hunting party; instead he joins Guinevere and her ladies in the forest, where the group encounters a mysterious knight and his surly dwarf. When first one of Guinevere's maidens and then Gereint ask the dwarf the identity of his companion, the dwarf responds by striking them. Such an insult needs to be avenged, but Gereint is not armed. He obtains Guinevere's permission to follow the miscreants and rides after them until he comes to a bustling town, where he seeks lodging from one Ynywl, a local nobleman.

Gereint will soon marry his host's daughter, but, as in *Owein*, love plays little part in their relationship, which stems from mutual convenience. Gereint pledges himself to Enid so that he can enter into a local competition in which a knight "claims" a sparrowhawk as the rightful property of his lady to prove that she is the fairest, and stands ready to assert her right against all comers. If Gereint has a lady for whom to claim the bird, he will be able to fight the knight that he has been following and thus avenge the insult he and Guinevere's maiden endured at the tale's beginning. In return, Ynywl finds a champion to restore his lands and wealth. The Welsh version of this tale explains Ynywl's poverty by adducing a specifically Welsh issue. Instead of impoverishment by wars—Chrétien's explanation, and a common enough complaint in twelfth-century France—Ynywl's financial problems arise out of a dispute over inheritance in a world governed by the Welsh practice of dividing the family's estate among heirs, as opposed to the English custom of primogeniture. Ynywl's nephew has seized much of his uncle's land and property, but Ynywl cannot avenge these losses by himself.

The bargain is made, without Chrétien's long description of two young people caught in Love's net. Indeed, Enid's role in this bargain is a completely silent one. As the excuse to enter into the tournament and the bond between her father and Gereint, she becomes both prize and chivalric badge. Gereint takes her to the contest the next morning, claims the sparrowhawk, and, after a pitched battle, defeats his enemy, both completing his initial quest for retribution and earning the right to the maiden. This episode, however, is more interested in politics, restoring Ynywl's domain to proper order, than in Gereint's acquisition of a bride; it explicitly addresses the need to change Welsh inheritance laws in such a way as to make the continuation of power possible. The chaos in Ynywl's earldom emerges from the lack of clear lines for the transmission of power and authority resulting from the practice of partible inheritance: if all male descendants are entitled to a piece of the inheritance, then the survivors are likely to attempt to increase their pieces by decreasing the number of heirs. In Ynywl's case Gereint ends the fight for property by instituting a clear line for the transmission of power, focusing on the rights of primogeniture and establishing Ynywl in undisputed authority, authorizing, as it were, Llewelyn's disinheriting of his own firstborn son, Gruffydd, who according to English law was illegitimate, in favor of Dafydd, his oldest son by John's daughter.

Gereint's marriage to the heiress apparent gives him a vested interest in reordering the affairs of the earldom so as to give the power back into Ynywl's hands. As he does so, he operates as the representative of a strong central government capable of enforcing his decision. When Ynywl's now-dispossessed nephew invites him to a celebratory feast, Gereint declines with an explicit threat: "Not I. . . . To Arthur's court will I go with this maiden to-morrow. And long enough I reckon the time that earl Ynywl has been in penury and tribulation; and mainly it is to seek to enhance his substance that I go" (240). The nephew wisely submits to Gereint and, through him, to the Arthurian order, empowering him to dictate the affairs of the earldom: "I will gladly abide by thy counsel, since thou art impartial as to justice between us" (240). Gereint's "impartial" counsel restores Ynywl to power and wealth, and, taking Enid with him, he rides back to court, where Arthur will formalize the union both between Gereint and Enid and between Arthur's kingdom and Ynywl's earldom by bestowing the maiden in marriage.

Gereint's initial episodes justify the power of the central government. The state of affairs in Ynywl's domain proves the need for such a government, and Gereint's victory in the contest for the sparrowhawk, combined with his threatened appeal to Arthur, confirms the court's strength—its ability to take what is not given freely. The text's concern with the balance between overt persuasion and implicit threat, and with the proper role of the central government, continues in the account of Gereint's return to his father's realm after his marriage. This realm could, potentially, suffer the same fate as had the earldom of Ynywl because it stands on the verge of a necessary transition of power: forces from the outside threaten its borders, and Gereint's father is an old man, no longer able to defend them. Yet, in this case, cousins and nephews do not pose a threat; instead they acknowledge primogeniture and send to Arthur's court for the rightful heir. Gereint arrives with an impressive Arthurian retinue, ostensibly as companions but effectively enforcing his claims. An orderly transition of power ensues in which the borders are established and Gereint's rule is ratified as his men pay homage to him and, through him, to Arthur. A feudal chain, the narrative argues, ensures a peaceful and profitable realm.

This chain still relies, however, on an implicit threat of violence, since feudal lords must prove their right to remain at the top of the chain through their ability to both coerce and protect those beneath them. Furthermore, the text must vindicate Arthur's, or any central government's, exercise of power by arguing that the realm is vulnerable to both internal and external threats. Thus the second half of *Gereint's* narrative is not about the proper function of women and the role of love in a man's life, as it is in Chrétien's *Erec and Enide*, but about the need to continually prove your right to the woman and, through her, to her dominions. If Gereint cannot hold Enid, he cannot hold her father's lands. Neither love nor fidelity is at stake, but prowess and power.

Gereint shares *Erec and Enide*'s pivotal scene in which Enide worries that people will blame her because Erec has abandoned tournaments for her bed. Enid in *Gereint* laments, "Woe is me . . . if it is through me that these arms and this breast are losing fame and prowess as great as was theirs" (251). Erec interprets Enide's words as a sign that she is contemplating an affair and precipitates the couple's mad ride through the forest, in which Enide, clothed in her shabbiest dress and forbidden to speak, endures her husband's gross mistreatment, threatened rape, and a forced engagement. In *Gereint*, however, this scene differs in a number of important ways. Gereint is not afflicted by an immoderate love; instead, his retreat from battle results from smug arrogance, "for there was none who was worth his fighting against him" (250). And Gereint's violent reaction to Enid's commentary is not designed as punishment for a presumptive wife but as proof that he can still hold her; his subsequent treatment of Enid is a threat: "And shame on me if thou come here till thou know whether I have so utterly lost my strength as thou reckonest" (251). Dalliance with another man will be unthinkable, not because she is constrained by love, but because she is constrained by violence and necessity.

The adventures that follow Enid's unfortunate observation—in which

Gereint forces her to ride silently and endlessly through the forest—reinforce the romance's concern with the need for a centralized government to impose order on an essentially unruly realm. These episodes multiply both external and internal threats in the form of marauding earls and stray robbers, all intent on snatching what is, through Gereint, Arthur's: the lady who, in true Welsh fashion, becomes the symbol of sovereignty. Gereint must defeat these threatening forces and protect Enid from both improper unions and outright rape. Here again, the text eschews the French love theme. Unlike Chrétien's heroine, this Enid does not agonize over her conduct or the potential loss of Gereint's love. She warns him of the impending dangers because it makes good sense to warn him; she is concerned with the well-being of her protector, and thus with her own safety. Similarly, the final episode, in which the hero must play a mysterious "game" that restores the "joy of the court" by forcing him to make his way through a thick mist and fight the knight he finds there, and, if victorious, to blow a magical horn, resonates differently in this narrative than it does in Chrétien's. In the French version, the hero's victory restores love and duty to their proper places; he releases the love-imprisoned knight from the mist to take his place in the male court. In the Welsh tale, Gereint earns his place in the golden chair next to a beautiful maiden—herself clearly a manifestation, like the empress in *Peredur*, of the Welsh sovereignty goddess. When he does so, he sounds the horn, disperses the mist, and ends the "game." The romance concludes as Gereint, Arthur's representative, restores order ("the joy of the court") to this fragmented land, where "peace was made between each one of them and his fellow," and then returns to his own realm, which "he ruled . . . from that time forth prosperously, he and his prowess and valor continuing with fame and renown" (273).

Owein and *Gereint* both conform to the standard romance narrative with its central marriage and happily-ever-after ending. However, the search for "proper marriage" is not about love but politics, not about the relationship between men and women, but about the relationship between ruler and realm. These tales are concerned with the question of survival, with who defends the fountain and who wins the sparrowhawk. In this context marriage is in itself a means to survive. *Owein* and *Gereint* argue for various sorts of marriages as practical compromises based on clear necessity. On the simplest level, there is the literal marriage: the union between the lady and her conqueror/protector, the marriage that buys a strong lord to defend her assets. On another level, there is the metaphoric marriage, the alliance between two political entities in which submission to the stronger power assures peace. On both, there is the implicit marriage of cultures, the compromise between the old ways and the new ways in which laws and customs are modified in the interest of survival.

These varying views of marriage combine to produce and affirm the ideal Wales at the heart of these romances—the realm of King Arthur. As *Owein* and *Gereint* return to the Arthurian past, they create a fictional history that bears no resemblance to the real past, which was closer to the plunder-and-pillage warrior economy depicted in *Culhwch and Olwen*. Instead, their Arthurian narratives argue for a centralized government that adopts English practices in the interest of Welsh survival. They confirm a feudal order, valorize English inheritance practices, and advocate overtly political marriage alliances. Such themes provided the Princes of Gwynedd with a theoretical justification for their new regime, depicting that regime as not new at all but rather a return to the good old days, when Wales was unified, strong, and independent and Arthur ruled in Caer Llion.

King Arthur in Medieval British Popular Culture

Both the Welsh and French romances discussed in the previous section assume an aristocratic audience. The Welsh narratives are clearly aimed at Wales's dominant warrior nobility. Highly charged and highly politicized, these tales explicitly examine the concerns of this class: conquest and colonization, resistance and assimilation. Chrétien's tales also address a privileged audience: an educated French aristocracy familiar with the themes and tropes of the medieval version of the "great books" canon. Just as the Welsh tales speak to the concerns of the thirteenth-century Welsh warrior elite, so Chrétien's romances explore the concerns of the French nobility in the late twelfth century: the connections between violence and power, the conflict between public duty and private desire, the role of women and marriage, and the nature of aristocratic identity. The audience is less clear for the somewhat later series of British Arthurian romances, written in Middle English and Middle Scots. Nonetheless, it appears that the romances discussed in this section, *The Knightly Tale of Gologras and Gawain, King Arthur and King Cornwall, Lancelot of the Laik, The Adventures of Arthur, Ywain and Gawain, Lybeaus Desconus, Sir Perceval, The Jeaste of Sir Gawain, The Avowyng of Arthur, Sir Corneus, Sir Launfal, The Wedding of Sir Gawain and Dame Ragnelle*, and *Sir Gawain and the Carle of Carlisle*, target a much wider audience. None of them is "dedicated" to a royal or noble patron, as are many of Chrétien's romances, and the very manuscripts in which they have been preserved argue against an exclusively aristocratic audience. These manuscripts are not luxury editions; instead they are serviceable, dog-eared, well-traveled, and possibly even marked for performance.

This manuscript evidence, combined with both anecdotal accounts that point to public performances of the tales in taverns, markets, and provincial barons' halls, and the derisive comments by "high-culture," literary authors such as Chaucer, whose Parson condemns such "rum raf rhyming," has, until recently, led scholars to dismiss popular Arthurian romances in much the same way that today's critics dismiss popular genre novels. However, just as popular novels often outsell their more literary rivals, so the British Arthurian romances seem to have enjoyed the medieval version of best-seller status. They survive in numerous manuscripts that attest to their wide geographic distribution, and many of these tales were recopied well into the seventeenth century, as evidenced by the Percy Folio, a shabby seventeenth-century compilation of romances. They were among the first printed books in both London and Edinburgh. And, as with modern best sellers and Hollywood blockbusters, it would be a mistake to assume that these romances were enjoyed only by a single group of readers. Popular texts can and do transcend class and education. These popular Arthurian romances may well have been the medieval equivalent of *Star Wars* or *Harry Potter*, tales that captured the imagination of the culture as a whole. Thus the many audiences proposed for these romances—rustic taverngoers, provincial barons, aspiring social climbers, and the upper nobility and their hangers-on—may indeed all have listened to, read, and enjoyed them.

What is clear is that the popular Arthurian romances were not exclusively intended for a literate, educated, and aristocratic audience. The choice to write in English, especially when retelling a French original, is in itself a bid for an audience that extends beyond the aristocratic court. As the author of *Of Arthour and of Merlin* explains: "Noble men use French, but every Englishman knows English" (lines 23–24). Furthermore, instead of intertextual references to the literary masterpieces to situate their tales, these narratives use formulae and clichés that place their texts not within the learned Continental and classical tradition but in the popular tradition of Britain. Even the romances that draw upon French originals become more British than French. Literary references, allegorical debates, long philosophical and psychological passages, and courtly irony all disappear, and action displaces courtly love to take center stage in a shorter narrative that aims straight for the happy ending.

Popular Arthurian romances provide very different pleasures than their

French counterparts. For the readers of Continental romance, pleasure stems from the self-conscious literariness of the text—the well-turned phrase, the learned comparison, and courtly sophistication—as much as it does from the plot. For the audience of the Middle English and Middle Scots romances, the pleasure comes from the comfort of recognition, the satisfaction of generic expectations, and the performance of a well-known and well-loved story that assures its audience that all is well with the world. For, like a mystery novel in which the murderer is unmasked and order restored, or a romance novel in which the heroine and hero are finally united, these Arthurian romances for the most part depict a world in which the hero's triumph valorizes and confirms the Arthurian order. This determined optimism, combined with the narratives' lack of literary ambitions, has led many critics to see them as, at best, prurient and hackneyed fantasies—the fourteenth- and fifteenth-century equivalent of a soap opera, replete with sex and violence—and, at worst, as tools of the dominant culture. For them, the popularity of the narratives indicates their audiences' ignorance in regard to their own oppression by the very chivalric class that the romances celebrate. However, more recent critics, including Thomas Hahn and Nicola McDonald, have pointed out that these narratives offer greater complexity than initially appears. They, like all popular narratives, also open up a space for exploration, critique, and negotiation.

These romances draw from both the Continental and Celtic traditions. Some are retellings of French originals, others have no obvious Continental source and rely heavily on Celtic imagery and motifs. They appear (if we can trust the evidence of the surviving manuscripts) relatively late in the development of the medieval Arthurian tradition. The earliest of them date from the fourteenth century, the majority from either late in that century or the fifteenth, and a few appear to date from the early sixteenth century. Readers can only speculate on the reason for the lag between the French and Welsh and the English and Scots in this genre; there are earlier popular romances written in English and Scottish—just not Arthurian ones. It may be that the earlier romances' aristocratic audience had no need for English translations of French texts; it may be that the more "popular" tales and their audiences relied upon oral performance rather than written manuscripts. Whatever the reasons were for their delayed introduction into the English and Scottish literary tradition, by the mid-fourteenth century circumstances had changed, and romances about Arthur and his knights, particularly Gawain, had become a vital part of that tradition.

While the French and Welsh Arthurian romances served the interests of an aristocratic class trying to retain its privileged position, these later popular Arthurian romances negotiated a path through the traditional aristocracy, the newly arrived gentry, the rising moneyed class, and the peasantry during two centuries of political and social upheaval in which questions of class antagonism, oppression, and social mobility played out against a background of war, famine, and plague. Our earlier look at this historical context focused on war and the ongoing struggle between the colonizer and the colonized; it began before the Norman Conquest and ended with the Battle of Bosworth Field to provide the background for the Arthurian chronicles' exploration of sovereignty, imperialism, political unity, and disintegration. The popular Arthurian romances, coming from the latter half of this history, also address questions and anxieties of their historical moment, but they focus less on "history" and "destiny"—past and future, national and global—than on the present and the domestic. Let us, then, take a moment to revisit England in the late thirteenth through the fifteenth century for a glimpse at the world that produced these popular tales.

As we saw in chapter 1, this period was in many ways dominated by war, both on the Continent over "English" territories in France and on the island as the reigning monarchs struggled against their nobles and among themselves to attain and maintain insular sovereignty, most notably in the Wars of the Roses. War, however, was also about status: national, class, and individual. When Henry III accepted the Treaty of Paris in 1259, he agreed to hold his Angevin lands from the French king, creating, at least in the eyes of his great-grandson Edward III, an untenable situation in which the sovereign king of England was also a vassal to the king of France. Edward's wars, first in Scotland and then in France, were as much about royal and national status as they were about territory; they united his nobles in a common cause, bolstering Edward's authority and power. They were also extremely expensive, and while martial victories created a national mood in which Parliament was more inclined to grant taxes and funds, ongoing warfare and agricultural crises combined in 1340 to deplete the king's coffers. Edward ramped up his rhetoric in pursuit of his ambitions; he claimed the French throne, added the fleur-de-lis to his coat of arms, and appealed to Parliament to grant him taxes to regain status and land, arguing, as David Green summarizes in his study of Edward, the Black Prince, that the "dignity of the crown and the country was at stake" (33).

Not only was warfare necessary to the assertion of royal and national status, it also defined, valorized, and justified the aristocratic elite in a society dominated by class distinctions that severely disenfranchised the lower classes. Power, land, and resources were concentrated in the hands of the aristocracy. Much of the population was attached to the lands of the nobility, to whom they owed compulsory service and who more or less controlled their lives, as indicated by the comprehensive and complicated list of duties, tolls, and fines connected to various aspects of life, from marriage and death to the education of sons and the misdemeanors of daughters. Serfs were completely subject to the lord, who could extract fees and fines, imprison and flog, and dictate their lives at will. In return, the lord, theoretically at least, provided peace, justice, and charity.

This state of affairs was justified by medieval social and political thought, which depicted society as divided into the Three Estates: those who pray (the clergy and church hierarchy), those who fight (the king and his nobles), and those who work (everyone else). It painted a just and peaceful society, in which the members of each estate performed vital functions that contributed to the welfare of the whole. Another medieval concept, the Great Chain of Being, argued that God had created the world based on a natural hierarchy that descended from God himself down to the smallest of stones, and this theory likewise emphasized the necessity of rank and hierarchy. To rebel against one's given place on the chain, or one's natural estate, was to reiterate Satan's own attempt to abandon his place in creation and aspire to godhood. From such rebellions, only chaos and disaster could ensue. While these social theories justified to the aristocracy and clergy their privileged status in the culture, whether they had any real relevance to the serfs or craftsmen is debatable. Economic and legal realities were what really enforced the status quo. In the fourteenth century, however, the material realities changed, and the ideological and legal framework that enforced class differences proved insufficient to maintain them.

In 1348 the Black Death arrived in England, and for the next two years it held the country in a literal death grip, wiping out, by some estimates, between one-third and one-half of the population. The psychological effects of such an epidemic can only be imagined, although the panic in our age of instant and constant information over every new possible pandemic may give us a hint of the terror that occurs when a deadly pathogen is on the loose. Looking at firsthand accounts, such as Boccaccio's famous preface to *The Decameron*, in which he describes the social disintegration, chaos, and helplessness that propels his noble storytellers from the city to the country, provides a glimpse of the panic and despair that pervaded society:

And against this pestilence no human wisdom or foresight was of any avail . . . Nor were the humble supplications, rendered not once but many times to God by pious people . . . in any way efficacious. . . . Neither a doctor's advice nor the strength of medicine could do anything to cure this illness . . . This pestilence was so powerful that it was communicated to the healthy by contact with the sick, the way a fire close to dry or oily things will set them aflame. And the evil of the plague went even further: not only did talking to or being around the sick bring infection and a common death, but also touching the clothes of the sick or anything touched or used by them seemed to communicate this very disease to the person involved. . . . From these . . . occurrences there came about such fear and such fantastic notions among those who remained alive that almost all of them took a very cruel attitude in the matter; that is, they completely avoided the sick. . . . And in this great affliction and misery of our city, the revered authority of the laws, both divine and human, had fallen and almost completely disappeared. (6–8)

Boccaccio's description of Florence in the grip of the plague is the closest we have to an eyewitness account of a medieval community's response to the Black Death. Note the tone of helplessness, both to prevent and to cure; note also that the plague leaves chaos and social disintegration in its wake, the abandonment, as Boccaccio observes, of all laws, human and divine. The psychological consequences of such an event must have been dire indeed: loss of faith, paranoia, instability. Certainly, those who survived would have been less inclined to place a blind trust in the way things were. The plague's material consequences also rent the fabric of the social order. Not surprisingly, given their lack of resources, the plague hit the lower classes harder than their noble counterparts—not that the nobility, not even the royal family, escaped entirely. And by the time the plague came to England, the country had already suffered the depredations of war and famine, resulting in conditions that left the population, particularly the lower classes, even more vulnerable to the disease. The death toll among workers had several ramifications for both the labor force and the aristocracy. A reduced workforce cut into the nobility's rent income, and those workers who survived became aware of the value of their labor and were much less inclined to accept unfavorable wages and working conditions, choosing rather to leave their manors to seek more profitable employment elsewhere. On top of this reduction in income and increase in labor costs, the nobility faced considerable losses in their own ranks. Nearly 30 percent of landlords died without any surviving child, and while 60 percent of their holdings passed to women in the collateral line, the need still existed to promote new families to aristocratic status to replace those that had been lost.

Thus, as the fourteenth century progressed, social change was inevitable. The aristocracy responded by desperately shoring up its prerogatives. As early as 1349, the Ordinance of Laborers was passed in an attempt to reassert aristocratic privileges and powers by regaining control over labor and the economy. This statute returned wages to pre-plague levels, forbade workers from leaving their manors to seek better wages elsewhere, and gave the nobility the power to force contracts favorable to their interests. This legislative trend continued into the fifteenth century. Of the seventy-seven parliaments convened between 1351 and 1430, more than a third passed labor laws aimed at limiting the ability of the workforce to take advantage of the economic opportunities made possible by the plague. In spite of legislative attempts to control wages, the lower class's rising income played havoc with one of the traditional markers of status: the ability to purchase luxury goods. Thus, hand in hand with the labor laws' attempts to control the economy, consumption laws, which made it illegal for anyone outside of the aristocracy to purchase certain luxury foods or wear luxury fabrics and furs, sought to preserve the distinctions between the nobility and a rising non-noble moneyed class. While there had been earlier attempts to limit the purchase of costly clothing and rare foods such as wine and spices, they had mostly been aimed at restricting foreign imports. As the fourteenth century progressed, these laws stemmed from the desire to maintain the distinctions of rank. Beginning in 1363 and undergoing several revisions over the next century or so, sumptuary laws dictated what could be worn and consumed according to rank and income. However, such laws were never terribly effective, and by 1483 lawmakers had mostly given up and seemed to be satisfied with reserving only the most expensive furs and fabrics for the top of the social ladder.

The nobility's precarious economic and social position in the fourteenth century was further complicated by developments in warfare introduced during the Hundred Years War, most notably at the battle of Crécy. As members of the military elite, aristocrats traditionally derived much of their status from their role on the battlefield. However, this position was threatened not only by the rise of mercenary armies but also by radical changes in warfare. On the battlefields of France, a scorched-earth policy and the archer's longbow, not the knight's sword or lance, became the keys to military success.

The aristocracy in fourteenth-century England thus faced multiple challenges to their identity and position. Changes in the technology of war had diminished their role as "those who fight." The plague had thinned their ranks, threatened their income, and loosened their traditional hold on the labor force. Rising incomes among other classes blurred the distinction between those who were noble and those who were rich. In addition to their attempts to police the borders between nobility and mere wealth through legislative acts, the aristocracy sought to preserve their privileges by asserting a noble identity in which valor, courtesy, and chivalric virtues passed through blood from father to son in an unbroken line that could, ultimately, be traced back to the Garden of Eden. "Chivalry," which referred both to a class of people (the chivalry of England) and the code that governed them, defined and justified an elite group associated with both military prowess and the violent acquisition and defense of lands and honor. As "chivalry" came to refer more to a code of conduct than to mere military prowess, it operated to distinguish those in the upper classes from those who merely fought. It added "courtesy" (refined manners and social skills), with its emphasis on *fin amor* (courtly love), to the definition of true knighthood. The code was also applied to the battlefield as chivalric values like prowess, loyalty, and courtesy justified warfare. A true knight proved himself in both arenas: the court and the battlefield.

This ideal of the complete knight dominated the education of young aristocratic males. From the elaborate feasts and ceremonies surrounding his birth, which celebrated the continuance of the noble line, the young heir was groomed to take his place among the chivalric elite of England. His early schoolbooks would have included books of battles and "deeds of worship." Evidence from the royal family also suggests that the future knight was provided early with the tools of his trade, swords and armor. Formal military training began at the age of fourteen. Groups of boys from great households trained together in horsemanship, jousting, and swordplay. The young men, however, were also trained in the etiquette of court and hunt. (Hunting, strictly reserved to the king and his elite, was another indicator of class, as was the consumption of the game that the hunt produced.) Table manners, courteous speech, the proper treatment of women, and, ironically, the restraint of aggression all indicated noble birth.

And noble birth became increasingly important as the aristocracy's economic privileges dwindled. The nobility argued that chivalric virtues were in the blood. Knights, the argument went, were born, not made, and heraldry (coats of arms), originally a way of identifying men in war, became proof of a family's noble history. However, despite the fact that nobility in theory depended upon lineage and passed, like chivalric deeds and virtues, from father to son, in practice it depended on wealth and land. Those who had land were usually assimilated into the nobility, and old families that lacked wealth were often granted gifts from the king to allow them to keep up appearances. As this happened, the makeup of the nobility changed. At the beginning of the thirteenth century, knighthood was a descriptive term identifying those who fought, from the social elite to the landless or nearly landless, and applied to 5,000 men; by the early fourteenth century, the term had been reserved for the landed elite and only about 1,500 men could claim the title. In addition, the aristocracy itself became increasingly stratified with the introduction of the peerage and the creation of the minor gentility or gentry, which resulted in an increasing distinction between those who were noble, from established aristocratic families, and those who were merely "gentle," of good breeding but not noble.

As the ranks of the aristocracy swelled and the old elite looked with disfavor on newly raised knights, kings such as Edward III created chivalric orders, including his Order of the Garter in 1348, which represented a scaled-down version of his original dream of an Arthurian Round Table. Elaborate tournaments were hosted in which knights could display their skills both on and off the field, and the courtly classes—old and new—could demonstrate their power and celebrate their virtues. For, as Thomas Hahn observes, the medieval English knight was theoretically "the ideal representative" of the society (4). However, Hahn continues, to retain their privileged position, the chivalric classes needed not merely their own approval but also the validation of the larger community, a validation that was by no means guaranteed. The popular Arthurian romances reflect this competition between chivalry as a "normative fantasy," grounded in an Arthurian golden age, and a "post-Arthurian" critique of the privileged classes in an England unsettled by its own shifts in class identity.

Thus, in these popular romances as well as the chronicles, the Arthurian legend is contested ground. As a group, these tales function as both fantasy and critique; they reflect the aspirations of the up-and-coming and the smug certainty of the arrived. For the disenfranchised, they offer a medieval version of a fantasy show exploring the lives of the rich and famous, and also a space for laughter, parody, and pointed commentary. Arthur and his knights appear both as noble paragons and as aristocratic jerks. His wide kingdom is seen either as his obvious right, the embodiment of a utopian ideal, or as the result of unjustified conquest, achieved and held by raw violence. Some narratives raise these issues only to contain them and reaffirm Arthurian order; others are less successful in their ultimate valorization of the Arthurian vision.

As a whole, the popular Arthurian romances are a motley lot: based on French originals and apparently native sources, spread over almost three centuries, from a wide range of geographic regions, radically different in style, tone, and focus. They could be organized for discussion in a variety of ways, each of which would yield interesting comparisons and analyses. For present purposes I have arranged them into four thematic units: "War and Conquest," which discusses four romances that explicitly address the Arthurian order's implication in an economy based on violence and plunder: *The Knightly Tale of Gologras and Gawain*, *King Arthur and King Cornwall*, *Lancelot of the Laik*, and *The Adventures of Arthur*; "Chivalric Adventures," which discusses four romances that examine a violent aristocratic identity in tales based on Continental sources: *Ywain and Gawain*, *Lybeaus Desconus*, *Sir Perceval*, and *The Jeaste of Sir Gawain*; "Chivalric Identities," which discusses two romances that question the traditional depictions of the Arthurian court and the "noble" knights who inhabit it: *The Avowing of Arthur* and *Sir Corneus*; and "Otherworldly Encounters," which discusses three romances that structure their exploration of class and chivalric privilege around the hero's adventures in a hostile otherworld associated with the Celtic margins of Arthur's realm: *Sir Launfal*, *The Wedding of Sir Gawain and Dame Ragnelle*, and *Sir Gawain and the Carle of Carlisle*.

War and Conquest

Although all Middle English romances deal, in some sense, with chivalric violence—after all, a knight's identity begins with his function as a warrior—the narratives examined in this section explicitly address the violence at the root of Arthur's claim to territory and kingdom. Some valorize its necessity, while others gloss it over. None, in the end, explicitly condemns the Round Table's modus operandi. At the same time, neither are these romances' attempts to close down the questions raised by the various challenges to Arthurian authority completely successful. Furthermore, although they are set in the Arthurian past, their focus on conquest and sovereignty, kingship and vassalage, would have resonated strongly in an English present both defined by the wars waged to maintain territories and to assert the crown's sovereign rights in Scotland, Wales, and France and governed by an aristocratic class that depended upon a celebration of martial violence to assert its identity and its privileges.

The Knightly Tale of Sir Gologras and Gawain provides a paradigmatic example of a romance centered on issues of war and conquest. Based loosely on an episode from a thirteenth-century French text, *The First Continuation* of *Chrétien's Perceval*, this tale survives in a book printed in Edinburgh in 1508—one of the first half-dozen books printed by that press. Its narrative opens with an assertion of Arthurian plenitude in the description of a court at the height of its military and economic power:

> Thus the Royale can remove, with his Round Tabill,
> Of all riches maist rike, in riall array.
> Wes never fundun on fold, but fenyeing or fabill,
> Ane farayr floure on ane feild of fresch men, in fay;
> Farand on thair stedis, stout men and stabill,
> [. . .]
> Thair baneris schane with the sone, of silver and sabill,
> And uthir glemyt as gold and gowlis so gay;
> Of silver and saphir schirly thai schane. (14–22)

> [Thus the King set out, in royal array, with his Round Table. Of all his nobles, he was the most kingly. In faith, there was never found on this earth—unless in a fairy story or fable—a fairer flower of bold men on any field, traveling on their steeds, stout and stable men. . . . Their banners of silver and sable shone with the sun, and their other gear gleamed with gold and gay red and brightly shone with silver and sapphire.]

Arthur's riches, his unparalleled fighting force, and his multitude of men—barons, dukes, other nobles, and client kings—prove his worth as a ruler. The action begins with the rather ambiguous assertion that Arthur "turnit on ane tyde towart Tuskane" (2) [journeyed once upon a time to Tuscany]. No reason is given for this journey, and as the first half of the tale unfolds, the king seems to bypass Tuscany in favor of a pilgrimage to the Holy Land. Remember, however, that in the chronicle tradition Arthur's progress through Italy is one of conquest, and indeed the description of the men leaving England depicts them as a fighting force "werryouris with wapinnis to wald" (7) [warriors with weapons to wield] not as a band of pilgrims. The events that follow their departure more address martial than pious motivations. Arthur arrives at the Holy City and makes his offering, but this event is passed over in four of the romance's 1,362 lines: "The Roy rial raid withoutin resting, / And socht to the cieté of Criste, ovr the salt flude. / With mekil honour in erd he maid his offering, / Syne buskit hame the samyne way that he before yude" (301–4) [The king rode without resting, and sought the City of Christ over the sea. With much honor on earth, he made his offering, and then hurried home the same way that he had come before]. Rather than focusing on Arthur's pilgrimage, the narrative concentrates on two incidents that explore the connection between power and resources, violence and territory, and also the courtly rituals that either negotiate or mask this connection.

The first incident occurs as Arthur's army, for all of its expensive and glittering gear, runs out of basic resources—a mere ten lines after its glorious departure. The land it travels through proves barren and inhospitable, and the men find themselves hungry and in search of shelter. They pass by a rich, well-guarded city, and Arthur proposes that they ask permission to enter and buy supplies. Kay volunteers to run the errand; however, instead of asking or paying for anything, he snatches a roast from a passing servant and eats. The lord of the castle, understandably outraged, accuses Kay of displaying reprehensible manners and demands reparation. Kay blusters, "Thi schore compt I noght ane caik" (103) [I don't give a cake for your threat], and the furious lord wallops him. Kay, rather than standing his ground, sneaks out the door and gallops back to camp, informing Arthur, "Lord, wendis on your way, / Yone berne nykis yow with nay; / To prise hym forthir to pray, / It helpis na thing" (115–17) [Lord, go on your way, the man said no; it won't help to ask him again].

Kay's encounter with the lord of the castle highlights standard features of his characterization as found in many romances. He is boorish, blustering, and incompetent. His comical encounters usually serve as a counterpoint to Gawain's courteous negotiations, as they do in this tale. After Kay's report, Gawain points out that sending Kay on this errand was an unwise decision, and that Arthur should try again with "ane man, mekar of mude" (120) [a man meeker of manner] so that his men do not starve. Arthur agrees and Gawain sets out for the castle, approaches the lord, and asks for permission to enter the city to buy supplies, promising that they will pay a good price. The lord declines, because it would be treasonous to sell Arthur what he already owns. He welcomes the entire army and claims kinship with Arthur, offering his fealty, his riches, and 30,000 well-armed warriors. Arthur accepts and, after four days of feasting, resumes his journey. While this episode follows the standard pattern for a Kay-Gawain story in which Kay is rebuked and humiliated and Gawain, with his superior courtesy and diplomatic skills, prevails, it explores more than good manners. It also attempts to mask the violence that produces Arthurian harmony by displacing that violence onto Kay. Kay is the one who simply takes what he wants or needs; Arthur and his knights, either through kinship or recognition of their essential merit, receive fealty, lands, and resources, not through violent appropriation but as free gifts. This episode argues for an ideal political unity based on the belief that one's individual resources and possessions should be offered in service to one's ruler.

The second major episode in *Gologras and Gawain*, conversely, explores what happens when aristocratic warriors cannot reach a harmonious resolution of their problems. As Arthur and his retinue journey toward Jerusalem, they spy a prime piece of real estate: a strong castle built on rising ground beside a fair river that controls extensive, beautiful lands on which thirty-three towns flourish. A deeply desirable land and one that, as the narrative emphasizes, is extremely well protected: a fortified wall, double moats, and sixty-seven boats docked on the river. For Arthur, to see is to covet. "Yone," he declares, "is the seymliast sicht that ever couth I se. / . . . / Quha is lord of yone land. / . . . / Or quham of is he haldand" (255–59) [Yonder is the most beautiful sight I have ever seen. . . . Who is the lord of that land . . . or from whom does he hold it?]. One of his knights, the oddly named Sir Spynagrose, replies, "Yone lord haldis of nane leid, that yone land aw, / Bot everlesting but legiance, to his leving, / As his eldaris has done, enduring his daw" (262–64) [That lord holds that land from no man; he rules it forever, without vassalage, until his death, as his ancestors have done]. Considering that Arthur himself originally raised the possibility that the land might be held by an independent lord, his shocked response—"how happynis this thing? / Herd thair ever ony sage sa selcouth ane saw!" (265–67) [How does this happen? Did any wise man ever hear such an odd law?!]—seems a bit disingenuous. It certainly serves as an excuse for conquest: "He sall at my agane cumyng / Mak homage and oblissing, / I mak myne avow!" (271–73) [I vow that, when I come back (from my pilgrimage), he shall make homage and obeisance!].

Presumably Arthur sees rich land and easy wealth ripe for the taking. With no overlord to defend him, the owner of the castle must rely on himself, whereas Arthur commands vast military resources from his vassals, including several crowned kings. Spynagrose tries to disabuse Arthur of this notion, pointing out that, unlike the lord of the previous castle, Gologras will not comply unless he is forced to do so, and the attempt would result in a futile loss of men and lives—no one has ever succeeded, not even the king of Macedonia. Spynagrose concludes with a lecture on the foolish exercise of power. If Arthur goes to war "quhen he wenys best" (287) [when he knows better], "your mycht and your majesté mesure but mys" (292) [your might and your majesty add up to nothing but trouble]. Not surprisingly, Arthur remains resolute, responding with the medieval equivalent of "I am the decider": "My hecht sall haldin be, for baill or for blis" (293) [My word shall stand, whether it bring sorrow or bliss]. At stake now are power and pride as well as the king's determination to annex this deeply desirable property. The exchange raises several troubling questions about the chivalric economy in which Arthur operates: Does, as a later Arthur will ask in Lerner and Loewe's *Camelot*, might make right? How many wars or conquests deploy ideology to justify simple covetousness? What about a king who will hazard his men so that "mony wedou / Ful wraithly sal weip" (297) [many widows shall grievously weep] in an unwise war, simply to get his way?

As promised, Arthur returns after his pilgrimage and sets up a camp calculated to demonstrate his wealth and power: fur, silk, gold, elaborate and costly decorative work, diamonds all on display. He calls his knights to a war council, and the debate between the king and Spynagrose continues. Spynagrose repeats his warning, insisting, "I knaw yone bauld berne better than ye" (343) [I know that bold man better than you], and lauds the knight's looks, manners, and strength, concluding that even if the strength of Arthur, Gawain, and Lancelot were rolled into one knight, Gologras would still defeat him. Spynagrose advises Arthur not to threaten the knight with violence but to offer an alliance and hope for the best. Not averse to achieving his objectives through diplomacy, Arthur sends Gawain to present the case for a nonviolent solution. Gawain's tact as he does so, however, rests upon the threat of violence. He does not come to the point about the king's desire for Gologras's "friendship" or "grant" until after he has listed the resources that Arthur can bring to compel compliance with this request: his riches, his land, the knights and kings he has at his beck and call. The words are polite, but the threat is clear. Gologras responds just as politely and just as firmly, promising every courtesy but refusing homage, pointing out that threats are useless; he "will noght bow me ane bak for berne that is borne" (449) [will not bow my own back to any man born].

Diplomacy fails, and Arthur and Gologras send for their armies. In a fit of pique, Arthur promises not only to take the castle but also to make it his residence; in the ensuing battle, Spynagrose provides an almost gleeful commentary as Arthur's knights fall one by one in the bloody combat and the outcome hangs in the balance. Finally Gologras himself takes the field, and Gawain meets him in single combat. After a drawn-out and hard-fought battle, Gawain prevails and makes the same offer to Gologras that he made at first: yield to Arthur and all will be well. Gologras's attitude, however, has also not changed. He responds that he would rather die than suffer the shame of defeat and forced vassalage. At this point, when it seems as though both parties have come up against a non-navigable gap between chivalric honor and military necessity, the narrative chronicles a series of submission gestures that both communicate across this gap and set the stage for the romance's unlikely happy ending. Gologras strikes a bargain: he asks Gawain to pretend that he, not Gologras, was defeated and return to the castle as the knight's apparent prisoner, assuring Gawain that, if he allows Gologras to save chivalric face, Gologras will submit to Arthur. Much to the horror of his companions, who conclude that Gawain's defeat represents the Round Table's humiliation, Gawain trusts the man's "gentrice," his birth, his chivalric character, and his honor. All does end well: having supposedly "won," Gologras agrees to Arthur's original offer and yields his castle and lands to the king. Arthur's response to Gawain's account of this deal with Gologras reverses the narrative's earlier emphasis on possessions, substituting an economy in which character, not wealth, bestows worth. Arthur claims that he would rather have the fealty of such a man than all the land from Gologras's domain to Roncevaux. Gologras's loyalty, Arthur asserts, has raised his "pris"—reputation, honor, worth.

What happens next is one of the strangest moments in Arthurian literature. So far, apart from Spynagrose's doom-saying, this romance has been a relatively straightforward Arthurian narrative in which various outlying territories have come, either through negotiation or coercion, to realize that allying themselves with the Arthurian order serves their best interest. A triumphant Arthur ends his, or his chivalric representative's, adventures with more land and resources. Yet in this text, departing from the narrative's source text, Arthur gives back what he has won, releasing Gologras from his vassalage and leaving him "Fre as I the first fand" (1361) [as free as I first found you]. This odd reversal in traditional Arthurian policy concludes the romance's attempt to close down the questions raised by Arthur's covetous vow and his subsequent refusal to listen to either Spynagrose's advice or the pessimistic knight's assessment of the Round Table's chances against the mighty Gologras. His (or Gawain's) victory over Gologras leaves Arthurian honor intact and the court's military supremacy unshaken. Arthur's war is not fruitless, nor, in spite of a few casualties, does it result in a bloodbath to make widows weep. The king achieves his ends; he gains both lands and homage. Furthermore, when Arthur returns these gains, he counters the charge of greedy conquest. Gologras, having proved his chivalric worth, is judged worthy to remain independent and to be Arthur's friend rather than his vassal. This ending, however, especially given the text's Scottish provenance, cuts two ways. On the one side, it vindicates Arthur, clearing him of the suspicions the text has raised about his addiction to war, riches, and conquest. On the other, it argues for an equal sovereignty—the possibility that an imperial power, in spite of its superior military force, might recognize an independent state's right to that independence based on factors other than its ability to resist invasion.

The Knightly Tale of Gologras and Gawain attempts to close down Spynagrose's pointed critique of the economy of war by narrating a tale in which an economy of honor displaces it. Whether that attempt is entirely successful depends upon the disposition and interpretation of the reader. Arthur's victory and subsequent magnanimity do not entirely erase his insistence on having his way even if it puts all of them in harm's way—and, in the end, violence succeeds in resolving disputes. Without Gawain's victory, Gologras would not have yielded and the war might well have continued until it reached the disastrous end that Spynagrose predicted. A reader not invested in an ideological glossing over of the violence inherent in the system might well latch onto these issues rather than the somewhat disingenuous ending in which everybody behaves well and everybody is happy.

A less idealistic version of ways in which military violence assures one's place in the royal and feudal hierarchy appears in an odd, fragmentary ballad-romance, *King Arthur and King Cornwall*. The surviving manuscript of this text is quite flawed, found only in the section of the Percy Folio where half of every page has been torn out by, according to Percy, seventeenth-century maids to kindle fires. Also, its date is uncertain. Is it a seventeenth-century rendering of a medieval tale or an example of medievalism? However, even in its fragmentary state, it is such an interesting exploration of power, violence, and status that it is worth at least a quick overview. It begins as Guinevere challenges Arthur's status, as symbolized by his possession of "one of the fairest Round Tables / That ever you see with your eye" (3–4). Tauntingly, she describes a realm whose wealth far outstrips Arthur's own:

"I know where a Round Table is, thou noble King,
Is worth thy Round Table and other such three.
The trestle that stands under this Round Table," she said,
"Lowe downe to the mould [ground]
It is worth thy Round Table, thou worthy King,
Thy halls, and all thy gold.
The place where this Round Table stands in,
It is worth thy castle, thy gold, thy fee;
And all good Litle Britaine." (7–15)

Guinevere's assertion that the room in which this table stands is worth more than all that Arthur possesses sets the rest of the narrative in motion. Just as Arthur had only to see Gologras's land to desire it, so he only has to hear of this realm to vow, "Ile never sleepe one night, there as I doe another, / Till that Round Table I see!" (24–25).

Arthur, of course, wants much more than merely to see this Round Table. He wants to possess it, its trestle, the room in which it stands, and everything else in the kingdom because only by doing so can he maintain his privileged position. Disguised as pilgrims, he and four knights set off and travel until they come to the king of Cornwall's castle, where a porter, clad in gold, boasts that no one is as rich or has so much gold as his master. The party barters for lodging and dines with the king, who, seeing that these men are from Little Britain, adds to Guinevere's litany of the ways in which this king surpasses Arthur, including the disclosure that he slept with Guinevere and is actually the father of Arthur's most beautiful daughter. Not only does the king of Cornwall threaten Arthur through his possessions, but he has invaded, as it were, Arthur's territory. Arthur can only regain his precedence by taking those possessions and exacting a fitting revenge. In the very odd sequence of magical events that follows, involving a seven-headed, fire-breathing sprite, a horse no one can ride, and a magic horn and sword, the superior might of Arthur and his knights affirms Arthur's position as the richest and the strongest of them all. They subdue and appropriate the sprite, tame the horse, and behead the king, and Gawain fulfills his own vow to "worke my will" (156) with the king's daughter. The manuscript breaks off as Arthur places the king of Cornwall's head on the tip of the magic sword, and from our knowledge of similar romances we can assume, as does the text's editor, Thomas Hahn, that the romance ends with the king and his knights returning triumphantly home, though we can only speculate as to what fate awaits the treacherous Guinevere upon that return.

Both *The Knightly Tale of Gologras and Gawain* and *King Arthur and King Cornwall* examine the connection between possessions, prestige, and conquest. A king, they argue, is defined by what he can take and hold. Those who submit willingly to superior force find themselves folded peacefully into the Arthurian order; those who do not, find their heads on a sword and their daughters despoiled. A Scottish romance based on a French original, *Lancelot of the Laik*, also explores violence, honor, and the chivalric economy, but in it Arthur occupies the antagonistic position of Gologras or the king of Cornwall. A single incomplete version of this narrative survives in a late-fifteenth-century manuscript; scholars posit both that the actual composition of the tale was not much earlier and that the romance's political advice was aimed at James III of Scotland. Between *Lancelot's* incompleteness and its lengthy political digression, the romance has been largely dismissed as an Arthurian narrative. However, when looked at in terms of the Arthurian tradition's exploration of violence, war, and sovereignty, this romance, even incomplete, contributes an interesting perspective to the dialogue. It allows Arthur to triumph, as he does in *King Arthur and King Cornwall*, at the same time that it criticizes Arthur's "utopia" and the economy that maintains it. And it does not close down that critique, as does the pat happy ending in *The Knightly Tale of Gologras and Gawain*.

Lancelot of the Laik is more aggressively literary than most of the medieval British Arthurian romances, even if it is a bit confused as to its exact genre. It begins as a classic love vision, in which a forlorn lover falls asleep and, in his dream, receives some friendly advice on how to win his lady. A helpful bird urges him to write something "Of love ore armys or of sum othir thing" (147) [of love, or arms, or some other thing] to woo her. After dithering about his lack of skill, his unworthiness, and the difficulty of finding good subject matter, the lover finally settles on a tale of both love and arms. The lover's tale is quite long, and so he proceeds to list all of the parts he is *not* going to tell, an extended rehearsal that functions much as the "last week on" segment that introduces weekly television dramas. It also functions, in spite of the poet's self-deprecation, to demonstrate his literary knowledge. He clearly knows his source text, the *Prose Lancelot*; his retelling represents a deliberate adaptation of the French material.

He begins his tale with Arthur and his knights gathered at his court in Carlisle, near the Scottish border. However, he also begins not with the standard description of Arthurian plenitude, but with lack. The knights, annoyed at a complete dearth of adventures, send Kay to the king to request a removal to Camelot where there should be more "of armys" to do (358).

Adventure and combat define knightly identity, and without either, Arthur's knights are restless and unhappy. The sense that not all is well in Arthur's kingdom, in spite of the planned journey to Camelot, is intensified when a dream disturbs the king's sleep: "It semyth that of al his hed the hore / Of fallith and maid desolat" (365–66) [all of the hair suddenly fell off his head and made him bald]. This vision of failing power and virility unsettles Arthur. He delays his trip and calls in his wise men, all of whom are reluctant to provide the king with an interpretation of his odd dream. It takes both Arthur's threat of violence and a promise of safety before these men agree to read the meaning of the king's sudden baldness: "All erdly honore ye nedist most forgo / And them the wich ye most affy intyll / Shal failye yow, magré of ther will" (498–500) [You must give up all earthly honor, and those whom you trust most will fail you, in spite of their will]. This dire prediction understandably upsets Arthur, as does one of the wise men's incomprehensible response to his request for a way to avoid this fate. The philosopher admits that they have seen a way, but it "is so obscure and dyrk til our clergye / That we wat not what it shal signefye" (511–12) [it is so obscure and dark that, in spite of our learning, we do not know what it might mean]. He then launches into a litany about a watery lion and a physician without medicine and a flower, concluding "God wot / What this shude menn" (521–22) [God knows what this might mean].

Thus, like the *Alliterative Morte Arthure* and the *Stanzaic Morte Arthur*, *Lancelot of the Laik* begins on the edge of Arthurian doom. The next episode brings the messenger of that doom into Arthur's court in a scene that echoes both Emperor Lucius's demand for tribute in the chronicles and Arthur's own message to Gologras. An aged knight enters the hall and states his errand:

Shir King, oneto yow am Y sende
Frome the worthiest that in world is kend
That levyth now of his tyme and age,
Of manhed, wisdome, and of hie curag,
Galiot, sone of the fare Gyande.
And thus, at short, he bidis yow your londe
Ye yald hyme ovr, without impedyment
Or of hyme holde, and if tribut and rent.
This is my charge at short, whilk if youe lest
For to fulfill, of al he haith conquest
He sais that he most tendir shal youe hald. (547–57)

[Sir King, I am sent to you from the worthiest man alive in the known world, Galiot, son of fair Gyand. He has more manhood and wisdom and great courage than anyone else of his age and, briefly, he orders you to yield your land to him without delay or to hold it from him and give tribute and rent. . . . And if you chose to do this, he says that he will hold you most dear of all (the kings) that he has conquered.]

Arthur's response also echoes Gologras's answer: "For I as yit, in tymys that ar gone, / Held never lond excep of God alone / Nore never thinkith til erthly lord to yef / Trybut nor rent, als long as I may lef" (561–64) [I have never, in all the time that has gone, held my land from anyone except God alone. Nor do I ever think to give tribute to any earthly lord as long as I live]. This discussion ends, just as it does in *Gologras and Gawain*, with a declaration of war to come.

The messenger departs and Arthur turns to his knights to determine the identity of this Galiot who dares to challenge the famous Arthur. They return with an answer that is not reassuring: he and his men are a good half-foot taller than anyone else; he has wisdom, manners, and courage; he has conquered many lands and has ten kings under his command; his men all love him; and he is only twenty-four. In fact, he sounds a lot like Arthur *should* sound. Here is a real threat, a rising young king, eager to prove his worth and extend his territory—just as Arthur did before him. Rather than preparing for war, Arthur rides out to hunt, and as he hunts, Galiot invades, destroying and conquering all in his path. Arthur finally realizes that he really must fight for his kingdom and sounds the call to arms, even though his counselors insist, "And ye ar here ovr few for to recist / Yone power and youre cuntré to defende" (660–61) [You have too few men to resist that powerful army and defend your country]. Arthur finds himself without men, without resources, and in danger of becoming, as he has made many rulers, a client king, vassal to a superior power.

Until this point, *Lancelot of the Laik* has told a reverse version of the *Gologras and Gawain* tale, in which Arthur and his kingdom function as the rich spoils for a glorious king to conquer. The narrative now turns to an introduction of its titular character. Lancelot of the Lake, imprisoned by the Lady of Melyholt for killing one of her knights, laments his literal and emotional incarceration, oppressed both by prison and by Love. However, *Lancelot of the Laik* is not a tale of "love and arms," it is a tale of arms and politics, in spite of both the narrative's stated subjects and its occasional forays into such courtly-love romance motifs as Guinevere's presence spurring

Lancelot to great deeds of arms and Lancelot's prowess kindling the Lady of Melyholt's own desire. The narrative shows Lancelot helplessly observing the bloodbath as Galiot's men invade and slaughter Arthur's hopelessly outnumbered troops, in spite of Gawain's amazing skills and courage. Desperately Lancelot strikes a bargain with his jailer, who lets him out to fight anonymously on the condition that he return to prison at night. Lancelot's presence on the field improves the Round Table's chances, but even he is insufficient to defeat Galiot. In fact, Galiot concludes that to continue his invasion against so weak an enemy would not be chivalric. He determines to withdraw and allow Arthur more time to gather his resources, for "than is mor worschip aganis hyme to ficht" (1164) [then there is more honor to be won fighting against him].

Galiot's dismissal of Arthur and his men as unworthy opponents is almost more devastating than an actual defeat. All the king can do now is obsess on "his deith, his confusioune, / And of his realme the opin distruccioune" (1285–86) [his death, his shame, and the open destruction of his realm]. His thoughts turn again to his disturbing dream of sudden baldness, and he realizes that the dream has come true: he has lost divine favor and, with it, the political and military potency that such favor brings. He calls for advice and receives perhaps more than he bargained for from Amytans, whose homily injects a political treatise on the responsibility of kings into the narrative, switching the focus from material and military resources as the source of royal power to a well-cared-for populace. What Arthur really needs, Amytans argues, is not more and better knights but the support of his God and his people, something that Arthur must earn by focusing on political and social justice. Instead of faithfully discharging the trust that God has placed in Arthur by ruling in such a way that the innocent are protected, the wicked punished, and the disenfranchised provided for, Amytans accuses the king of being concerned with nothing but his own pleasure, ruling over a suffering kingdom in which justice is absent and the oppressed poor have no one to hear their complaints or right their wrongs. And so, Amytans continues, Arthur's warriors have failed him because they do not serve him out of love but out of fear, concluding:

> Of al thi puple the hartis ben ylost
> And tynt richt throw thyne awn mysgovernans
> Of averice and of thyne errogans.
> What is o prince, quhat is o governoure
> Withouten fame of worschip and honour?

[. . .]
May he his rigne, may he his holl empire
Susten al only of his owne desyre
In servyng of his wrechit appetit
Of averice and of his awn delyt
And hald his men wncherist in thraldome?
Nay! that shal sone his hie estat consome,
For many o knycht therby is broght ydoune
[. . .]
For oft it makith uther kingis by
To wer on them in trast of victory.
And oft als throw his peple is distroyth
That fyndith them agrevit or anoyth. (1520–38)

[You have lost the heart of all your people, squandered it through
your misconduct of avarice and arrogance. What is a prince or a governor without a reputation for worship and honor? . . . Can he sustain
his reign and his empire when he serves only his own desire and his
wretched appetite for acquisition and his own delight while he keeps
his men, unloved, in servitude? No, he will soon consume his own
high standing. . . . For often it encourages other kings nearby to make
war on them, assured of victory; and often also he is destroyed by his
own people, who find themselves aggrieved and annoyed.]

Arthur's true problem, according to Amytans, is not Galiot but himself. His
lack of resources is directly related to his bad stewardship. To prepare for
battle, he needs not to gather more knights but to work on amending his
ways: to wage a battle for the hearts and minds of his own people.

A messenger from Galiot, repeating the young lord's determination not
to invade in light of the shockingly feeble defense Arthur has mounted, interrupts Amytans's lecture: "That of this world the uorthiest king wor yhe,
/ Gretest of men and of awtoritee. / Wharof he has gret wonder that yhe ar
/ So feblé cummyne into his contrare / For to defend your cuntré and your
londe" (1557–61) [You were the worthiest king in the world, the greatest in
men and authority; therefore he is greatly surprised by how feebly you have
come against him to defend your country and your land]. When the messenger departs, Amytans lays out Arthur's new "battle plan": appoint hon-
est ministers and counselors, avoid flatterers and greedy people with quick
tempers, punish abuse of power, distribute justice equally to the rich and

the poor, make sure all subjects have access to the king, travel the kingdom and meet the subjects of the land, give great feasts, support the poor, give interesting gifts to the rich, do not usurp nobles' goods and lands, and do this all happily. Only then will the people love Arthur and happily fight for him.

Amytans's advice represents standard medieval political doctrine, yet it seems out of place in an Arthurian narrative. After all, his long speech is about neither love nor arms. However, it does add an interesting twist to the genre's exploration of political legitimacy. If Arthur's power depends on his ability to attract and keep the best knights, then he must have something to offer them, and the author of this text suggests that Arthur's best coin is good governance. When this section of the romance ends, Arthur has successfully followed Amytans's program and "thar hartis holy haith conquerit" (2158) [has wholly conquered his people's hearts].

The text then turns to a specific battle for "hearts and minds"—the question of the Red Knight, or Lancelot. When Galiot's messenger offered Arthur a year's reprieve to mount a strong defense, he also announced his lord's determination to acquire the services of the mysterious Red Knight. Arthur realizes that his own possession of this knight is crucial to his standing and his victory:

And sumtyme it preswmyt was and said
That in my houshold of al this world I had
The flour of knychthed and of chevalry.
Bot now tharof Y se the contrarye,
Sen that the flour of knychthed is away. (2181–85)

[Once it was presumed and reputed that in my household I had the flower of the world's knighthood and chivalry. But now I see that it is not so, since the flower of chivalry is away.]

Gawain, much to Arthur's dismay, gathers the Round Table for a quest to seek the Red Knight and restore Arthurian honor. When Galiot returns, neither he nor Gawain has been successful. Lancelot remains in prison, pleading with the lady to release him for war. The battle seems likely to end as it did in the last round, with Arthur's forces overcome until the lady finally relents. Lancelot, clad in black armor, joins the fray and rallies Arthur's failing troops. Here, as Galiot attempts to reinvigorate his own troops, the manuscript breaks off. We can, of course, use our knowledge of Arthurian legend and the romance's source text to speculate on how it would have ended: with Arthur, through Lancelot, triumphant, Galiot assimilated into the Arthurian order, and Lancelot receiving his reward in the arms of the Guinevere.

Lancelot of the Laik, however, is more than just a rather odd version of this standard Arthurian story because of its focus on the relationship between sovereign power and good governance. If *The Knightly Tale of Gologras and Gawain* seeks to mitigate criticism aimed at a king who could conceivably be accused of an acquisitive lust for power, possessions, and land, *Lancelot* allows such criticism to stand and centers its narrative on Arthur's necessary conversion from the avaricious king of the few to the just ruler of the many. If *Gologras* assures us that might is right, *Lancelot* argues that without right there is no might. This message is pointed; as such, it seems that the text turns to the Arthurian past to make a statement about the Scottish present. In fact, many critics argue that this text's Arthurian narrative functions merely as a frame for its "real" material, Amytans's political homily, which is aimed, they feel, directly at James III.

Similar accusations of avarice, indifference, and isolation are made against Arthur and his court in *The Awntyrs off Arthur*, or *The Adventures of Arthur*, another late-fifteenth-century romance from the North, although its dialect is from the area around Carlisle rather than as far north as Scotland. This alliterative romance survives in four manuscripts copied in various parts of England, a fact that seems to indicate that the tale was a popular one. It is also an odd one. Not based on any obvious source and with an atmosphere more Celtic than French, the *Adventures* consists of two episodes that seem to be only tangentially related: Guinevere and Gawain's encounter with the grisly ghost of Guinevere's mother, and Gawain's victorious combat with Galaron of Galway to prove Arthur's right to that land. Nonetheless, the second episode functions as a direct commentary on and refutation of the critique of the Round Table that the ghost makes in the first.

The action begins, as it does in many of the romances that draw from the Celtic rather than the French tradition, as Arthur and his court hunt in the woods around Tarn Wathelene. This landmark clearly harks back to Celtic Otherworld traditions; it is a magical site marking the border between the primary world of the court and the secondary world of the supernatural. While Arthur's hunting party, smugly decked out in gold and jewels, pursues its prey, Gawain and Guinevere linger in a pleasant grove. At midmorning a "marvel" occurs: midnight darkness descends, stinging hail falls, and a ghost glides, howling, toward Gawain and the distressed queen. Gawain, somewhat comically, tries to comfort Guinevere by interpreting these bizarre events as an eclipse. The queen does not believe him; she insists that all of the other knights have abandoned her to die at the hands of the "grisselist goost that ever herd I grede" (99) [the grisliest ghost I ever heard moan]. Gawain, ever courteous, offers to go and speak to the ghost.

The description of the ghost that follows provides an interesting and deliberate contrast to the description of the courtly hunting party with which the romance began. Both focus concretely on the details of apparel, that which "clads" the body. The court and its mounts, including Guinevere, glitter with gold and jewels and silks; the ghost is obscured by dirt and "clethyng unclere" (119) [unfathomable shrouds], surrounded by serpents and toads. This contrast between the ghost and the court sets up the spirit's tale, in which, like Jacob Marley in Charles Dickens's *A Christmas Carol* several hundred years later, she presents her fate as a warning to the living:

> Quene was I somwile, brighter of browes
> Then Berell or Brangwayn . . .
> Gretter then Dame Gaynour, of garson and golde,
> Of palaies, of parkes, of pondes, of plowes,
> Of townes, of toures, of tresour untolde,
> Of castelles, of contreyes, of cragges, of clowes.
> Now . . .
> Into care am I caught and couched in clay. (144–52)

> [Once I was a queen more beautiful than Berell and Brangwane. . . . I had more treasure and gold, palaces, parks, enclosures, estates, towns, towers, untold treasures, castles, countries, mountains, and valleys than Lady Guinevere. Now . . . I am trapped in despair and laid out in the earth.]

She identifies herself as Guinevere's mother and urges her daughter to "muse on my mirrour" (167) and change her ways before it is too late. Again, the similarities to *A Christmas Carol* are striking; the ghost's warning boils down to "mankind is your business." She tells Guinevere that those in power must have pity on the poor, for it is only the prayers of the poor that will be able to save them after death. The ghost then launches into a scathing indictment of the Arthurian court and its conspicuous consumption, including Guinevere's feasting on rich foods while her own mother is dogged by fiends from hell. She warns her daughter to be charitable and chaste and to use her position to give alms to succor those in need, including her mother, whose plight can be relieved by a number of bought masses for her soul. So far, the

ghost's diatribe includes fairly standard morality fare. However, when Gawain enters the discussion, the romance raises issues that its second episode
explicitly addresses, which are the same issues at the heart of *Golagros and
Gawain*: "How shal we fare . . . that fonden to fight, / And thus defoulen the
folke on fele kinges londes, / And riches over reymes withouten eny right, /
Wynnen worshipp in werre thorgh wightnesse of hondes?" (261–64) [What
will happen to us that fight and injure the people on many kings' lands, and
conquer realms, without any right, to win fame in war through the might
of our hands?]. The ghost does not hesitate to agree with Gawain's assessment of his dilemma, asserting, "Your King is to covetous" (265). She then
predicts Arthur's doom—providing a quick summary of the final events
chronicled in Geoffrey and the various Death of Arthur narratives. She
concludes her glimpse into future tragedy, rather incongruously, by telling
Gawain and Guinevere to "Have gode day" (313) and not to forget to order
those masses for her soul. She glides away, the sun comes out, the queen and
Gawain rejoin the court and tell their tale, and they all retire to their pavilion for an elaborate dinner. It appears that the odd events of the morning
have been dismissed or forgotten.

This feast sets the stage for the romance's second adventure. As Arthur,
splendidly appareled in embroidered love-knots and topazes, sits at his
meal, a woman, also richly attired, enters the hall and asks Arthur give justice to the man who will follow her to court. Arthur promises to do so, and
an equally splendidly and richly armed knight presents himself to the king.
The description of the three actors in this drama—king, damsel, knight—
reads more like a fashion column than a chivalric romance. However, in the
Middle Ages, clothing represented wealth, power, and status, as indicated
both by romance narratives' detailed attention to clothing and by legislative
attempts to regulate people's attire. Each character's elaborate costume announces its wearer's status, and the two petitioners are presented as equals
by their clothes. Arthur recognizes the challenge implicit in the knight's
elaborate armor and demands an explanation; the knight replies, "Whether
thou be cayser or king, her I the becalle / Fore to finde me a freke to fight
with my fille. / Fighting to fraist I fonded fro home" (410–12) [I don't care if
you are an emperor or a king. I challenge you here to find me an opponent
to fight with until I have achieved satisfaction; I came here from my home
to seek combat]. Arthur points out that a courteous knight would provide
a few more details, his name for instance. The armed man identifies himself
as Galeron of Galway and lodges a complaint against the court that seems
to support both Gawain's anxieties about seizing lands without any right

and the ghost's accusation of Arthurian covetousness. He lists a half dozen territories, saying that Arthur has "wonen hem in werre with a wrange wile / And geven hem to Sir Gawayn" (421–22) [won them in war with unjust strategems and given them to Sir Gawain] and concludes with a demand that Gawain win them from him again—this time in a fair fight, to restore Arthurian honor.

Gawain does not hesitate to accept the challenge, reassuring Arthur that God will "stond with the right" (471), echoing other Arthurian assertions of the court's divine mandate and endowing the upcoming battle with the ideological weight of these philosophies. The next day dawns and the two knights take to the field with their gold and jewels flashing. They fight long and viciously; blood and jewels fly from them, mixing in the mud. The court watches anxiously, for—as it does in Gawain's battle with Gologras—the fate of the Arthurian court hangs in the balance. In fact, Galeron's damsel is so distressed that she enlists Guinevere to plead with Arthur to end the battle and "make thes knightes accorde" (635). But before Arthur has a chance to intervene, Galeron himself recognizes Arthur's rights and yields to Gawain's superior might: "[I] resynge the my ryghte; / And sithen make the monraden with a mylde mode" (641–42) [I resign my rights to you, and from this day forward I will, with good will, pay homage to you]. He breaks off fighting and goes to kneel at Arthur's feet.

This victory and the events that follow in its wake disprove both Gawain's and the ghost's earlier assertions that Arthur is a covetous king who takes realms without any right. Arthur redistributes his land and organizes his kingdom with its levels of vassalage. To Gawain he gives Glamorganshire, Wales, Carlisle, and bits of Ireland and Brittany, thus granting Gawain the Celtic territories that always seemed to evade the English monarch's grasp. These lands are bestowed on Gawain with the understanding that he will, in turn, grant lands to Galeron. Gawain does so, restoring Galeron's lands to him as feudal fiefs. Arthur's rights are affirmed, order restored, and Galeron assimilated into the Round Table. Guinevere then commissions a million masses for her mother's soul. The romance ends in the Arthurian plenitude with which it began, with both the ghost of Guinevere's mother and her accusations—theoretically—laid to rest.

Chivalric Adventures

The Adventures of Arthur and *King Arthur and King Cornwall* explore the motivational force of supremacy and sovereignty that lie behind the chivalric adventures chronicled in *Ywain and Gawain, Lybeaus Desconus, Sir Perceval,* and *The Jeaste of Sir Gawain.* The first three of these romances loosely follow the generic expectations of chivalric romance as established by Chrétien de Troyes, who, indeed, authored the source texts for *Ywain and Gawain* and *Perceval,* and focus not on Arthur and his wars but on a single knight's education, exploits, and eventual triumphant return to the Round Table. However, as they do so, their heroes' adventures still center on the assertion of Arthurian superiority at the heart of *The Knightly Tale of Gologras and Gawain, King Arthur and King Cornwall, Sir Lancelot,* and *The Adventures of Arthur.* Each knight spends his days destroying giants, defeating hostile knights, assimilating outlying realms, and generally bringing the forest world into line with Arthur's political order.

Ywain and Gawain was probably composed in the late fourteenth century; written in a northern dialect, it is a reasonably faithful adaptation of Chrétien de Troyes's *Yvain,* and thus recounts the same basic narrative as the Welsh tale *Owein.* Like *Owein, Ywain and Gawain* follows Chrétien's double-course structure, providing two moments of Arthurian triumph: Ywain's marriage, and his eventual reunion with his lady—and thus the reunion of her lands with Arthur's kingdom. As it does so, the romance also explores the questions of violence and sovereignty embedded in both *Owein* and *Yvain* that are rarely absent from an Arthurian narrative. In fact, the tale of Ywain's marriage, for all its talk of love, presents a pragmatic argument for politic submission to a superior force and resignedly advocates making a virtue of necessity. Although it recounts the same events related in both the French and Welsh versions of the tale, this version focuses more explicitly on the threats posed by Arthur's court to the lady's domain and, subsequently, on the absolute necessity of having access to military prowess in a world defined by violence.

The narrative begins with a romance within a romance as Arthur's knights, well fed and happy, listen to a tale of chivalric exploits. These exploits, however, ended badly, making the knight, Colgrevance, reluctant to tell the story before the queen, who unexpectedly joins them, explaining it "towches me to ill" (115) [makes me look bad]. His companions prevail upon him to continue, and the tale that follows does indeed undermine the reputation of both Colgrevance and the Arthurian court. In quest of adventure, "my body to asai and fande" (316) [to test and try my strength], Colgrevance followed the directions of a bestial herdsman to a magical well, where, according to instructions, he poured water into a golden basin. As promised, a storm arose and provided him with a chance to prove his might. A gigantic knight appeared, accused him of recklessly destroying his property, and challenged him to a retributive duel. Rather than proving his might, however, Colgrevance was humiliated: the knight quickly knocked him down and stole his horse, leaving the stunned Arthurian knight so woeful that he "wist noght [didn't know] what was what" (432).

When Arthur hears this tale, he swears that he will go "se . . . that syght" (523). "See" here is, of course, a euphemism for "conquer." Arthur and his knights travel to the magic well to defeat its guardian and prove their right to his territories, as becomes abundantly clear in the events that follow. Before Arthur and the court can set out, however, Ywain, seeking to prove his worth, sneaks out on his own, since he knows that if he waits to go with the court, Arthur will grant the battle to one of the more experienced knights. He traces Colgrevance's path back to the magic well, pours water in the basin, endures the storm, and encounters the same outraged knight. Ywain, however, proves to be the mightier, mortally wounding his foe after a pitched battle. The dying defender flees. Ywain follows, but as he enters the gates of the knight's castle, the portcullis slams down, slicing his mount in two and cutting the spurs from Ywain's own heels. Our hero finds himself trapped in the enemy's castle, pursued by men bent on revenge.

The sequence that follows highlights the chivalric violence at the root of the knight-errant's adventures. Ywain escapes his murderous pursuers with the aid of a maiden, Lunette, who recognizes him as the one knight who was polite to her when she was a young and inexperienced visitor at court. She provides him with a ring of invisibility. Later, after Ywain has seen and fallen in love with the woman he widowed—knowing that it "wroght ful mekyl ogayns resowne / To set his luf in swilk a stede, / Whare thai hated him to the dede" (904–6) [was completely against reason to fall in love in a place where they hated him to the point of death]—Lunette agrees to woo the lady for him. Lunette may be the original "best friend" in romance: the sensible, pragmatic woman who stands in the shadow of her more desirable friend and never wins the heart of the handsome male lead. Here she offers her lady, Laudine, surprisingly frank advice: Arthur is on his way; he wants your lands, and unless you find someone to defend them, "yowre landes er lorn, this es sertayn" (958) [your lands will certainly be lost]. Lunette spells out the purpose of chivalric adventures, which is the gaining of land and riches. To survive in this economy, one needs to meet violence with violence, to ally oneself with a knight capable of defending one's property. Love cannot win battles, and so Lunette chides Laudine that it is as easy to love a strong man as a weak one:

. . . Chastise thi hert, madame;
To swilk a lady it es grete shame
Thus to wepe and make slike cry;
Think opon thi grete gentri.
Trowes thou the flowre of chevalry
Sold al with thi lord dy
And with him be put in molde?
God forbede that it so solde!
Als gude als he and better bene. (977–85)

[Get hold of yourself, madam. It is a great shame for a lady like you to
weep and make such a fuss. Remember your high status. Do you think
that all of the good knights should die with your lord and be put with
him in the grave? God forbid that it should be so! There are knights as
good as—and even better than—he was.]

Lunette clearly argues that lords and husbands are replaceable. "The knyght
that lifes es mare of maine / Than yowre lord that was slayne" (1005–6) [The
knight that's still alive is more powerful than your lord who was killed],
she concludes bluntly. Realizing that not a single knight in her entourage
is capable of standing up to Arthurian might, Laudine finally admits the
wisdom of Lunette's argument. When she puts the question to her council,
they willingly agree with her; certainly none of them volunteers to "defend /
Yowre well, yowre land, kastel, and towrre / Ogayns the nobil King Arthure"
(1080–82) [defend your well, your land, castle, and tower against the noble
king Arthur].

In the love scene that follows, the English poem, like the Welsh adaptation, plays down the courtly love elements that in Chrétien's *Yvain* somewhat mask the brutal necessity of Laudine's second marriage. Ywain tries
to declare his undying love, but Laudine cuts straight to the heart of the
bargain: "Dar thou wele undertake / In my land pese forto make / And forto
maintene al mi rightes / Ogayns King Arthure and his knyghtes?" (1169–72)
[Do you dare to undertake / to keep peace in my land / and maintain all of
my rights / against King Arthur and his knights?]. Ywain's promise to do
so is, of course, disingenuous. As Arthur's knight, he can hardly defend the
land against his lord's men. In fact, their marriage glosses over the fact that
the land has already been conquered and annexed to Arthur's realm. Ywain's
battle against Kay when he, like Colgrevance and Ywain before him, challenges the fountain, is pure window-dressing, and perhaps comeuppance for

Kay's earlier snide comments to Colgrevance. After he defeats Kay, Ywain reveals his identity and his marriage and invites the entire Arthurian party to the feast, where they all admire the lady and the land that Ywain has won through his chivalric prowess.

Thus ends the first movement of *Ywain and Gawain*, with the valiant and triumphant knight suitably rewarded and the renegade realm integrated into the Arthurian order. The next section returns to the issues of vulnerability and protection raised in Lunette's frank discussion with her lady. The episode begins with Gawain's claim that a knight can only maintain his position, and thus his lady's love, by continually proving his martial prowess. Laudine gives her newlywed protector permission to accompany Gawain on the tournament circuit for a year. Ironically, she can do this because the primary threat to her lands and property came from the Round Table and now—thanks to Ywain—she is a part of it. Ywain rides off without a backwards glance, and he and Gawain enjoy a remarkably successful run. The year passes; Laudine sends a message to her errant husband that calls his status as a knight and a king's son into question. This accusation strips Ywain of his identity, and he flees, mad, into the forest, where he subsists until a passing lady recognizes him and restores him to sanity through the use of a magical ointment.

Once restored, Ywain embarks on a second series of adventures that both prove his worth as a knight and demonstrate the necessity of such Arthurian protectors. The forests he rides through are rife with marauding earls, ravaging giants, and demonic opponents, all harassing their innocent inhabitants. Ywain begins by defeating the earl who has been destroying the lands of his benefactress, ordering him to rebuild what he has destroyed and to swear allegiance to the lady. He then rescues a lion from the jaws of a dragon, acquiring a faithful companion for the rest of his adventures. The lion aids him as he rescues a man who has a serious problem with a marauding giant (six sons slain, four to go, and a daughter who risks becoming the plaything of kitchen knaves), defends Lunette against a charge of treason (for recommending his marriage in the first place), frees exploited embroidery workers from two sons begotten by the devil in the shape of a ram, and defends the rights of a younger sister whose older sister refuses to yield her share of the family estate to her.

A common theme ties together this second set of adventures: they all depict vulnerable women needing rescue from various forms of harassment, imprisonment, and injustice. The message is clear: those without an Arthurian knight to defend them are at risk, and Ywain's sin was not so much against love as against responsibility. By leaving Laudine's well unguarded for so long, he placed both lady and domain at risk. In these adventures, he proves his ability to defend her rights over and over again; as he does so, he is offered multiple ladies and lands in return, but he refuses them all. Having proved his worthiness, he sets off to regain his own realm and wife. He achieves this not by appearing contrite before her but by reminding her of the circumstances that originally forced her to accept him. He goes back to the well and raises a terrifying storm. Lunette, on hand to reconcile knight and lady, points out the obvious: "ye have no knight, / That dar wende to yowre wel and fight / With him that cumes yow to asaile" (3859–61) [you don't have a knight who will dare to go to your well and fight against him who comes to attack you]. Laudine faces the same dilemma as earlier in the romance, and again Lunette promises to provide a defender, under certain conditions. Laudine has to promise to reconcile this unnamed defender and his lady. She does. Ywain appears, apologizes, and they all live happily ever after—including, the English version of this tale assures us, Laudine and the lion. In spite of this upbeat ending, however, the romance's second triumphant sequence is also one in which love and marriage mask necessity. Ywain has the power to take what he asks for, but the romance sugarcoats that power by casting its hero and his Arthurian cohort as knights in shining armor, establishing peace and order in a hostile world.

While the Welsh version of this tale, *Owein*, uses its hero's adventures to argue for political centralization, *Ywain and Gawain* focuses on the valorization of an aristocratic masculine identity based on martial violence and demonstrates this class's essential function in the maintenance of peace and prosperity. By the end of the romance, the monsters are destroyed, all hostile knights are either assimilated or dead, and the mysterious realm, whose separate existence so troubled Arthur and his knights at the beginning, has been successfully incorporated into Arthur's kingdom, achieving an insular unity that actual historical British monarchs very seldom grasped and never held for long.

Lybeaus Desconus repeats this process of elimination and assimilation as it follows the adventures of an unknown knight, illegitimately fathered by Sir Gawain, the text informs us "by a forest syde" (9). This romance, which bears marked similarities to a French romance, *Le Bel Inconnu*, has been traditionally attributed to Thomas Chestre, whose *Sir Launfal* will be discussed later in this chapter. The attribution, however, is based on inconclusive philological evidence and has been called into question by several scholars. Whether written by Chestre or not, it is clear that this late-four-teenth-century narrative, which survives in five manuscripts, was reason-ably popular.

While *Ywain and Gawain* follows two established knights who are already well integrated into the Arthurian court, *Lybeaus Desconus* chronicles the assimilation and domestication of an outsider while simultaneously argu-ing for the innate possession of chivalric virtues by the English aristocracy. The romance does not present a proto-democratic view of the medieval past in which the son of a serf can prove to be a great knight; rather, its "fair unknown" is fair, possessing the necessary qualities of an Arthurian knight, precisely because he is the son of Gawain and a lady, despite the unortho-dox circumstances surrounding his conception. Even though a bastard, the narrator makes clear, he was beautiful, and this beauty codes him as noble as soon as he blunders into Arthur's court. He also possesses another trait necessary to chivalric success: the potential for violence. This trait alarms his mother, who shelters him from all contact with knights, "For he was so savage" (19). However, by keeping her son from his true heritage, she denies him the chance to learn how to control and judiciously exercise his savage-ness. He needs to learn to be a man among men and to become a productive member of the Arthurian order.

As a lusty ten-year-old, the unnamed boy comes across a knight in the forest who has been "sleyn and made full tame" (36) [killed and rendered harmless]. He strips the dead knight of his armor, dons it himself, and pro-ceeds to Arthur's court. (Readers should not expect narrative consistency or logical plot and/or character motivation in many romances: How can a ten-year-old wear a grown man's armor? How does this hero know about Arthur and Glastonbury and how to travel there?) Once at court, he identifies him-self as a "childe uncouthe" (49) [unknown or uncivilized youth], and asks to be made a knight. Arthur, recognizing the child's beauty as an indication of his worthiness, in spite of the boy's lack of a name, christens him Lybeaus Desconus (the Fair Unknown), knights him, provides him with armor and sword, and hands him over to Gawain for training. The new knight asks the king for a boon: that he be given the first "fight" that comes to the Round Table.

The fight arrives immediately after the court sits down to feast, when a fair maiden and a dwarf come as supplicants to the king:

My Lady of Synadon
Is brought in gret prison,

That was of grete valour,
And prays yow of a knyght
That in werre ware wyght
To wyne hyr with honour (163–68)

[My Lady of Synadon, who has great valor, is incarcerated in a strong prison. She begs you for a knight who is mighty in war to honorably free her.]

Maidens in distress and hostile knights preying on vulnerable properties: Arthur's fame and power rest upon his ability to provide a knight with the proper battle skills to rescue the imprisoned lady. Lybeaus Desconus volunteers for the battle, but the lady and her dwarf are not amused. "Alas," the maiden chides,

That I was hether sende!
This wyll spryng wyde
And lorne is, kyng, thi pride,
And all thy lordys is schent
That thou wold send a chyld
That is wytteles and wyld
To dele mannes dynte,
And hast knyghtys of mayn,
Persyvall and Ser Gawayn,
Full wyse in tournament. (182–92)

[Alas . . . that I was sent here! People will hear about this, King; your reputation will be lost and all of your lords will be shamed because you would send a witless and wild child to strike a man's blow when you have strong knights—Perceval and Sir Gawain—well versed in tournaments.]

If the best Arthur can offer is an inexperienced child, in spite of the fact that he has a table full of good knights, then his reputation will be seriously compromised.

Arthur, however, remains obdurate, declaring, "Here getys thou non other knyght. / . . . / If thou thinke not hym wyght, / Get thee another were thou myght" (230–33) [You won't get any other knight here. If you think he is not mighty enough, get yourself another one wherever you can find one]. Arthur takes a bit of a gamble here, but if the child succeeds, how much greater glory goes to a court where even ten-year-olds, provided that they have the right father, can defeat Arthur's enemies and enforce Arthurian order. Of course, to accept the rest of the narrative, the audience must forget that the hero is ten and see, instead, a teen on the brink of manhood. The series of adventures that follow depict the "unknown" boy handily defeating a dizzying array of hostile forces, each more daunting than the last. From the dour guard at the Perilous Bridge (shaved and sent to Arthur), through his three vengeful nephews (also packed off to court), to two dastardly maiden-abducting giants (only their heads are sent back), the boy proves his natural martial talents, talents that win him several nights of "game and grete solace" (474) [entertainment and great pleasure] with his beautiful escort, by name Elaine or Elyn.

The maiden's acceptance of Lybeaus Desconus as a lover signifies his chivalric worthiness; he has earned the right to a courtly maiden's love and body. His next series of adventures affirm that right. He enters a contest on her behalf, asserting that she is the fairest maiden and should be awarded a hunting bird (a contest also found in *Gereint* and *Erec and Enide*). He defeats his opponent and sends the bird to join the defeated knights and severed heads at Arthur's court. Next his lady expresses a desire for a magical hunting dog, whose color consists of all the flowers that bloom between May and midsummer. Lybeaus Desconus sets out to procure it for her, but he offends a powerful lord in the process. In spite of being ambushed by the lord and eleven of his knights, Lybeaus emerges from the fight triumphant, in possession of the dog, "Tresoure, londys, and rente / Castellus, halle and boure" (1249–50) [treasure, lands and rents, castles, hall and bower). He sends the lord to Arthur's court to join the rest of his conquests, and his defeated enemy becomes a knight of the Round Table.

At this point in the narrative, Lybeaus Desconus has successfully performed all the requisite acts of a knight: he has defeated a host of Arthurian enemies, won a fair lady, assimilated men into Arthur's court, and appropriated wealth for Arthur's coffers. He has not, however, accomplished his original quest: Lady Synadon remains a prisoner. He continues on his adventures and kills another giant, who has also kidnapped a noble lady. This lady, once rescued, offers him herself and her castle, and Lybeaus Desconus happily accepts her offer and lingers with her for more than a year, removing himself from the Arthurian order and thus committing the evil that Gawain warns Ywain of, substituting love—in fact, the lady's name is Dame Amour—for manly duties. The original maiden finally locates this recreant hero and recalls him to his duty and his quest. He escapes from the sorceress Amour and travels until he comes upon a castle with an odd custom:

all knights must joust with its lord to earn their lodgings, and if they lose, the ladies and boys will pelt them with excrement, a graphic and public humiliation. Lybeaus Desconus wins and, once again, demonstrates his—and, through him, Arthur's—martial superiority. Here at last he gains knowledge of his lineage: the defeated knight recognizes him as Gawain's kin and, as such, the right man to rescue his lady, Synadon.

Until now, Lybeaus Desconus has battled a predictable assortment of Arthurian villains, including renegade knights and ravenous giants. This battle, however, is against subtler and more worrisome forces: two enchanters, Mabon and Irain, whose magical castle, filled with traps and illusions, feels more like the Celtic otherworld of the king of Cornwall's realm in *King Arthur and King Cornwall* than the straightforward military strongholds of Lybeaus Desconus's earlier adventures. And, in spite of his proven military prowess, the young man is not entirely successful here. He does kills Mabon and free the lady with a kiss, a rescue that also marks him as either Gawain or one of his kin, since only kisses given by a member of that bloodline are effective against the spell that has transformed her into a dragon. However, whether or not he kills Irain is uncertain. In the manuscript from the TEAMS Middle English Texts edition, Lybeaus Desconus cuts off Irain's head, but the text also retains lines that identify Mabon as slain and Irain as wounded. Other manuscripts explicitly state that Lybeaus Desconus fears Irain's return.

In spite of this ambiguity, *Lybeaus Desconus* ends with Arthurian triumph. The "uncouth child" has freed the lady and gained both her and her fifty-five castles in marriage. (It appears that Elaine was merely a "starter wife.") His mother comes to the ceremony and identifies Gawain as Lybeaus Desconus's father, and Gawain welcomes his son into the family. The boy's success has affirmed Arthur's position, subjugated renegade and outlying knights, annexed properties, and added to the kingdom's wealth. Irain or no Irain, all is well with the Arthurian world, until the next challenge arises. Despite this happy ending, the romance has not contradicted Lybeaus Desconus's mother's initial assessment of her son as worryingly savage; instead it valorizes that very savageness as the defining trait of chivalric identity. Not only does the romance argue that such savageness is natural—boys will be boys—but it also demonstrates that this inherent tendency to violence is necessary to the survival of Arthur's utopia.

Like *Ywain and Gawain*, *Sir Perceval of Galles* (that is, of Wales) is based, although much more loosely, on one of Chrétien's tales, and, like *Perceval*, it takes a mother's rejection of chivalric violence and her attempts to shield her son from his knightly nature and chivalric inheritance as its starting point. The English version of *Perceval* dates from the mid-to-late fourteenth century and survives in a single fifteenth-century manuscript; it both radically simplifies and alters Chrétien's unfinished tale, excising Gawain's adventures, which occupy most of the second half of Chrétien's version, and concluding Perceval's adventures with a tidy and happy ending. It is thus not so much an adaptation of Chrétien's romance as it is a whole new tale, and it is unfair, as many critics have done, to dismiss it as a crude and inferior version of that tale. Neither is it, as others have asserted, entirely a parody of the romance genre. Think of it as the fairy-tale version: the story of an earnest local boy who makes good, achieves riches and success, and lives happily ever after. It begins with an extended prequel to its hero's tale that introduces the romance's exploration of violence as the primary means to chivalric identity, social recognition, and material rewards, which includes access to women in the world of Arthurian romance. This prequel tells the tale of Perceval's father: his early career, his marriage (to Arthur's sister, who is given to him, along with lands and riches, as a reward for his prowess), the tournament at which he humiliates the Red Knight by unhorsing him, the Red Knight's vow of revenge, the birth of Perceval, and the father's death at the hands of the vengeful Red Knight. As the Red Knight rides blithely away, no one has the courage to stop the man who just killed Arthur's best knight, and Perceval's mother vows to leave the world of chivalry and chivalric deeds. She abandons her attendants and her goods, taking with her only one maiden, a flock of goats, and a short Scottish sword, and secludes herself and her son in the woods, thus rejecting the Arthurian court's unbreakable cycle of violence. Rather than connecting her son's honor and identity to his ability to avenge his father, she chooses instead to raise her son with "Nowther nurture ne lare" (231) [neither training nor education].

This rejection of her son's chivalric heritage both critiques Arthurian violence and shapes an alternative vision of masculine identity. Perceval becomes a skilled hunter and woodsman, able to provide for the members of this household that has left the court for the simpler pleasures of a country life. All goes well until Perceval reaches his fifteenth birthday and his mother suddenly attends to his religious education, urging him to pray to God's son for guidance. This is the first time that the wild boy, apparently, has heard anything about God. When Perceval asks for clarification, his mother answers, conventionally, that God is the one who created the world in seven days. Impressed, Perceval replies that he will certainly pray to such a man and runs off to look for him. Instead he finds three Arthurian knights.

Contrasting the knights' rich green robes to his own makeshift goatskin tunic, he assumes that such richly clothed beings must be gods. The knights point out that none of them is a god, but Perceval threatens to kill them all if they do not tell him "Whatkyns thynges that ye bee" (295) [what kind of things you are]. He is placated only when he learns that they are Arthur's knights and that, if he wants to be one too, he must journey to court and ask Arthur to make him one.

Perceval's instinctive response to the first knights he meets is to offer violence as a way of accomplishing his ends and establishing his position; "kynde [nature]," as his mother realizes when her son returns to her riding a wild mare, "wolde oute sprynge" (355). Indeed, in spite of his mother's attempts to instill in him a code of conduct that might control his violent impulses, an instinctive and inspired violence marks Perceval's subsequent adventures. His mother's words urge measure and manners, "Lyttill thou can of nurtoure: / Luke thou be of mesure / Bothe in haulle and in boure" (397–99) [You know little of good manners. Be careful to behave moderately in hall and bedroom], but Perceval disregards this advice in favor of blunt force.

Perceval's manners are certainly lacking when he rides into Arthur's banquet hall and threatens to slay the king if he does not immediately knight him. Furthermore, after hearing the story of the Red Knight's constant harassment of the court—openly insulting Arthur and slaying his knights—and of the Round Table's helplessness in the face of these onslaughts, Perceval orders the king to "late bi thi jangleynge!" (575) [stop your nattering!]. In spite of Perceval's rude manners, Arthur does not dismiss his request to be knighted, mostly because his beauty marks him as of noble blood. The king, the narrator informs us, understands that the child is a wild man who knows nothing of good or evil, a condition that does not appear to disturb Arthur in the least. When the Red Knight rides into court to repeat his challenge to Arthurian authority, Arthur happily agrees to knight the wild boy if he defeats the Red Knight. For Arthur, prowess, not manners, makes a knight.

In the adventures that follow, Perceval proves both his abundance of prowess and his shocking lack of manners. In fact, he becomes so proud of his martial abilities that, after defeating the Red Knight, he decides to dispense with Arthur altogether, declaring, "I am als grete a lorde als he" (814) [I am as great a lord as he]. At this point the English romance diverges from its source text and explores the threat that Perceval poses to Arthur's court and Arthur's subsequent successful quest to integrate him into the

Arthurian order. When Perceval fails to return to the court after slaying the Red Knight, Arthur first takes to his bed in despair. Later he and the court ride off in search of Perceval, inspired, the narrative insists, by love, but, one suspects, also by the fear of a potentially renegade knight. As they search for him, Perceval appropriates a quest, and potentially a kingdom, from Arthur. The Lady of Maidenland seeks Arthur to protect her from the Sultan who desires her person and her riches, and Perceval rides off to the rescue, refusing to wait for the king. Once there, he proves his worth by single-handedly slaughtering so many Saracens that their "hede-bones / Hoppe als dose hayle-stones / Abowtte one the gres" (1190–92) [skulls hop about on the grass like hailstones]. This victory earns Perceval the admiration of the lady and her promise that, if he defeats the Sultan, he will be rewarded with both her and the kingdom.

If Perceval succeeds and gains the lady and her lands without being integrated into Arthur's court, he will forever pose a threat to that court. For this romance to end happily for Arthur, Perceval must serve as a knight and join the Round Table. Fortunately, Gawain is still allied with Arthur, and he fights Perceval to a stalemate. At this point, as happens in *Ywain and Gawain*, the two knights recognize each other and return to Arthur as good friends. Perceval's upcoming fight with the Sultan now becomes his way to prove his knightly prowess as well as to win the maiden, and he does so only after Arthur knights him, urging his new knight to be "hende and curtayse" (1642) [well-behaved and courteous]. These instructions are, however, secondary to Perceval's real mission: find the enemy and give him no peace.

Readers never see Perceval's courtesy and good manners, but they do watch him find and defeat the enemy, thus winning "that wymman, / With maystry and myghte" (1735–36) [that woman with mastery and might] and becoming "kyng full righte / Of alle that lande brade. / . . . / For he had with a ryng / The mayden that it hade" (1747–56) [the rightful king of that broad land, . . . because with a ring he claimed the maiden it belonged to]. This wedding brings the narrative back to the Arthurian plenitude that was initially disrupted when the Red Knight killed Perceval's father and sent mother and son into exile. Although Perceval's marriage concludes the first movement of the romance, a loose end remains: Perceval's mother, Arthur's sister, remains in exile. In most versions of the Perceval story, her absence can never be remedied because she dies of grief after Perceval's departure. The Middle English tale, however, insists on a happy ending for all, and the romance's abbreviated second movement sends Perceval off in quest of his mother, whom he rescues from both the Sultan's giant-ogre brother and her own madness, brought about by the conviction that her son has died. He returns with her to his new kingdom for a second triumphant celebration.

Taken as a whole, these three chivalric adventures, *Ywain and Gawain*, *Lybeaus Desconus*, and *Sir Perceval of Galles*, tell stories—part action-adventure, part celebrations of courtly life—that glorify martial violence, affirm aristocratic identity, and argue for a return to a status quo in which the upper classes, by virtue of their natural talents, rule and protect the land. The final tale discussed in this section, the fifteenth-century *Jeaste of Sir Gawain*, is not as sanguine about the violence at the heart of chivalric identity. It chronicles the events surrounding Lybeaus Desconus's begetting in a forest glade, as it also tells a tale of Gawain's brief relationship with the boy's mother. This romance compresses two events from a twelfth-century continuation of *Perceval*, removing them from the larger context of the Grail quest and focusing instead on Gawain's repeated battles with the male relations of his paramour/victim. As it does so, it explores the centrality of violence in an aristocratic man's identity and social position, and makes explicit the role of women in the chivalric economy as markers of male prowess and honor. Although the sole surviving copy of the *Jeaste* lacks an opening, the first lines make the circumstances quite clear: Gawain has stumbled across an unaccompanied maiden in the forest, and he immediately pursues her sexually until, the narrator assures us, "he had her countenaunce [favor] withoute any more delaye" (9–10).

Whether escapade or assault, Gawain's sexual encounter is not the prelude to a love story; rather, it sets in motion a series of fierce jousts. The maiden's father discovers his daughter in Gawain's arms, and the focus immediately shifts to the men. Gawain, the maiden's father insists, has dishonored *him* and should prepare to fight. Gawain agrees that he owes the man something, and offers to make retribution for his violation of the man's daughter and property. The outraged father, however, insists that the only way his honor can be restored is in battle. Unfortunately for the aggrieved father, Gawain handily defeats him, takes his horse, and grants him mercy on two conditions: that he not punish his daughter and that he promise never to seek to avenge his defeat. This defeat, and Gawain's conditions, further jeopardize the family honor, as the lord's eldest son recognizes. This man also challenges Gawain, adding the insult to his father to his sister's dishonoring in his accusations. Gawain again admits the offense and offers to make amends; again he is told that no amends can be made that do not involve a battle. The young man suffers the same fate as his father and returns horseless from the combat, concluding that this knight must be "of the Rounde Table / For . . . he ys both stronge and hable" (194–95).

This assessment of Gawain's identity ties his seduction and rape of the maiden to Arthur's various martial conquests. Because Gawain is "strong and able," he can take what he wants without consequences, just as the Round Table can, since they can later gloss over their actions as "favor" or compliance. The lady in *The Jeaste of Sir Gawain* stands in the same position as the castles and lands in the martial tales: she is subject to "annexation" if her relatives/knights cannot defend her by force. The story continues, and her second brother is no more successful than the first. The third brother, Brandles (Bran de Lys in the French), is bigger and stronger than his father and siblings; he can stand up to Gawain. The contest between the two is cast explicitly in terms of "manliness" and their respective places in the chivalric hierarchy. In response to Gawain's jeers—"ys that youre boast greate? / I wende youe woulde have foughten tyll ye had sweate! / Ys youre strenght all done?" (275–77) [Is this what you boasted about? I thought you would at least have fought until you broke a sweat! Are you out of strength?]—the second brother responds that if Gawain beats his brother, then he will admit Gawain's preeminence as a knight. Brandles insists upon trying his own strength against Gawain, in spite of his father's fear that he will not survive the contest. "Thoughe he have done wronge, lett hym goo" (378) [Even though he has done wrong, let him go], his father pleads, but Brandles replies, "Sone shall we see yf he be a manne" (390) [soon we shall see if he is a (real) man]. Upon seeing Brandles, Gawain recognizes him as a worthy opponent, a manly man such as he has not seen for three years. The two knights repeat the ritual of challenge, Gawain's offer to pay amends, the rejection of that offer, and the combat that we have seen in Gawain's three earlier jousts. In this one, however, the opponents are equally matched. When their dispute has not been resolved at sunset, they agree to part with the understanding that their match has only been suspended; when they meet again, the question of who is the better knight will be resolved in a battle to the death. Gawain urges his opponent to be kind to the maiden and trudges home, without his horse or his armor. Brandles beats his sister soundly for causing the trouble, and she flees into the forest and out of this version of her story. Brandles then returns, semi-triumphant, to his father and brothers:

... I have beate my syster,
And the knyght, I made hym sweare
That whan we mete agayne,
He and I wyll together fyght
Tyll that we have spended our myght,
And that one of us be slayne. (515–20)

[I have beaten my sister. As for the knight, I made him swear that when we meet again, he and I will fight until we have expended all our might and one of us is slain.]

This ending is unconventional in three ways: the knight does not return triumphantly to Arthur's court; no marriage—only a missing maiden—commemorates the knight's successful performance of chivalric identity; and a defeated, hostile knight is not integrated as a member of the Round Table. Gawain and Brandles remain schoolyard bullies who use their might to jockey for position; the lady herself, rather than look to either for protection, flees altogether. If this is her experience of knights, no wonder she fears that the son she bears as a result of this day's events will be too "savage."

Chivalric Identities

Unlike *Ywain and Gawain*, *Lybeaus Desconus*, and *Sir Perceval of Galles*, *The Jeaste of Sir Gawain* exposes the limitations of a chivalry defined by martial violence; its repeated battles and suspended resolution call attention to the endless cycle of violence upon which such a definition depends. Nonetheless, *The Jeaste* is the exception rather than the rule; *Ywain and Gawain*, *Lybeaus Desconus*, and *Sir Perceval* all, in the end, valorize prowess and battle skills as knights' primary virtues. In spite of the dismay of Perceval's eventual wife at his lack of manners, and his mother's admonition that he behave himself in "hall and bower," there is very little hall or bower in the English adaptations of Chrétien's romances, which are considerably more concerned with courtly behavior; in the English tales, a lack of manners can certainly be overlooked if the knight is successful on the battlefield. The two narratives that we will discuss in this section—*The Avowyng of Arthur* and *Sir Corneus*, however, take place more in hall and bower than on the field, and thereby add to the definition of true knighthood by arguing that chivalric identity depends on more than the ability to be the biggest bully in the forest.

Interestingly enough, Arthur and his court do not prove as adept at negotiating the world of hall and bower as they are at winning on the battlefield. In the first of these romances, the late-fourteenth- or early-fifteenth-century *Avowyng of Arthur*, the court receives a lesson in chivalric behavior from Baldwin, one of the Round Table's lesser-known knights. This romance begins as its narrator identifies King Arthur and his knights as "elders" of this land, men who were wise, wary, bold, and powerful. He invokes these men as real—"no fantum ne no fabull" (17) [not phantoms nor fables]—reminding his audience that they "wote wele of the Rowun Tabull" (18) [well know about the Round Table] and the sterling reputation of its knights. Having thus established both Arthurian plenitude and reputation, the narrator begins a tale that explores the truth of the Arthurian reputation with which he begins.

As in tales like *Ywain and Gawain*, *Sir Perceval*, and *Lybeaus Desconus*, a challenge to the court occasions the plot. A huntsman interrupts Arthur's gathering, announcing that a monstrous boar—fierce, destructive, as big as a horse—is destroying the countryside and terrorizing all would-be hunters. "Quo durst abide him a buffe," the huntsman concludes, "Iwisse he were wighte" (63–64) [Who dares to attack him, surely, he is a strong man]. The boar bears a striking resemblance to Twrch Trwyth, the otherworldly boar that challenges Arthur's authority in *Culhwch and Olwen*, and its appearance in this narrative, along with the mysterious Tarn Wathelene, may well indicate that this tale stems from Welsh, rather than French, origins. As in the Celtic tale, the boar threatens Arthur's authority; as in French narratives, it presents an opportunity for Arthur and his knights to affirm their prowess. The king and three of his men, Gawain, Kay, and Baldwin, take up the challenge and ride off into the forest, where they discover that the boar is every bit as unnatural and formidable as the huntsman reported.

At this point in the romance, Arthur and his knights swear individual vows, each man intent on proving proving his chivalric worth, but the scene unfolds almost comically, as if a bunch of kids were engaged in playground one-upmanship. Arthur begins, swearing that he will bring down that satanic boar single-handedly, and then turns to the others: "I cummaunde yo / To do as I have done nowe: / Ichone make your avowe" (125–27) [I command you, do as I have just done; each one of you make your vow]. Gawain vows to sit all night beside Tarn Wathelene, the site of troubling and supernatural occurrences, as it was as well in *The Adventures of Arthur*, and Kay swears to ride throughout the forest and kill anyone who gets in his way. Arthur's, Gawain's, and Kay's vows conform to chivalric expectations in numerous romances: a knight proves his worth through bravery and prowess, conquest and destruction. Baldwin's vow, on the other hand, seems out of place in this context:

> Nevyr to be jelus of my wife,
> Ne of no birde bryghte;
> Nere werne no mon my mete
> Quen I gode may gete;
> Ne drede my dethe for no threte
> Nauthir of king ner knyghte. (139–44)

> [Never to be jealous of my wife, nor of any other beautiful woman; never to deny any man my food when I may get plenty, nor dread my death for any threat of king or knight.]

Baldwin's vow focuses not on bravery and combat but on behavior; not on proving himself, but on his relationship with others. Even his final promise not to fear death focuses more on someone else—the threat of king or knight—and on his reaction to that threat, rather than on proving his martial skills as the three others intend.

The companions separate, and the narrative turns to the first three vows. Arthur, in a fierce battle cast as a chivalric contest, defeats and expertly butchers the boar, but he accomplishes this feat through divine assistance. Kay fails miserably to defeat Menealfe, the only knight he encounters, and must be rescued by Gawain, who not only frees Kay but also wins the lady who was won by his opponent in an earlier encounter. Since Kay and his conqueror seek Gawain out at Tarn Wathelene, Gawain's fight with Menealfe counts as fulfillment of his vow. By the end of this sequence, Arthur's court has proved that it cannot uphold the chivalric values at its core. Arthur's victory was not single-handed, but required divine intervention, and Kay himself admits that his reputation is based more on bombast than on knightly abilities. Only Gawain has upheld his vow. In spite of this, the three, along with Menealfe, the lady, and the boar meat, return to court for a moment of Arthurian triumph in which Menealfe becomes a member of the Round Table.

In the second half of *The Avowyng of Arthur*, Arthur and Kay conspire to trick Baldwin into breaking his vow. Since this is Kay's idea, one can only assume he hopes to make himself feel better by embarrassing another knight. He begins by arranging an ambush, and six men accost Baldwin on his return to court. Rather than fleeing, Baldwin handily defeats them all and, when he arrives at court, reports that he had an uneventful journey. Next, the court sends a minstrel to spy on Baldwin's hall, and that minstrel remains a fortnight. He learns that Baldwin indeed denies no man meat; his tables are never bare, wine is never lacking, and no man is turned away. Finally, Arthur plants a naked knight in Baldwin's wife's bed and waits for his anger to explode, but instead Baldwin calmly explains:

> . . . hitte was atte hur awen wille:
> Els thurt no mon comun hur tille.
> And gif I take hitte thenne to ille,
> Muche maugreve have I.
> For mony wyntur togedur we have bene,
> And yette ho dyd me nevyr no tene. (897–902)

[No man would dare approach her unless she permitted it. And if I take it the wrong way, then I am to blame, because we have been together for many years and she has never been unfaithful.]

Such odd—and, by their lights, not altogether knightly—behavior puzzles Arthur and his knights, and they require further explanation of Baldwin's values. Baldwin tells them a tale of his time at war in Spain. Besieged, with five hundred men and three women servants, he learned, as the women killed each other out of jealousy, that one woman is perfectly capable of both doing the housework and seeing to the sexual needs of five hundred men—a disturbing instance of a standard trope in medieval misogyny that asserts that, when it comes to sex, women have an insatiable appetite, and one that seems at odds with Baldwin's earlier evaluation of his wife's virtue. Thus Baldwin concludes that a good woman, well supervised and with plenty to do, will be meek and mild, and there is no need to be jealous. He then goes on to explain that he does not fear death because one's "day" is appointed unless, through "wontyng of witte" (1040) [lack of good sense], one casts life away, a comment that sounds suspiciously like a jibe at Kay, and he illustrates his point with the tale of a coward who stays home from battle only to be killed in a freak accident. Finally, he elaborates on his earlier explanation for his generous hospitality as a means of sharing God's generosity with an illustration of the rhetorical power of conspicuous consumption: just as they were about to run out of provisions, he hosted an elaborate feast, causing his enemy's messenger to advise his lord to call off the siege, since the castle had an abundance of provisions, a scene that recalls Arthur's riotous party in the *Alliterative Morte*. After hearing these tales, Arthur affirms that Baldwin has kept his vow and proved himself to be all that a knight should be. The romance ends here, without the expected return to the Round Table. By ending the narrative with an affirmation of Baldwin's style of knighthood, *The Avowing of Arthur* shifts ideal chivalric identity from martial aggression to politic resignation and an ability to accept with equanimity life's vicissitudes. Above all, Baldwin seems to argue, one should not take one's honor too seriously.

Sir Corneus, identified as an Arthurian "bowrd" (4) [joke], develops themes similar to those in *The Avowyng of Arthur*. While the narrator begins with a quick nod to Arthurian plenitude, Arthur's many castles and towers and his great renown, he immediately focuses on an odd feature of this plenitude—the many beloved cuckolds at Arthur's court. As was also apparent in *The Avowyng of Arthur* and *The Jeaste of Sir Gawain*, female chastity and male honor and identity are tightly intertwined in the chivalric economy. Successful knights either win or are given women; defeated knights have their women taken by other men; despoiled daughters and sisters dishonor their fathers and brothers; and husbands whose wives deceive them lose chivalric honor. Medieval romances frequently explore the cultural anxieties attached to the specter of the cheating wife, stemming from both the threat such wives pose to one's masculinity and the fear that they will foist a false heir on the unsuspecting husband. There is Arthur's own fate, in which the adulterous relationship between Guinevere and Lancelot leads to the fall of the Round Table; there is the "wager romance," in which a man, often a traveling minstrel, leads an unwary husband to bet his possessions on his wife's chastity and then sets out to seduce her; and there is the chastity-test narrative, usually aimed not at the potentially unfaithful wife but at her husband, in which a magical device identifies those whose wives have been unfaithful. *Sir Corneus* belongs to this last category. However, while the repercussions from these chastity tests in other narratives are often quite dire for both husband and wife, *Sir Corneus* ends with a celebration of a new kind of chivalric brotherhood.

This narrative joke begins with an Arthurian feast, the moment that, in a standard romance, would introduce the adventure—a hostile knight, a chivalric challenge, a damsel in distress. In the narrative position of this challenge, readers find not one of these standard plot devices but an extraordinary drinking vessel: "If any cokwold dryke of it, / Spyll he schuld withouten lette" (31–32) [If any cuckold drinks from it, he will spill without fail]. Arthur amuses himself with this drinking horn, deriving "solas and game" (39) [pleasure and amusement] from ordering his men to drink without spilling wine on their tunics and thus establishing a new sort of chivalric hierarchy: instead of a Round Table, a Cuckold's Table. He crowns the cuckolds with willow garlands as a sign of their bad romantic fortunes and consoles this unlucky brotherhood with the best food and wine from the High Table. Arthur coyly admonishes them not to be angry with their wives because, even if women have compromised their husbands' masculine identities, without women there would be no manhood at all. The romance then focuses on a particular moment in which, the narrator informs us, "bygynnes game" (84) [the game begins], the arrival of the Duke of Gloucester on a visit to his monarch.

The duke, dining with Arthur, takes note of the Cuckold's Table and asks its meaning. Arthur takes great delight in describing the unhappy chance, or adventure, that has befallen these men, dwelling pruriently on their wives' self-marketing, their cheap and easy availability, their bawdy body language, and concluding gleefully that the men are cuckolds. The duke is amazed that Arthur is able to identify them as such, and Arthur, looking to add another knight to his table, orders the horn to be fetched and offers it to his guest. The duke, no fool, refuses to drink before Arthur. Arthur, defending his own honor, obliges, but gets a rude shock: "sone he spyllyd on hys brest" (179) [soon he spilled on his own breast]. King Arthur, as the narrator asserts, "for all hys grete honour, / Cokwold was" (94–95) [for all his great honor, was a cuckold]. His erstwhile victims gloatingly observe that the man who has spent so much time and effort scorning them is now their brother and Guinevere attempts to flee in shame. Arthur, however, accepts his humiliation in good humor, redefining cuckoldry from a badge of shame to a sign of chivalric brotherhood. He thanks the man who amused his wife while he was gone and seats the cuckolds beside him at the High Table, and the adventure ends in merriment. The narrator insists that Arthur "lyved and dyghed with honour" (251) [lived and died with honor].

In many ways, *Sir Corneus* is exactly what it claims to be, an Arthurian joke. (In fact variations on this theme still circulate today, including a rather crude one involving Lancelot and a chastity belt.) In other ways, its narrative presents a pointed critique of both chivalric honor and chivalric reputation. Arthur's separation of his court into manly men and cuckolds plays comically by arguing that a knight's identity depends solely on his wife, removing the chivalric deeds at the center of most romances from the equation.

Arthur's convenient redefining of cuckoldry and honor once he spills wine on his tunic suggests that honor is in the eye of the beholder—or in the dictates of the man who has the power to define it. Finally, the fact that Arthur and his court, for all their honor and reputation, are a merry brotherhood of cuckolds brings the renowned king and his famous knights down to the level of the lascivious clerks, unfaithful wives, and befuddled husbands who populate another popular and decidedly un-Arthurian medieval genre, the fabliau, best known today from Chaucer's *Miller's Tale*. While the romance focuses on highborn knights who earn their courtly ladies' favors through chivalric deeds (as Ywain wins Laudine), the fabliau focuses on cuckolded merchants and millers deceived by clever clerks. In romances, the emphasis is on love; in fabliaux, it is on sex. In both, women function as a marker of masculine accomplishment. As *Sir Corneus* strays into the realm of the fabliau, it suggests that Arthurian identity is a myth disseminated by the dominant class, a mask to hide the fact that there are no differences between the high and the low—that, indeed, they are "all of a freyry [brotherhood]" (215).

Taken together, *Sir Corneus* and *The Jeaste of Sir Gawain* undermine the high chivalric mythos of the more serious medieval British Arthurian romances. By focusing, to the exclusion of other themes, on the roles played by women and violence in the achievement and retention of chivalric identity, these tales reveal this chivalric identity to be tenuous and Arthur's utopia to be built on an unstable foundation: one battle, one treacherous knight, one unfaithful queen away from dissolution.

Otherworldly Encounters

The forests of adventure in many Arthurian romances, containing such marvels as Laudine's magic fountain, giants and ogres, demonic jailers, random maidens, and disappearing castles, owe their origin to tales of the Celtic otherworld. Arthurian romances often chronicle the interaction between the primary world of Arthur's court and the secondary world of the forest. The Arthurian use of the Celtic otherworld takes two distinct forms. In romances such as Chrétien's *Yvain* and its Middle English adaptation *Ywain and Gawain*, the otherworld figures as an outlying territory to be annexed, and the interaction between the two worlds centers on Arthurian conquest of it; these romances provide an insular version of Arthur's continental exploits. In other Arthurian romances, among them the short version of *Peredur*, the Celtic otherworld functions not as a kingdom to be conquered but as an alternative realm that serves to criticize the Arthurian order's values and mores. Ultimately, this Celtic otherworld challenges the Arthurian court's moral and ideological prerogatives, questioning the reputation that both defines and supports the Round Table's claims to supremacy. This section examines three such romances: Thomas Chestre's adaptation of Marie de France's *Lanval* and two popular Gawain romances, *The Wedding of Sir Gawain and Dame Ragnelle* and *Sir Gawain and the Carle of Carlisle*. These narratives use the interaction between a mysterious otherworld and Arthur's court to explore questions of class and gender.

Dating from the late fourteenth century, *Sir Launfal* is one of the few signed Middle English popular romances. "Thomas Chestre," the author informs us, "made thys tale" (1039). The second of two Middle English adaptations of Marie's twelfth-century narrative *Lanval*, it demonstrates the author's familiarity with both the earlier Middle English tale, *Sir Landevale*, and the genre that Marie herself classified as the Breton lai: short romances derived, according to Marie, from ancient oral tales told by the Celtic minstrels living in Brittany. The medieval versions of these tales are characterized by the interaction between the primary world of the court and a secondary world of faerie and magic. Unlike chivalric romances such as *Lybeaus Desconus*, *Sir Perceval*, *Sir Lancelot*, and *Ywain and Gawain*, these tales focus not on martial deeds and masculine honor but on a private world of love and desire that is often in direct competition with the needs and mores of the court. Marie's lais criticize Arthur's chivalric utopia more often than they celebrate it, and Chestre's adaptation of *Lanval* loses none of Marie's disenchantment with Arthur's famous Round Table. While *Sir Corneus*, which also demonstrates that the Arthurian Court may not live up to its chivalric reputation, ends in a raucous and good-humored cuckold's dance affirming the court's flawed community, *Sir Launfal* concludes with the self-exile of its hero and the befuddled court he leaves behind.

Written near the time of the Peasants' Revolt of 1381, Chestre's tale demonstrates none of the reverence for the golden Arthurian past apparent in so many other romances. The tale begins conventionally enough, with the evocation of an Arthurian once-upon-a-time: "By doughty Artours dawes / That helde Engelond yn good lawes" (1–2) [In days of mighty Arthur, who governed England with good laws]. It continues with the expected vision of Arthurian plenitude: great and famous knights, many riches, and a generous king. But it quickly introduces the snake in Arthur's paradise: his new bride. The traditional challenge to Arthur's authority comes in its established narrative slot—at a great feast—only in this case it comes from inside rather than from outside his walls. At the wedding feast, Guinevere distributes rich gifts to all of the Round Table's knights except one, Launfal, who—along with other unspecified knights—disliked her, "For the lady bar los of swych word / That sche hadde lemmannys under her lord, / So fele ther nas noon ende" (46–48) [for the lady had this reputation: she had lovers in addition to her lord, so many there was no end to them]. Launfal, saddened by this slight to his honor and what it predicts for his future position at court, fabricates a plausible excuse to remove himself from the Round Table. Arthur, regretful but unaware of Launfal's motivation, gives the knight money for his support and two of his own nephews for company, and sends him on his way.

This opening sequence establishes that Chestre is not merely translating Marie's tale; he shifts the blame for Launfal's departure from Arthur to Guinevere. In Marie's version of the narrative, Arthur "forgets" to distribute goods to Launfal, in spite of his dedicated service, and he neglects to pay him, leaving Launfal without the means to support himself at court. By exonerating Arthur and, from the very day of her wedding, casting Guinevere as a trollop, not just as Lancelot's adulterous lover but as a women with many lovers, Chestre overshadows Marie's critique of Arthur's flawed order with a misogynist diatribe. From beginning to end, Guinevere bears responsibility for the disruptions to the court, and subsequent Arthurian failings can be laid squarely at her feet.

Upon leaving the king's service, Launfal forfeits both social position and power, as he discovers when he requests lodgings from the mayor of Caerleon. Launfal discloses his new status:

I am departyd fram the Kyng,
And that rewyth me sore.
Ne ther thar no man, benethe ne above,
For the Kyng Artours love
Onowre me never more. (101–5).

[I am departed from the king, and I greatly regret it. Nor is there any man, of low or high class, who will ever honor me again for the love of King Arthur.]

He reminds the mayor of their former friendship, but this man responds, hardly persuasively, that his rooms are reserved. Launfal remarks scornfully that men with no position can expect these kinds of slights. Abashed, the mayor offers him an outbuilding in the orchard as lodgings, and Launfal accepts. A year passes; Launfal spends all of his money and finds himself not only without position but also without income or the means to procure any income. Arthur's nephews, wearing rags because Launfal cannot replace them with new clothes, return to court, leaving Arthur's former knight in poverty.

While Arthur's nephews do not divulge Launful's penury at court, excusing their threadbare robes as old hunting clothes, Launfal's misery increases. He finds himself excluded from the community of the town altogether: in danger of starving, uninvited to the religious festival, and unable to go to church in his shabby clothing. He begs a saddle and bridle from the mayor's daughter, saddles his horse, and rides out of the city; however, he and his horse are in such a sorry state that the horse slips and Launfal falls into the mud, with the narrator remarking, "Wherefore hym scornede many men / Abowte hym fer and wyde" (215–16) [Because of this, many men scorned him, near him and far and wide]. At this point in the romance, Launfal has lost his identity, lacking all markers that would identify him as a member of the aristocratic class, including an association with the royal court, the financial means to maintain his position, his sense of honor, such bare necessities as saddle, bridle, and food, and even the ability to stay on his horse.

In this state of deprivation, Launfal, the hero, finds his heroine. Resting under a tree, he spies two beautiful and richly attired maidens approaching him. He greets them, and they issue an invitation to visit their mistress, Dame Tryamour. Launfal, ever courteous, agrees and follows them into the forest. What he finds there changes his fortunes entirely: a pavilion, lavishly ornamented in jewels that surpass all King Arthur's possessions and decorated in crystal, enamel, and gold, presided over by an eagle with ruby eyes. In the pavilion stands a rich bed with costly purple linens, and on the bed is a stunning half-naked lady, the daughter of the King of Faerie, declaring her undying love for him. What more could any knight desire? Dame Tryamour proves to be Guinevere's foil in numerous respects. Whereas Guinevere withholds and hinders him, Tryamour bestows and enables Launfal to prosper as a knight. "Ryche I wyll make the," (318) [I will make you rich], she promises, as she gives him a purse that produces gold magically, a new horse, a squire, and an enchanted banner to protect him from the blows of other knights. She seals her promise by feeding him lavishly and taking him to bed. When Launfal rises to take his leave, she reveals her one condition: he must not boast, or even speak, of her. The minute he does so, he will lose her love, as well as, one assumes, the material benefits that she provides.

Launfal returns to the city in a much happier state than when he left, and Tryamour continually bestows bountiful gifts upon him. Ten richly armed knights arrive bearing gifts for Launfal, including elaborate and expensive clothes. When they ask a passing boy where he is to be found, the boy sneers, "Nys he but a wrecche! / What thar any man of hym recche?" (394–95) [He is nothing but a bum! Why would any man take notice of him?]. The boy nonetheless directs the knights and their treasure to the mayor's house, and the riches they carry make the mayor regret his treatment of the formerly impoverished knight. In a speech as unconvincing as his previous one when he asserted that his rooms were reserved, the mayor claims he "forgot" to invite Launfal to yesterday's festivities and begs him to come to dinner. Launfal refuses, commenting that the mayor neglected him in poverty and seeks his friendship only now that Launfal has "more gold and fe / . . . / Than thou and alle thyne" (412–14) [more gold and riches than you and all of your relatives].

Launfal repays his debts and sets up a rival court. He dresses himself in purple and ermine and holds elaborate feasts, feeding rich and poor alike, freeing prisoners, rewarding clerics, clothing minstrels, distributing lavish gifts, and bestowing honors on men from many countries. As he does so, he places himself in King Arthur's position: giver of feasts, distributor of goods, bestower of honor. Finally, he takes on all comers at a tournament designed to showcase his prowess. Sir Launfal easily takes the prize, and, emulating Arthur's generosity, he throws

> . . . a feste ryche and ryall
> That leste fourtenyght.
> Erles and barouns fale
> Semely wer sette yn sale
> And ryaly wer adyght. (494–98)

[a rich and royal feast that lasted a fortnight. Many earls and barons, royally dressed, were properly seated in the hall.]

His success reaches the ears of Sir Valentine of Lombardy, who sends his messenger to Launfal's court to issue a challenge, which Launfal readily accepts. He travels to Italy, kills Valentine, defeats his outraged lords, and returns triumphantly home.

Not surprisingly, this rival court attracts Arthur's attention. Moving quickly to assure Launfal's loyalty to the Round Table, Arthur announces a plenary feast that reasserts his royal position: forty days of elaborate entertainments for a court full of aristocratic men and beautiful ladies. At the end of these forty days, Arthur's supremacy and reputation for generosity are reestablished, as is Launfal's position at court. He has been appointed steward in recognition of his own knowledge of "largesse." Guinevere, however, reenters the story and disrupts Arthur's newly reinstituted utopia. She offers herself, in no uncertain terms, to Launfal, who, horrified, declares that he would never betray his lord. Guinevere launches into a tirade that alternates between death threats and slurs on his masculinity, concluding, "Thou lovyst no woman, ne no woman the— / Thou were worthy forlore!" (689–90) [You don't love any woman, and no woman loves you. You deserve to be destroyed!].

If Guinevere's initial failure to recognize Launfal in her distribution of gifts posed a threat to his position at court, her thinly veiled accusation in this tirade poses a threat to his chivalric reputation. The love of a woman signifies a man's worth and accomplishments: the more beautiful and wealthy the lady, the more worthy the knight. In the face of this second threat, Launfal does not leave quietly; he lashes out, affirming that his position is secure. After all, he loves a fairer woman than any she has seen in seven years. Yet, Launfal asserts, since his lady's ugliest maidservant is more worthy to be a queen than Guinevere herself, her position is not nearly as enviable. Unfortunately, this assertion reflects upon Arthur, as it suggests that Launfal's lady, and therefore Launfal's worth, exceeds the king's own. This suggestion truly inflames the king even more than Guinevere's assertion that Launfal propositioned her. When Arthur confronts the bound and accused knight, he identifies Launfal's boast about his lover's maids' beauty as vile treachery, but attributes his supposed propositioning of the queen to mere arrogance.

Fortunately for Launfal, Guinevere's reputation for promiscuity inclines the knights who must judge his claims to favor him, and they rule that Launfal merely needs to produce his lover and her beautiful maids to prove his innocence. Unfortunately, Launfal's boast has broken Tryamour's prohibition, and she, along with her riches, horse, and squire, have vanished, leaving Launfal materially and emotionally destitute. The span of a year and a fortnight granted Launfal to prove his case passes with no sign of Tryamour, and Launfal seems doomed to death or exile. Then comes the procession of richly clad maidens in two sets of ten, the second more beautiful than the first, to announce the arrival of their lady. Finally the lady herself arrives, dressed in dazzling jewels and rare cloth, riding a horse bedecked in gold and wearing a breastplate worth an earldom, and accompanied by a train of expensive hunting birds and hounds. This display of beauty, wealth, and power stuns Arthur's court, as does Tryamour's exoneration of her lover: "He bad naght her, but sche bad hym / Here lemman for to be" (998–99) [He did not proposition her; rather she asked him to be her lover]. Even Arthur admits the truth of Launfal's boast, an admission that seals Guinevere's fate, since she has bet her eyes that no one would prove more beautiful than her. Tryamour now forces her to fulfill her promise, blinding the queen with a magical breath. As Arthur's Round Table is plunged into disarray, Launfal escapes the court that has twice proved to be corrupt, unable to fulfill the promise of plenitude and honor that it makes to its knights. This noble knight exiles himself to Faerie, from which, the narrator tells us, Launfal offers a perpetual challenge to the knights of Arthur's court: a joust to prove their worth.

In this romance, the Round Table has been held up to the otherworld and found wanting. Rather than integrating the otherworld into the Arthurian order, as Ywain and Lybeaus Desconus do, Launfal abandons that order and chooses to exist on its borders. This reversal stands as a scathing commentary on Arthur's court, and on the aristocratic world that uses arguments about chivalry, noblesse oblige, and benevolent monarchy to justify its rights and privileges. Beneath its pomp, glitter, and brave knights, the court is a hollow place, ruled not by the king but by a queen who is little better than a whore. Arthur's inability to see through Guinevere breaks up the fellowship of the Round Table and threatens his entire kingdom. In addition to its misogynist portrayal of Guinevere and its equally misogynist valorization of the perfect woman, the one who will make a knight fabulously rich, appear in his bed whenever he calls, and then leave him to his masculine amusements, *Sir Launfal*'s portrayal of this failed utopia resonates on many levels, all of them a direct critique on the ruling class whose interests Arthurian romances generally support. A commentary that would have been particularly pointed during the reign of Richard II, *Sir Launfal* skewers a society that equates wealth with worth, and it ridicules a king ruled by a corrupt and self-interested favorite.

In *Sir Launfal*, the lady from the otherworld represents all that Arthur's world is not; she is and remains of Faerie. In the various versions of *The Wedding of Sir Gawain and Dame Ragnelle*, however, the otherworldly bride becomes the means of a possible reconciliation between the primary and secondary worlds. This bride first appears as repulsive as Tryamour is desirable, but, like the Beast in the well-known fairy tale *Beauty and the Beast*, she merely awaits the civilizing touch that will reveal her true form. This narrative was extremely popular in late medieval Britain. In addition to the romance discussed here, the Percy Folio contains an incomplete ballad-version, both John Gower and Geoffrey Chaucer composed renditions of the tale (Gower's *Tale of Florent* and Chaucer's *Wife of Bath's Tale*), and documents attest to a performance of the tale in 1299 at one of Edward I's Round Tables. Clearly this story struck a chord with its original audiences—for both its potential for comic burlesque and its own brand of fairy-tale wish fulfillment.

The tale opens with the standard establishment of the Arthurian good old days, introducing Arthur as the flower of kings and the best of knights, and his land as a paradise of chivalry. As in many Celtic otherworld romances, the action begins not in the court but in the woods. Arthur, stalking a hart, is separated from his retinue. He kills his prey, but as he advances on it, a fully armed knight accosts him, saying:

Welle imet, Kyng Arthour!
Thou hast me done wrong many a yere
And wofully I shall quytte the here;
I hold thy lyfe days nyghe done.
Thou hast gevyn my landes in certayn
With greatt wrong unto Sir Gawen.
Whate sayest thou, Kyng alone? (54–60)

[Well met, King Arthur! You have done me wrong for many years, and I will make you pay for it here. I consider your lifetime nearly over. For truly, you have given my lands, with great wrong, to Sir Gawain. What do you say, King, now that you are alone?]

We have certainly heard this challenge before, most explicitly in another Gawain romance, *The Adventures of Arthur*. In that case the challenging knight, Galeron, identified his lands as real places on the Celtic borders of England. In this instance Sir Gromer Somer Jour, clearly a denizen of the Celtic forests, is less specific about the lands' geographical location, but the accusation of unlawful conquest and redistribution is the same as the one made by Galeron. Interestingly, Arthur neither answers nor denies the accusation; instead he points out that if Sir Gromer insists on fighting an unarmed man, he will endanger his own status and reputation. The king promises that "that is amys I shalle amend itt" (71) [I'll fix what is wrong], but Gromer refuses to be bought off with gold or land. What he demands moves the romance from the world of chivalric contest to the world of courtly romance and, from there, into the territory of parody and satire:

To shewe me att thy comyng whate wemen love best in feld and town
And thou shalt mete me here withouten send
Evyn att this day twelfe monethes end;
[. . .]
And yf thou bryng nott answere withoute faylle,
Thyne hed thou shalt lose for thy travaylle. (91–98)

[To show me, when you come back, what women, both in field and
town, love best. And you shall meet me here, without me sending for
you, on this very day at the end of twelve months. . . . And if you do
not, without fail, bring me an answer, you will lose your head for your
trouble.]

Sir Gromer's request makes no sense in terms of the chivalric economy apparent in other romances. It could simply be seen as an impossible quest,
established to ensure Arthur's failure and subsequent execution. It could
also merely function as a narrative trigger for the tale's true interest—misogynist burlesque. Or it could be read more complexly as a fitting lesson
on conquest and colonization in which women, as they so often do, symbol-
ize land, territories, and masculine status. As the romance continues, these
various possibilities remain in play.

Arthur despondently rides back to court, where he confides in Gawain,
who offers a practical solution: he and the king should ride through the
country, asking everyone they meet, "What do women want?" and recording the answers in a book. Arthur agrees, and the two men spend the next
several months collecting two great books full of data. Gawain cheerfully
concludes that one of these answers must be right, but Arthur is uncertain; he rides back into the forest to search for more answers. There he
meets Dame Ragnelle, whose hideous appearance is allotted several lines
of vivid description: her yellow, protruding teeth, humped back, barrel-
shaped body, pendulous breasts. Arthur is appalled when she points out
that his life is in her hands and is even more appalled when she names
her price: Sir Gawain's hand in marriage. Arthur finds himself in quite
a dilemma. Gawain, ever loyal to king, kin, and brotherhood, is sure to
marry her to save Arthur's life, yet to marry such a foul wife, in spite of her
insistence that she is a lady, would damage Gawain's status and reputation
in the courtly world. Gawain, when presented with the situation, immediately agrees to the marriage, "thowghe she were as foulle as Belsabub (345)
[even if she were as ugly as the devil], pointing out that the bonds between
king and knight demand it.

Arthur rides back to Ragnelle with Gawain's consent. Ragnelle dismisses the standard misogynistic litany of possible answers to the question of what women want—beauty, many men, youth, flattery—insisting:

Butt there is one thyng is alle oure fantasye,
And that nowe shalle ye knowe.
We desyren of men above alle maner thyng
To have the sovereynté, withoute lesyng,
Of alle, bothe hyghe and lowe.
For where we have sovereynté, alle is ourys,
Thoughe a knyght be nevere so ferys,
And evere the mastry wynne.
Of the moste manlyest is oure desyre:
To have the sovereynté of suche a syre,
Suche is oure crafte and gynne. (420–30)

[But one thing is all of our fantasy, and now you shall know it. We desire, above all things, to have sovereignty over all men, both the highborn and the lowborn. I am not lying. For when we have sovereignty, everything is ours, even if a knight is very fierce and always wins the prize. We desire the manliest man: to have control over such a man, that is our craft and art.]

Women, Ragnelle argues, want sovereignty over men and, above all, over the manliest men. Ragnelle's revelation is, of course, a distillation of misogynist fears: what women really want is to emasculate men. However, the answer lies in the eye of the beholder. And, presiding over this case, those eyes belong not to an impartial justice or another woman but, the text reveals, to her brother, Gromer. Arthur certainly feels that he gives Gromer the true answer, but Gromer's response to losing reveals his own prejudices. He curses his "nag" of a sister, consigns her to the fire, and, swearing he will always be Arthur's mortal enemy, rides off in a rage.

Gromer may accept Ragnelle's answer as the true one, but in order to really determine the truth of her answer, we must look at her behavior once she acquires the manliest man. At first it does look as though Ragnelle desires sovereignty. In spite of the court's dismay and Guinevere's impolite hints that a private wedding would be best, Ragnelle insists on an elaborate ceremony and feast "before alle thy chyvalry" (529). An Arthurian feast follows, yet it is one in which the plenitude that marks Arthur's court is marred by Ragnelle's ugliness, her lack of manners, and her ravenous appetite. Here Ragnelle, the hideous and uncivilized bride from the conquered territories, is manifestly unfit for Arthur's court. At this point a page is missing from the manuscript, but as the narrative continues, it is clear that the bride and groom have retired to bed in the missing lines. Ragnelle chides Gawain for not performing his marital duty and asks, for Arthur's sake, that he at least kiss her. Gawain, ever dutiful, promises more than a kiss and, when he turns toward her, finds himself in bed with a gorgeous woman. Not surprisingly, he is both dumbfounded and ecstatic. His joy, however, is short-lived, as the lady informs him that her beauty "wolle nott hold" (658) [will not hold]; he must choose whether he will have her fair by night or by day. This forces Gawain to decide between his public reputation and his private pleasures. Unable to choose, he lets her make the decision, yielding sovereignty over her body and fate to her.

Ironically, Gawain's failure to decide offers the correct resolution to the dilemma. Since he has honored her, she honors him, and she will be fair both day and night. She then explains that she was under an evil enchantment, one that could be broken only when the best of men had both married her and given her sovereignty. Gawain's actions have freed her to be both beautiful and submissive, and this tale ends in the Arthurian plenitude disrupted first by Gromer's challenge and then by Ragnelle's perverse wedding feast. Gawain's courtesy and loyalty have tamed the "monstrous" on the borders of Arthur's kingdom, civilizing and assimilating it into the dominant order. Arthur even promises to leave Gromer alone for Ragnelle's sake. Despite the happy ending, it is clear that the author of *The Wedding of Sir Gawain and Dame Ragnelle* had problems with the contradiction between his tale's conclusion of Gawain's marital bliss and the multiple wives Gawain takes in the course of his literary adventures; he circumvents this narrative snag by explaining that they were married only five years but, nonetheless, she was his favorite wife.

Gawain's courtesy and integrity and his subsequent taking of a wife also serve the Arthurian court well in *Sir Gawain and the Carle of Carlisle*, in which a challenger from the Celtic borders again questions Arthur's right to sovereignty; this romance also ends with Gawain married to a woman from the forest realms. *Sir Gawain and the Carle of Carlisle*, like *The Wedding of Sir Gawain and Dame Ragnelle*, tells what was clearly a popular tale. In addition to the romance examined here, the tale exists in a later ballad version called simply *The Carle of Carlisle* and is connected both to the popular version of *Gawain and the Green Knight* and to the fourteenth-century al-literative poem, canonized as one of the masterpieces of Middle English literature, *Sir Gawain and the Green Knight*.

Sir Gawain and the Carle of Carlisle begins with a slightly different per-spective on Arthurian plenitude, one more in line with the chronicle tradi-tion, in which Arthur's supremacy lies not in his wealth and his knights but in his sovereignty over the Isle of Britain, including its Celtic margins. Then, like other Gawain and otherworld romances, the tale segues into a hunt. As it does in the *Adventures of Arthur*, a mysterious mist descends, separating the hunters from one another and setting the stage for an interaction with the otherworld. Gawain, Kay, and Baldwin, stranded in the forest, decide to seek shelter in the castle of a "carl," or churl, in spite of Baldwin's warning that most guests have not fared well at his hands. By identifying the owner of the castle as a "carl" rather than a lord, the romance invokes questions of class. This man may hold land and wealth, but he does not have a noble lineage; he does not belong to the privileged classes, nor does he necessarily share their values, customs, and manners. Yet the narrative comments more on Arthur's knights' manners, or lack thereof, than on the carl's. With the same arrogance he displays in *The Knightly Tale of Gologras and Gawain*, Kay declares that if the carl dares to treat them badly, he will beat the man until he stinks. Also true to character, Gawain points out that asking politely for shelter would probably yield better results.

The contrast between the two knights—Kay, who recognizes no man's rights but his own and will take what he wants by force, and Gawain, who accords each man his property and relies on manners and negotiation to achieve his ends—continues throughout their stay at the castle. That they are indeed in a place beyond the borders of Arthur's kingdom becomes ap-parent from the moment they meet their host, a giant surrounded by wild beasts. They find him drinking wine from a nine-gallon gold cup as he warns them that "her no corttessy thou schalt have, / But carllus corttessy" (277–78) [here you shall have no courtesy except a churl's courtesy]. Kay and Baldwin neither show appreciation for this churl's courtesy nor display much of their own. In spite of that, they find their horses well cared for, but still they turn out their host's own foal from the stall. They sit down without an invitation, and Kay declares that the carl's beautiful wife is inappropriately wed.

Gawain, on the other hand, puts the foal in the stall with his own horse and feeds it, then politely waits to be asked to sit at the table, and although he too lusts after the carl's beautiful wife, he shows proper shame when the man orders him to squelch his unseemly desires and drink his wine instead. Gawain also complies with a number of odd requests from his host, beginning with the carl's demand that Gawain take a spear from the wall and throw it at his face, and continuing with his request for Gawain to climb naked into bed with the aforementioned wife and kiss her. The carl stops this game when it goes beyond kissing, crying, "Whoo ther! / That game I the forbede" (467–68) [Whoa there! I forbade you to play that game]. Having proved his obedience and courtesy, Gawain is rewarded. The wife leaves and the carl's equally beautiful daughter appears; the father orders the daughter to "wern hyme nott to playe" (477) [do not deny him his play], assuring Gawain that he should enjoy her throughout the night. Gawain happily does as he is bid.

Gawain's exceptional courtesy and compliance to a man's desires in his own house succeeds in contrast to the violence offered by countless dead knights, who now reside as a pile of bones on the carl's lands. Gawain's manners tame the carl, transforming him from an enemy in the forest who offers violence and villainy to errant knights into a functioning member of Arthur's community. The carl repents his previous behavior, promises to "forsake mi wyckyd lawys" (541) [forsake my wicked ways], and vows to have masses said for the souls of the knights he destroyed. He welcomes Arthur to an elaborate feast, and the romance ends as the carl becomes a knight of the Round Table and builds an abbey. This edifice signifies his assimilation into both the political and the religious order, and Gawain weds the daughter to cement further the bond between their realms.

The later ballad version, *The Carle of Carlisle*, adds an episode that both ties it to the Gawain and the Green Knight romances and makes the transformative powers of Arthur's court more clear. At the same time, it takes away its source text's underlying theme of social mobility. In this version, the key point in the plot is a "beheading game" in which the carl orders Gawain to cut off his head. When Gawain obeys, he frees from the carl's form a nobleman who, like Ragnelle, was under a curse—in this case one that could be broken only when one of Arthur's knights agreed to behead him. Arthur's court here possesses the power to free and transform the disenfranchised. However, Gawain's blow merely reveals what was there all along. The carl does not climb to the ranks of the nobility; rather, he returns to his true form—an addition that mitigates the earlier romance's exploration of social assimilation.

In each of these three narratives, *Sir Launfal*, *The Wedding of Sir Gawaine and Dame Ragnelle*, and *Sir Gawain and the Carle of Carlisle*, an otherworld, based on Celtic traditions and identified with the Celtic margins of England, presents a challenge to Arthur's court. In all but *Launfal*, the court, through

Gawain, proves itself up to the challenge. Its values, mores, and reputation are affirmed. Gawain, through his successful adventures, hands Arthur's reputation back to him, allowing the narrative to end where it began: in Arthurian plenitude.

"Is This Arthur's House?" Sir Gawain and the Green Knight

In contemporary Arthurian cinema, including such films as *Camelot, Monty Python and the Holy Grail,* and *Excalibur,* Lancelot is the "star" of Arthur's Round Table. However, as a look back at the romances we have discussed demonstrates, in medieval Britain that role belonged to Gawain. Even in romances adapted from French sources, such as *The Knightly Tale of Gologras and Gawain, Lybeaus Desconus, Ywain and Gawain, Sir Perceval, Sir Lancelot,* and *The Jeaste of Sir Gawain,* the medieval British texts either select episodes that feature Gawain or highlight his participation in the narrative. In these tales Gawain occupies the position of Arthur's right-hand man, both on the battlefield and at the bargaining table. He forfeits this position only in *Lancelot,* where, in spite of his best efforts, he cannot defend Arthur's borders. In the romances of British origin, *The Adventures of Arthur, The Avowyng of Arthur, Sir Gawain and the Carle of Carlisle,* and *The Wedding of Sir Gawain and Dame Ragnelle,* Gawain goes beyond being Arthur's right-hand man to represent both the epitome and the future of Arthurian ideals. Through his courtesy he redresses Kay's boorishness and ineptitude; through his prowess he silences those who would challenge or criticize Arthur's authority—such as Galeron, Sir Gromer, and the carl, who all claim that Arthur wrongly appropriated their lands—and integrates renegade territories, assuring Arthur's control over a unified island of Britain.

Thus it is not surprising that Gawain, not Lancelot, is the hero of the most widely praised Middle English Arthurian romance, *Sir Gawain and the Green Knight,* a courtly text that draws on popular romances chronicling Gawain's interactions with the otherworld. In fact, we can reasonably speculate that a more popular version of this tale was much better known in the Middle Ages than its canonized counterpart. For instance, William Paston, a lawyer of humble origins who rose to land and respectability in the early fifteenth century and founded the family now famous for the Paston letters, a vivid record of life in fifteenth-century England, lists a *Green Knight* in his library catalogue. This text, however, was almost certainly closer to the straightforward romp called *The Greene Knight,* compiled in the Percy folio, than to the elaborate alliterative poem found in modern anthologies.

Sir Gawain and the Green Knight entered the literary canon when it was edited in the nineteenth century, and since then has been elevated until it is considered almost equal to the works of Chaucer. It remains, along with Malory's *Morte Darthur*, the medieval Arthurian text most likely to be taught in an undergraduate survey. The fact that *Sir Gawain and the Green Knight* has found its way into the canon reflects the assumptions and prejudices of literary studies. Unlike the popular romances, *Sir Gawain and the Green Knight* tells a complex and ambiguous tale that lends itself to scholarly analysis and has, indeed, supported a critical industry. Its structure, symbolic resonances, and use of language are highly wrought and beautifully executed. If the popular romances are the equivalent of today's genre fiction, *Sir Gawain and the Green Knight* is the equivalent of a Pulitzer Prize–winning novel: literary, artistic, and sophisticated. It survives, along with three other alliterative poems, *Pearl*, *Patience*, and *Cleanness*, in a single manuscript. Critics conventionally attribute these four poems to a single author, often characterized as a "clerk" or secretary attached to a provincial court that sits, on the evidence of the poems' dialect, in the northwest of England; this poet is referred to either as the *Pearl* Poet or the *Gawain* Poet. However, no concrete evidence supports assigning the four texts to a single author, merely speculation based upon the fact that they were all copied by the same hand, in the same dialect, and all use an alliterative verse form. Arguments based on similarities of theme are even less convincing because they fail to consider the poem's secular concerns, requiring a heavily allegorical reading of *Sir Gawain and the Green Knight* as primarily a religious poem.

In fact, *Sir Gawain and the Green Knight*'s Arthurian themes clearly distinguish it from the three religious-themed poems in the manuscript. Like other Arthurian texts, the romance takes readers back to the Arthurian past to explore issues of conquest, honor, sovereignty, and power. *Sir Gawain and the Green Knight* begins with a historical overview of Britain, narrating a romance of origins drawn from the chronicles that ties Britain firmly to the classical tradition. The opening stanza includes the siege of Troy and the founding of Rome, as the narrator traces the sovereignty of the island to Brutus, the great-grandson of Aeneas. This overview deftly writes the original Celtic inhabitants out of the story. The narrator then focuses on Britain and its tumultuous and troubled past—"Bolde bredden thereinne, baret that lofden, / In mony turned tyme tene that wroghten" (21–22) [Valiant men bred there, who thrived on battle. / In many an age bygone, they brought about trouble (trans. Winny, here and throughout)]. He succinctly sums up the island's history:

Where werre and wrake and wonder
Bi sythez hatz wont therinne,
And oft both blysse and blunder
Ful skete hatz skyfted synne. (16–19)

[Where war and grief and wonder
Have visited by turns,
And often joy and turmoil
Have alternated since.]

The poem presents the British past as an endless cycle of "joy and turmoil," troubled by valiant men and wars, setting the scene for the entrance of Arthur and his utopia: a moment of wonder and joy in a history of war and trouble. By placing Arthur's court within this larger picture, *Sir Gawain and the Green Knight* from its very beginning calls attention to the fact that this moment in history is both transcendent and transient. Of all British kings, the poem tells us, Arthur was "the hendest" (25) [noblest].

After introducing this noblest of kings, the narrator settles into telling his tale "as I in toun herde" (31) and describes Arthur's Christmas court. As readers might expect in an Arthurian romance, this description establishes Arthurian plenitude, and this version of that plenitude focuses insistently on the court at play, the "rych revel oryght and rechles merthes" (40) [rich revelry and carefree amusements], fifteen days of tournaments and jousts, "Dere dyn upon day, daunsyng on nyghtes" (47) [Days full of uproar, dancing at night]. The narrator summarizes the plentiful pleasures of Arthur's feast:

With all the wel of the worlde thay woned ther samen,
The most kyd knyghtez under Krystes selven,
And the lovelokkest ladies that ever lif haden,
And he the comlokest kyng that the court haldes;
For al watz this fayre folk in her first age,
        On sille,
    The hapnest under heven. (50–56)

[With all of life's best, they spent that time together,
The most famous warriors in Christendom,
And the loveliest ladies who ever drew breath,
And he the finest king who rules the court.
For these fair people were then in the flower of youth
        In the hall.
    Luckiest under heaven.]

This court is not the martial entourage of chivalric romances, as in *The Knightly Tale of Gologras and Gawain*, nor the settled center to which a new knight journeys to seek recognition, as in *Lybeaus Desconus* and *Sir Perceval*. Instead it is a virtually endless party, occupied by the beautiful people, smug and snug in their wealth and reputation, hosting an over-the-top holiday bash.

As they settle down to their New Year's feast, gorgeously dressed and exclaiming excitedly over their gifts, they wait expectantly for the next amusement. None is more eager than Arthur, who is "joly of his joyfnes, and sumquat childgered" (86) [lively in his youth, and a little boyish] and fidgety with his "yonge blod and his brayn wylde" (89) [young blood and restless mind]. Before eating on feast days, he demands entertainment: a good story, a challenge, a joust. Arthur stands while the elaborate feast is served and soon finds more entertainment than he bargained for:

> Ther hales in at the halle dor an aghlich mayster,
> On the most on the molde on mesure hyghe;
> Fro the swyre to the swange so sware and so thik,
> And his lyndes and his lymes so longe and so grete,
> Half etayn in erde I hope that he were,
> [. . .]
>> For wonder of his hwe men hade,
>> Set in his semblant sene;
>> He ferde as freke were fade,
>> And overal enker-grene. (136–50)

> [When there bursts in at the hall door a terrible figure,
> In his stature the very tallest on earth.
> From the waist to the neck so thick-set and square,
> And his loins and his limbs so massive and long,
> In truth half a giant I believe he was,
> [. . .]
>> His hue astounded them,
>> Set in his looks so keen;
>> For boldly he rode in,
>> Completely emerald green.]

The Green Knight's precipitous arrival at Arthur's court conventionally signals the beginning of the romance's major plot, the adventures that follow a challenge to Arthur's court and its authority. But even from the first moment, this challenge is out of the range of Arthurian experience. The challenger himself is otherworldly: half a giant, disturbingly green. Furthermore, he defies categorization. Giants in other Arthurian romances are clearly monstrous in their savagery. Even the Carl of Carlisle, with all his his riches, is also surrounded by wild beasts and marked as "churlish." The Green Knight, on the other hand, apart from his size and color, epitomizes chivalric masculinity. He is well-made and elegant; both he and his horse wear elaborate and costly garments and trappings, intricately embroidered in the latest fashion, whose materials and workmanship declare their wearer's wealth and aristocratic social position. The knight's highly civilized apparel contrasts with his long hair, his beard "like a bush," and his intimidating size: "Hit semed as no mon myght / Under his dynttez dryghe" (201–2) [It seemed that no one could / His massive blows endure]. Furthermore, although Arthur's knights might well expect such an unearthly challenger to arrive armed to the hilt, this man wears no armor and carries no chivalric weapon, spear, or shield. Instead he bears a holly branch in one hand and an axe in the other. The Green Knight lies outside the court's experience, and they can only watch in astonished silence as he makes his way to the high table and demands, "Wher is . . . the governour of this gyng?" (224–25) [Where is . . . the governor of this crowd?]. "For uch mon had mervayle," the narrator explains, "quat hit mene myght / That a hathel and a horse myght such a hwe lach" (233–34) [For everyone marvelled what it could mean / That a knight and a horse might take such a colour]. Stunned by this challenger, who they conclude can only be a phantom or a fairy, Arthur's self-satisfied knights and ladies finds themselves struck dumb with fear. The court that a moment ago pealed with laughter and games falls silent, "As al were slypped upon slepe" (244) [As though everyone fell asleep].

Although the narrator qualifies his assertion that the knights have been silenced by fear, pointing out that he thinks a few might merely have been acting politely, his speculation is unconvincing, particularly in light of the events that follow. Arthur alone stands and courteously greets his visitor, inviting him to join the feast. The Green Knight refuses, baldly stating his business at Arthur's court:

> Bot for the los of the, lede, is lyft up so hyghe,
> And thy burgh and thy burnes best ar holden,
> [. . .]
> The wyghtest and worthyest of the worlds kynde,
> [. . .]
> And here is kydde cortayse as I haf herd carp,

And that hatz wayned me hider, iwyis, at this tyme.
[. . .]
Bot for I wolde no were, my wedez ar softer.
Bot if thou be so bold as alle burnez tellen,
Thou wyl grant me godly the gomen that I ask. (258–73)

[But because your name, sir, is so highly regarded,
And your city and warriors reputed the best,
[. . .]
The most valiant and excellent of all living men,
[. . .]
And here courtesy is displayed, as I have heard tell,
And that has brought me here, truly, on this day.
[. . .]
But since I look for no combat I am not dressed for battle.
But if you are as courageous as everyone says,
You will graciously grant me the game that I ask for.]

Again the Green Knight confounds the court's expectations; he comes to challenge them and to force them to uphold their reputation, but he explicitly states that he does not come looking for combat, only a game. Arthur does not even listen to the Green Knight's speech; he immediately leaps up and assures his visitor that they are ready and willing to fight him, armor or no armor. The Green Knight's response dismisses both the knights and their vaunted reputation. He points out that he cannot possibly fight "berdlez chylder" (280) [beardless children] and again proposes his odd "Chrystemas gomen" (283) [Christmas game]:

If any so hardy in this hous holdez hymselven,
Be so bolde in his blod, brayn in his hede,
That dar stifly strike a strok for an other,
I schal gif hym of my gyft thys giserne ryche. (285–88)

[If anyone in this hall thinks himself bold enough,
So doughty in body and reckless in mind
As to strike a blow fearlessly and take one in return,
I shall give him this marvellous battle-axe as a gift.]

This game, like the Green Knight himself, confounds boundaries: a ritual exchange of blows with a deadly battle-axe as the prize is hardly the equivalent of chess. Additionally, having dismissed Arthur's knights as beardless boys, too young for real combat, he implies that there may not even be anyone in the court manly enough to play his game.

The Green Knight is very nearly proved right, since the response to his proposition is less than enthusiastic: "If he hem stouned upon fyrst, stiller were thanne / Alle the heredmen in halle, the hyghe and the lowe" (301–2) [If he petrified them at first, even stiller were then / All the courtiers in that place, the great and the small]. Contemptuously he asks them:

> What, is this Arthures hous? . . .
> That al the rous rennes of thurgh ryalmes so mony?
> Where is now your sourquydrye and your conquestes,
> Your gryndellayk and your greme, and your grete wordes?
> Now is the revel and the renoun of the Rounde Table
> Overwalt wyth a worde of on wyghes speche,
> For al dares for drede withoute dynt schewed! (309–15)

> [What, is this Arthur's house? . . .
> That everyone talks of in so many kingdoms?
> Where are now your arrogance and your victories,
> Your fierceness and wrath and your great speeches?
> Now the revelry and repute of the Round Table
> Are overthrown with a word from one man's mouth,
> For you all cower in fear before a blow has been struck.]

The Green Knight punctuates his assessment with unbridled laughter, dismissing the court that so recently celebrated its unmatched reputation as not worthy of its renown and not entitled to either its arrogance or its boasting. Much more is now at stake than a Christmas game; the entire legend of Arthur and his knights is at risk. Arthur, enraged, agrees to the Green Knight's "folly" and takes up the axe. However, if Arthur is forced to meet the challenge himself, the court is still compromised, because Arthur's reputation depends upon having a houseful of brave knights ready to take on all foes. Gawain therefore steps forward and deftly requests "the game," arguing that, since his worth lies solely in his relationship to the king, the court has the least to lose by his death. As Gawain makes his argument, he reaffirms the bravery and courtesy of the Arthurian court, values that the Green Knight's challenge has called into question.

Arthur advises his nephew to make sure to strike his blow "aright," pointing out that, if he does so, he will not need to worry about the return blow to be given, according to the Green Knight's initial challenge, in a year and a day. Note that the Green Knight has not specified that the blows exchanged be deadly; in fact, he has explicitly called this exchange a game and not a battle. Gawain could simply tap the knight, or hit him with the blunt edge of the axe. Arthur, however, decides that violence will silence the Green Knight and his laughter forever, allowing the court to return to its amusements. After agreeing to the terms of the challenge, Gawain steps up and beheads the unarmed and passive knight. The Green Knight's head, streaming blood, flies to the floor; Arthur's courtiers kick it as it rolls past, and by all laws of nature as the court knows them, the episode should be over.

To the courtiers' surprise, the headless knight swoops up his head, mounts his horse, and, holding his head by the hair, turns its face toward the high table and orders Gawain to keep his bargain, to come to the Green Chapel to receive his return blow. A moment later he has jerked the reins and "Halled out at the hal dor, his hed in his hande" (458) [hurtled out of the hall door, his head in his hand]. Arthur's court should be astonished, ashamed, even abashed. Ignoring that they have, at best, behaved badly, and the fact that Gawain's future is uncertain, the court glosses over these bizarre events with laughter, deciding that this "interlude," fitting for Christmas, was arranged for Arthur's appreciation; he has seen a marvel and can now enjoy the feast. The king tells his nephew to hang up his axe, joking that it "hatz innogh hewen" (477) [has severed enough]. The incident is domesticated as one of the marvelous tales of the Round Table, and the knights and ladies return to the party that the Green Knight so rudely disrupted.

Unlike other romances, in which the return to the feast marks the successful completion of the knight's quest and either the elimination or integration of the challenger, in *Sir Gawain and the Green Knight* none of these events has occurred. The feast is mere whistling in the dark—men "mery quen thay han mayn drynk" (497) [light-hearted when they have strong drink]. The second part of the romance swiftly leaves the feast to chronicle the changing seasons as Gawain's year's respite draws inexorably to a close. That Gawain might ignore his commitment to meet the Green Knight is never an option. Both his honor and the court's reputation depend upon his fulfillment of his vow. The court may grumble about the loss of such a man to a strange game, but they realize that the bargain must be kept. When the time comes, Arthur's court carefully arms its representative, equipping him as best it can to face the challenges that lie ahead.

This arming sequence dwells on the costly and rare materials of Gawain's robes, their intricate embroidery, the circlet of diamonds on his brow, the craftsmanship of his armor—its bright gold and polished steel—and the elaborate decoration of his horse's tack. These descriptions are in keeping with the emphasis on wealth and power in countless romances, in which the ideal knight is defined as a strong warrior, richly and beautifully armed. Once Gawain is armed and waiting, the courtiers bring him his shield, and the definition of ideal knighthood shifts, adding a dimension absent from those festivities. The narrator spends two stanzas describing Gawain's shield, going into great detail about the symbolism of the gold pentangle painted upon it. The pentangle, in its endless knot, represents faultless virtue, "Voyded of uche vylany (634) [Devoid of all vice]. Its five points refer to the five "fives" that make an ideal knight: perfect in the five senses, dexterous in five fingers, putting one's faith in the five wounds of Christ, drawing one's strength from the five joys of Mary, whose image, painted on the inside of Gawain's shield, keeps his courage from failing, and possessing the five essential chivalric virtues of generosity, fellowship, purity, courtesy, and compassion. These interlocking fives, as the unbroken lines of the pentangle indicate, are crucial to perfect knighthood; if a knight lacks one, the whole design is broken. Gawain, the narrator insists, embodies the values of the shield's design.

Many critics take this lengthy description of the pentangle and Gawain's association with it as a statement of the romance's religious concerns, allegorizing Gawain's adventures as a kind of *Pilgrim's Progress* in which the Christian knight battles and either defeats or succumbs to temptation. In these readings of the poem, *Sir Gawain and the Green Knight* measures an explicitly Christian chivalry against a secular chivalry that is found wanting. However, the reduction of the romance to strictly a Christian allegory or religious tract misses the poem's secular concerns, including its exploration of power and reputation. Such readings accept the court's evaluation of Gawain and, through him, of itself. Remember, this is the same court we saw in the first part of the romance, where reputation and reality proved to be seriously unaligned. When Gawain sallies forth as Mary's Knight or the Knight of the Pentangle, the substance behind the title has yet to be proved. So far this definition of Arthurian virtue, like the court's reputation for bravery and courtesy, is merely hype. What happens to Gawain in the rest of the poem, like the Green Knight's Christmas game, tests the truth of Arthur's court's self-definition.

Gawain's adventures begin as he journeys into a hostile wilderness, inhabited only by dragons, wolves, and wild men, in which he wanders in the freezing rain and sleeps on the bare rocks. This harsh journey, away from the glamour and comfort of the court, can be read in support of allegorizing the tale as rough equivalent to Jesus's temptation in the wilderness, or a time of solitude and purification. It can also be read literally as a journey away from the capital, through the uncharted wilds of Britain and north into the Celtic borderlands. Christmas approaches as Gawain stumbles through a dense, wild, desolate forest; desperate for a place to observe the festival and hear mass, Gawain prays to find lodging. He has hardly finished crossing himself when his prayers appear to be answered. Seemingly out of nowhere, a splendid, shining castle appears, ornately built in the latest fashion. Delighted, Gawain rides toward it and asks for lodging, which is readily granted. Courteous knights care for his horse and lead him to the castle's lord, eventually identified as Bertilak, who welcomes him and escorts him to a richly appointed bedchamber, where Gawain is provided with costly robes. He changes and sits down to an elaborate feast, replete with rare and expensive dishes and fine wines.

Wandering in the forest, Gawain has stumbled upon an otherworldly court, one that clearly rivals Arthur's in its architecture, material abundance, and hospitality. Its inhabitants also rival the lords and ladies of the Round Table: a handsome lord in the prime of his life, strong and impressive knights, and the fairest lady Gawain has ever seen—lovelier than Guinevere, he judges (945). Such otherworldly courts in Arthurian romance serve to challenge Arthur's court, testing the mettle of the Arthurian knights who stumble upon them. And this court is no exception. Once they realize that "Gawain himself" (906) is in their midst, the lord laughs and his knights are delighted to have among them the man whose reputation as a paragon of good manners, master of conversation, and expert at "love-talking" precedes him. Unfortunately, this reputation belongs to the Gawain of the glittering Christmas court and not to the Knight of the Pentangle, who left the safety of that court to face almost certain death. With his New Year's Day appointment looming, Gawain does not want to be defined by his considerable success as a ladies' man (as demonstrated in romances such as *The Jeaste of Sir Gawain* and *King Arthur and King Cornwall*). The Knight of the Pentangle owes his chaste allegiance to the Virgin and numbers "purity" among his unassailable virtues.

Included in these virtues are also "courtesy," the ability to negotiate social situations gracefully without giving offence, and "fellowship," loyalty to the male bonds at the foundation of aristocratic society. The bargain that Gawain strikes with his host at the end of the evening's merriment will test these three chivalric virtues and also his adherence to the mandate to put his faith in the five wounds of Christ and draw his courage from the five joys of Mary. When Gawain declares that he is seeking the elusive Green Chapel, which he must find or else be false to his oath, his host assures him that he knows exactly where to find it and that Gawain can, with a clear conscience, stay with them until New Year's Day. When the host proposes a bargain, Gawain promptly replies, echoing the events in *Sir Gawain and the Carle of Carlisle*, that he knows his duty as a guest and will happily do as he is bid. The bargain is quite attractive for a knight who has spent months roughing it in the wilderness: for the next three days he will sleep in, attend mass, eat nice meals, and keep company with his host's wife, while the host arises before dawn to go hunting. The two men will also swap their winnings at the end of each day. Gawain readily agrees, and they drink to seal the bargain. The exchange of winnings, like the exchange of blows in part I, tests Gawain and, through him as its representative, the exalted reputation of the Arthurian court. If the Green Knight's challenge and the court's decidedly lackluster response to that challenge has called its bravery and courtesy into question, the exchange-of-winnings bargain will give Gawain a chance to prove that he possesses the qualities that he advertises with the pentangle on his shield.

The game begins the next morning, as part III of the romance opens with Gawain in his bed. His host's wife sneaks into the room and seats herself at the slumbering knight's bedside. Taken aback, Gawain pretends to be asleep and hopes she will leave; when she stays, he reluctantly opens his eyes to spar with the very determined suitor. Claiming him as her prisoner, the lady says she can think of numerous activities they can enjoy in bed while her husband and his men are off hunting and all the house servants are still asleep. She calls upon his reputation, "hym that al lykez" (1234) [the man everyone loves], and assures him that he is "welcum to my cors" (1236) [welcome to me].

Her blatant offer poses a threat to both fellowship and purity, but it also requires Gawain to juggle words desperately to retain his courtesy. He demurs, saying he is unworthy, and offers to amuse her in other ways. The debate that follows makes explicit a theme introduced by Gawain when he asks to take on the Green Knight's challenge: the question of a knight's worth, what it is based on, and who determines it. In the first part of the romance, worth derives from adherence to a secular courtly chivalry—noble blood, valor, loyalty, courtesy—and when Gawain describes himself as of little worth, he actually proves himself very valuable. Furthermore, if he is the most worthless of knights—"lest lur of my lyf" (355) [my death would be the least loss]—then his successful defense of Arthurian reputation is worth even more. In the second part, the terms for judging Gawain's worth shift to the values represented by the pentangle, adding a religious dimension to the chivalric identity explored in the poem. Held up to these standards, Gawain is valued "as golde pured" (633) [like refined gold]. Once he enters Bertilak's castle, the terms of evaluation shift yet again, adding "love-talking," a virtue best judged by the lady, to his range of chivalric traits. The lady explicitly values Gawain, arguing that there "ar ladyes innoghe" (1251) [a great many ladies] who would rather have Gawain at their beck and call than "much of the garysoun other golde that thay haven" (1255) [much of the treasure or wealth they possess]. Later in the conversation, she reiterates her evaluation of Gawain as desirable merchandise:

> For were I worth al the wone of wymmen alyve,
> And al the wele of the worlde were in my honde,
> And I schulde chepen and chose to cheve me a lorde,
> For the costes that I haf knowen upon the, knyght, here
> Of bewté and debonerté and blythe semblaunt,
> And that I haf er herkkened and halde hit here trwee,
> Ther schulde no freke upon folde bifore yow be chosen. (1269–75)

> [For if I were the worthiest of all women alive,
> And held all the riches of the earth in my hand,
> And could bargain and pick a lord for myself,
> For the virtues I have seen in you, sir knight, here,
> Of good looks and courtesy and charming manner—
> All that I have previously heard and now know to be true—
> No man on earth would be picked before you.]

Gawain finds himself caught between three systems of chivalric evaluation, desperately trying to meet the requirements of each. He must manage to placate the lady, behave honorably toward his host, and maintain the pentangle's virtues unbroken. This task becomes harder as the days pass and the lady grows more blatant in her seductions, coming into his room in increasing states of undress, suggesting that a man of his many virtues can use force if he likes, and calling into question his very identity—"Bot that ye be Gawan, hit gotz in mynde" (1293) [But that you should be Gawain I very much doubt]—when he fails to beg at least a kiss. For two days Gawain upholds his values, fending the lady off with "virtuous" banter and "allowable" kisses that he exchanges for his host's killings at the end of each day.

The scenes between Gawain and the lady are comical, with Gawain peering through his lashes, begging to get up and dressed, confounded by the lady's alarmingly scant clothing and even more alarming offers.

As Gawain lies and, sometimes, cowers in bed "conversing" with his hostess, Bertilak rides into the forest, enthusiastically hunting his prey. These hunting scenes parallel the bedroom scenes, thus providing a stark contrast between the silken, feminine world that Gawain inhabits and the vigorous, masculine world of the hunt. In the forest, Bertilak is in control; he pursues. In the bedroom, the lady is in control, and Gawain flees. Next to Bertilak's larger-than-life masculinity, Gawain, with his good looks and courtly manners, seems boyish at best as he huddles in bed like a coy maiden. The vivid and bloody descriptions of the hunt, kill, and butchering of the prey have often been read as an allegorical commentary on the action in the bedroom. The first day, the Lord and his men pursue deer; the second day, a boar; the third day, a fox. Deer, or *harts*, are often associated with the lady pursued by the courtly lover; the boar here has been read as the increasing use of force, and the fox as deception and wiliness. Indeed, the tenor of the bedroom conversation changes each day as the lady becomes more and more determined, until she gives up on blatant seduction and changes her tactics.

The lady offers Gawain an exchange of love tokens, first a ring, which Gawain refuses since he has nothing to give her in return, and then, taking it from her body, a girdle, or belt. Gawain again refuses, and the lady, to use a hunting metaphor, closes in for the kill:

> For quat gome so is gorde with this grene lace,
> While he hit hade hemely halched aboute
> Ther is no hathel under heven tohewe hym that myght,
> For he myght not be slayn for slyght upon erthe. (1851–54)

> [For whoever is buckled in this green belt,
> As long as it is tightly fastened about him
> There is no man on earth who can strike him down,
> For he cannot be killed by any trick in the world.]

Gawain's resolve leaves him. He grabs onto the magical belt, hoping that it will save his life, and promises the lady to "loyally" conceal it from her husband—utterly violating, of course, his previous obligation, the oath he has sworn to Bertilak.

By entering into this new bargain with the lady, Gawain forfeits his claims to both secular and religious chivalric perfection. He violates the terms both of the bargain between him and his host and of his "contract" to place his faith and find his courage in Christ and Mary. When, in part IV, he sets out on the final leg of his journey to the Green Chapel, the narrator makes no mention of the pentangle, but does assure us that Gawain did not forget to bring along the lady's gift. Ironically, given his motives for accepting the girdle, Gawain rejects his guide's advice to flee, even though the man promises to tell no one, because it would be a cowardly act he could never live with. He rides stoutly on until he reaches the dismal, mist-shrouded meeting place, a cave where, he laments, "Here myght aboute mydnyght / The dele his matynnes telle!" (2186–87) [Here probably at midnight / The devil his matins says!]. Gawain steels himself and holds to his bargain, agreeing to expose his neck for the return blow. The Green Knight slashes the axe through the air, but checks his blow when Gawain flinches. "Thou art not Gawayn . . . that is so goud halden" (2270) [You are not Gawain . . . who is reputed so good], he accuses; how can a man with such a reputation for bravery flinch before he has even been hit? Gawain accepts the rebuke and assures him that he will not flinch a second time. The Green Knight swings again, and again checks. Gawain has refrained from flinching, but his opponent mocks him, saying that now that Gawain has found his courage, it is time for the real blow. He swings a third time, nicking the back of Gawain's neck. Gawain springs to his feet, draws his sword, and exclaims that he has fulfilled his bargain and the Green Knight strikes again at his own peril.

The events that follow constitute one of the strangest reversals in Arthurian legend. The Green Knight soothes his outraged opponent, telling him the potentially bloody exchange was all playful and in good fun. He then reveals his identity: he is both the Green Knight and the lord of the castle, Bertilak. He explains that the testing of Gawain and Arthur's court was actually twofold: the original Christmas game and the bargain between guest and host. The two blows that he withheld correspond to the two days that Gawain faithfully kept his bargain; the gash punishes him for the day he did not. For, the Green Knight points out, "hit is my wede that thou werez" (2358) [it is my belt you are wearing]. His wife, he claims, acted at his direction, to test Gawain and prove his worth. In the end, at least in Bertilak's evaluation, Gawain has done well: "As perle bi the quite pese is of prys more, / So is Gawayn, in god fayth, bi other gay knyghtez" (2364) [As pearls are more valuable than the white peas, / So is Gawain, in all truth, before other fair knights]. He blames Gawain's lapse not on lust or avarice but on his love of his life, and concludes, "the lasse I yow blame" (2368).

The Green Knight, however, fails to understand the values of secular chivalry: to love one's life puts the whole economy at risk. Knights become great as a result of their willingness to hazard their lives on a regular basis. Furthermore, by taking the girdle and abandoning the values of the pentangle, Gawain has violated the most basic tenet of Christian knighthood, for he has lacked faith. Gawain is mortified because in his eyes he has become, indeed, "not Gawain": guilty of cowardice, covetousness, treachery, and deceit. Gawain is also quick to assign blame, and explodes into a misogynist tirade against deceitful women, from Eve to Bertilak's wife. He then agrees to accept the girdle, not, as Bertilak suggests, as a souvenir of his adventures at the Green Chapel, but as a "syngne of my surfet" (2433) [a sign of my failing]. Gawain rides home in despair and confesses his failings to the court, concluding that "mon may hyden his harme bot unhap ne may hit" (2511) [a man may hide his misdeed, but never erase it]. More is at stake in Gawain's quest than Gawain's own conscience: the reputation, and with it the power and privileges, of the Round Table are on the line, and the court refuses to accept Gawain's self-evaluation. Just as it redefined the Green Knight's initial visit as a fitting Christmas marvel, it redefines the green girdle as a token of victory. Arthur declares that "Uche burne of the brotherhede, a bauderyk schulde have, / A bende abelef hym aboute of a bryght grene, / . . . / For that watz acorded the renoun of the Rounde Table" (2516–19) [Each member of the brotherhood, should wear such a belt, / A baldric of bright green crosswise on the body. / . . . / And that became part of the renown of the Round Table].

As the courtiers adopt the girdle as a sign of Arthurian renown, *Sir Gawain and the Green Knight* ends, as it began, in Arthurian plenitude. In spite of this upbeat ending, the romance also points inexorably forward to Arthurian doom. Before Gawain hurries back to court, Bertilak offers another revelation: the whole plot originated with Morgan the goddess, whose enmity will ultimately bring about the fall of the Round Table through her son Mordred. The other piece in the puzzle of Arthurian doom is foreshadowed by Bertilak's wife's suggestion that women themselves may go to the marketplace to judge chivalric worth and "buy" the best knights. And the audience knows that Guinevere, seen at the beginning of the poem safely seated at the high table, will soon go to market herself and choose Lancelot over Arthur.

As *Sir Gawain and the Green Knight* foreshadows the tragic fate of Arthur's young court, it also questions that court, and through it the ruling class of fourteenth-century England that often based its claims to power and privilege on chivalric ideals. While the popular version of the same tale clearly blames Bertilak's lustful wife for trying to disrupt homosocial bonds, and ends with Gawain and Bertilak reconciling and returning to Arthur's court, *Sir Gawain and the Green Knight* offers no such valorization of the Arthurian order. In this rendition of the story, Arthur's court, as its response to the Green Knight's challenge proved, is more reputation than substance, and it uses that reputation and the concomitant power to insist on its own version of events. The court redefines the grisly beheading game as an amusing Christmas interlude and the green girdle as a sign of victory. Furthermore, the poem exposes chivalric virtues, which were often used to bolster the aristocracy's claim to power and privilege, to be convenient rather than constant. Gawain's "virtue" changes with his situation. He is Arthur's brave nephew at court, Mary's pious knight when he sets out on his dangerous quest, a loyal guest to his host, and a courteous gentleman in bed with the lady; in the end, however, all of these virtues mean little in the face of the common human condition: mortality. When Gawain takes the girdle, he is not brave, pious, loyal, or courtly. He is simply scared. By exposing the faults of Arthur's court, the unfounded rhetorical basis for its power, and the fact that chivalric virtue is not an innate quality, *Sir Gawain and the Green Knight* played right into the debates about class and power in post-plague England. The fact that, in this poem, the splendor, vigor, and honesty of Bertilak's otherwordly court expose Arthur's famous court as much less than it is reputed to be can be read as the commentary of a provincial court on Richard II's court's excesses, manners, and pretensions, or as the opinion of the rural gentry that the elite nobility was more hype than reality.

3

"This Noble and Joyous Book Entitled Le Morte Darthur"

CAXTON'S MALORY

Sir Thomas Malory's *Morte Darthur* stands at the end of the medieval Arthurian tradition and at the beginning of the modern one. Writing during the Wars of the Roses, Malory adapts the French *Prose Lancelot*, the English chronicle tradition, and the *Stanzaic Morte* to present his own version of Arthurian themes and history. From the chronicles Malory draws a political Arthur who offers the dream of a unified England to an island both at war with France and divided by its colonial past between English and Welsh, English and Scots, and Norman and Saxon. From the romances he takes the adventures of Arthur's knights, which test, hone, and valorize ideal aristocratic masculinity. This combination of the chronicle and romance traditions turns to the Arthurian past to find answers for one of the most troubled moments of England's troubled history.

On the home front, the country was still embroiled in civil war. The Wars of the Roses had supposedly ended with the accession of Edward IV in 1460, but Henry VI had escaped to France, and Edward never sat easily on his throne. Indeed, Edward was temporarily ousted in 1470 and Henry held the throne for six months. On the Continent, England had lost all of its French territories except Calais in 1453. And socially, both the upheaval caused by the civil war and the loss of the French territories exacerbated the ongoing conflict between classes. Without French territories to exploit and defend, the aristocratic class—already threatened by the economic conditions following the Black Death—further lost position and prospects. The personal and financial tolls exacted in the Wars of the Roses were heavy; men were killed or imprisoned, properties lost or confiscated. To make matters worse, the steady rise of the moneyed class in the towns and an increasing distance between royalty, nobility, and the country gentry resulted in a land-based military class that desperately clung to its traditional rights and privileges in the larger culture, despite being even less sure of its identity and function than it had been in the late fourteenth century.

Malory's return to the Arthurian past offers, to a fragmented England, a chronicle that presents what Patricia Ingham calls a "fantasy of insular union" and, to a dispossessed class, a romance that promises a privileged place in the social order. His tale comes down to us in two distinct versions: the Winchester Manuscript of 1469, first exhibited in 1934, and William Caxton's 1485 printed edition. Many academics feel that the Winchester Manuscript is closer to Malory's original intentions, but since Caxton's version of the *Morte Darthur* shaped the Anglo-American Arthurian tradition from Tennyson to Disney, we will base our discussion of Malory on the Caxton edition in this study.

Caxton begins with a preface that extends the narrative's audience beyond Malory's own class, to the moneyed townsfolk that threatened the aristocracy, and also provides a template for the proper reading of the tale that follows. He frames Malory's Arthurian narrative by justifying it, arguing that the book responds to popular demand. "Noble and divers gentleman of this realm of England," he claims, have consistently requested a history of "the most renowned Christian king," the best of the three Christian Worthies, the one that "ought most to be remembered among us Englishmen" (xv). Caxton's emphasis in this opening section is on both Arthur's Englishness and his historicity. Not to have an edition of the Arthurian legend is, according to Caxton's likely fictitious petitioners, un-English, especially since French versions of the tale abound. Arguing like an academic, Caxton presents the debate about the "real" Arthur: his nonappearance in some chronicles, countered by his inclusion in others; archaeological evidence: his tomb, his seal, Gawain's skull, the stones of Camelot; and the vast number of Arthurian tales in several languages. Caxton declares himself convinced and announces that he has taken it upon himself to print the tale that Sir Thomas Malory translated from French into English. He directs his work to "noble lords and ladies, with all other estates, of what estate or degree they be of," casting a wide net that includes the audiences of both courtly literary texts and popular romances, envisioning his tale as the object of private reading and shared entertainment: "to read or hear read of the noble and joyous history of the great conqueror and excellent King Arthur, sometime king of this noble realm" (xviii).

Perhaps because he envisions such a diverse audience, Caxton also exhibits some anxiety about his readers' response to his narrative, so he provides them with both a guide to their experience of it and an admonition about their response:

> That they take the good and honest acts in their remembrance and to follow the same. Wherein they shall find many joyous and pleasant histories, and noble and renowned acts of humanity, gentleness and chivalry. For herein may be seen noble Chivalry, Courtesy, Humanity, Friendliness, Hardiness, Love, Friendship, Cowardice, Murder, Hate, Virtue, and Sin. Do after the good and leave the evil, and it shall bring you to good fame and renown. And for to pass the time this book shall be pleasant to read it, but for to give faith and believe that all is true that is contained herein, ye be at your liberty, but all is written for our doctrine and for to beware that we fall not to vice nor sin, but to exercise and follow virtue. (xviii)

Caxton appeals to several audiences with these words. At the same time that he leaves it up to his readers ("ye be at liberty") to determine the truth value of this "pleasant" reading, he invokes biblical language ("all is written for our doctrine") to describe it. While he recognizes the potential of this text to, in Chaucer's words, "lead into sin," he leaves it up to his audience to read critically, determining the good and the evil. In the end, he presents this "joyous and pleasant history" to them as an exemplum from which they can learn a lesson about their own conduct that will bring them to "good fame." Given the sweep of Caxton's audience, his emphasis on the pedagogical potential of Arthur's history can be seen as a primer for a newly arrived class on noble manners and mores, a reminder to the aristocracy of proper chivalric behavior, and a warning to all about the dangers that threaten political and social unity.

Caxton ends his preface by outlining the *Morte*, dividing it into books and chapters complete with plot-summary headings. The shape he provides in his table of contents edits and, arguably, radically changes Malory's work; he presents it as something akin to a modern-day novel, in which all parts are connected, and in which the events should be read as a "history," with a clear beginning, middle, and end, inextricably woven together. In this reading, the earlier books set in motion the events that lead to the work's final tragedy, and thus should be interpreted in light of Arthur's ultimate fate. No brief discussion of Caxton's Malory can begin to address the complexities presented by this nearly one-thousand-page Arthurian history. The focus here will be on what arguably leads to Arthur's final tragedy: the incompatibility of the values of the world of the chronicle and those of the romance. The chronicle's vision of insular union is premised on successful conquest, binding treaties, and a resulting period of peace and plenty. The romance's valorization of the privileged place of a military class stems from the assumption of a continual violence that both creates and justifies masculine chivalric identity.

Centering on the familiar motif of a realm brought from chaos into order by its true king, the *Morte* begins as a chronicle, retelling the conception, birth, recognition, and coronation of Arthur. Malory opens this narrative, as did Geoffrey, with Uther's lust for Igraine (Ygerne), the wife of the Duke of Cornwall, introducing one of his text's main themes: the disruptive potential of personal desire. Uther's frustrated desire for Igraine leads to "pure anger," causing him to break his "accord" with the duke and plunge the country into war. Poised against Uther's desire for a woman is Merlin's desire for Uther's heir to bring the country out of chaos. When Uther falls ill from lust and rage, Merlin proposes an exchange: "So ye will be sworn . . . to fulfil my desire, ye shall have your desire" (3). Uther wins his night with Igraine, while Merlin wins the child born of that night. Uther, in the guise of the duke, begets Arthur. The duke is killed in battle, Uther weds Igraine, and Arthur is born to a puzzled woman who knows only that she slept with a man who looked like her husband when her husband was already dead.

Malory emphasizes Arthur's legitimacy, making changes to his source text, the *Prose Lancelot,* to assure that the line of descent is and always was clear, a fantasy that must have been particularly attractive to a man who lived through the chaos of the Wars of the Roses. When Igraine admits that she does not know who fathered her child, Uther assures her, "I am father of the child" (5). No mystery arises about where the infant prince is taken—Merlin tells Uther who will foster the boy and what his qualifications are—and before Uther dies, he calls his barons to him and declares Arthur his heir. When, in the next chapter, "stood the realm in great jeopardy long while, for every lord that was mighty of men made him strong and many weened to have been king" (7), the chaos is caused not by the lack of the king's son but by powerful men's desire to appropriate the crown by force. A sign from God temporarily ends their campaign: the appearance in London of the sword in the stone with the inscription "Whoso pulleth out this sword of this stone . . . is rightwise king born of all England" (7). In the events that follow, Malory repeatedly emphasizes Arthur's legitimacy, the fact that he is "rightwise king" (7). Only Arthur can draw the sword from the stone, as he proves numerous times. Finally the "commons" band together against the lords to proclaim Arthur king. They, of course, have much to lose and nothing to gain in a continued contest for power among the great.

In spite of Merlin's assurances and Uther's own designation of him as his heir, many of the lords remain unconvinced by this "beardless boy," claiming that Arthur is "of low blood" (12). They disrupt the coronation feast and begin a series of battles in which Arthur, with the aid of Merlin, both asserts his sovereignty and reunites the island of Britain. In this sequence drawn from the chronicles, Malory, while recounting Arthur's successful internal military campaigns, dwells upon the devastation caused by a civil war that leaves the kingdom vulnerable to its enemies. In addition, the episodes that follow these campaigns foreshadow Arthurian doom. After Arthur's successful rescue of King Leodegrance, he first seduces King Lot's wife, not knowing that she is his sister, and then sets out on a series of adventures that ironically prove him to be an incompetent knight. In the forest, Arthur encounters King Pellinore, who humiliates him in combat, nearly kills him, steals his horse, and leaves Arthur "in a study" (37). After this unpromising encounter, book I concludes with two key events: Arthur's trip with Merlin to the Lady of the Lake, who gives the king Excalibur, and his infamous May Day slaughter, when Arthur, Herod-like, orders the killing of all children born on May Day in a desperate attempt to forestall his prophesied death at the hands of his son.

This first book of Caxton's Malory valorizes the violence necessary to bring order and prosperity to a kingdom; it also deplores that necessity. Violence stems from the immoderate pursuit of personal desires: for a woman, for a kingdom, for possessions, for honor, to save one's own skin. Arthur in this first book appears as the hero, the "rightwise king born" (7), capable of controlling his fractious lords, but he also embodies numerous faults, including desire, arrogance, and a tendency to resort to violence when thwarted. Furthermore, as Malory demonstrates repeatedly, any victory in a world ruled and ordered by violence is only provisional. Book I may chronicle Arthur's more-or-less-successful unification of his kingdom, but as book II begins, the young king is beset on all sides: by his restless barons; by Rience, who has demanded the king's beard to complete his trophy-mantle; by the emperor of Rome, who has demanded tribute; and by Mordred, his intimate enemy and son born of his incestuous relationship with his sister.

Book II transitions from chronicle to romance, exploring the pitfalls of a chivalric identity and economy based on an honor maintained by violence. It opens as a messenger appears at Arthur's court, announcing that "King

Rience of North Wales had reared a great number of people, and were entered into the land, and burnt and slew the king's true liege people" (49), but before the military response of the chronicle can unfold, the romance world enters in the person of a damsel girded with a magical sword that can only be drawn by "a passing good man of his hands and of his deeds" (50). She has come, she says, from the court of King Rience, where she found no knight able to accomplish the task. When Balin successfully draws the sword, he proves not only his own worth but also that of Arthur's court. This success, unfortunately, is soon followed by a series of events that reduce the court to chaos and question Arthur's ability to rule his knights, let alone the kingdom. First, Balin insists on keeping the sword, even though the damsel warns him that it is not "wise" to do so: she prophesies that he will "slay with the sword the best friend that ye have . . . and the sword shall be your destruction" (52). He sees the sword and the adventure it promises— even with her dire warning—as a way to prove his worth and to redeem the position that he lost when he slew Arthur's cousin. Then, claims of blood feud fly. The Lady of the Lake rides into the court and demands the gift that Arthur promised her in return for Excalibur: "I ask the head of the knight that hath won the sword, or else the damosel's head that brought it; I take no force though I have both their heads, for he slew my brother . . . and that gentlewoman was causer of my father's death" (53). Arthur points out that he cannot give her either head "with my worship" and begs her to choose another gift. "I will ask none other thing," the lady declares, but before she can continue, Balin calmly beheads her in front of the high table, claiming she caused the death of his mother and was furthermore the "destroyer of many good knights" (54). Since Balin's act of violence in Arthur's presence has "shamed me and all my court," the king banishes his knight (53). In this episode Arthur's desperate attempt to control a violent response to previous acts of violence, to insist on an order at his court in which the honor of king and court trumps personal and familial honor, utterly fails.

Balin's subsequent journey both exposes the cycle of violence that the aristocratic ethos of honor and revenge perpetuates and insists that martial violence is necessary to maintain an orderly kingdom. Blood feud follows blood feud, leaving the forest littered with dead bodies, including, in the end, those of Balin and his brother Balan. But along the way Balin also defeats multiple Arthurian enemies, including Rience, and reinforces the romance's ethical emphasis on the essential function of a military aristocracy. A lone knight, not the king and his army, clears the way for Arthur's marriage to Guinevere and the establishment of the Round Table.

Yet even as Balin triumphs over Arthur's enemies, his adventures also look toward Arthur's final doom. The tone of this book is melancholy, not triumphant; "me repenteth," Balin frequently states, and this pithy expression of regret is the dominant, if futile, reading of the adventures. Merlin—or mysterious golden writing—periodically appears to tie events into a series of causes and effects that lead to future tragedies: the dolorous stroke that will plunge three kingdoms into "great poverty, misery and wretchedness" (60); Gawain's slaying of King Pellinore to avenge his father; and the Grail quest itself, which signals the beginning of the end for the Round Table. Book II concludes as Merlin buries the hapless brothers in one tomb and sends the sword that sparked the adventures downstream, where it will "by adventure" appear in Camelot to set the Grail quest in motion.

Book III begins in (guarded) Arthurian triumph as Arthur weds Guinevere. But even this wedding feast, which should mark a moment of unalloyed festivity, devolves into a reminder that Arthur's order is fragile indeed. The unruly borders of the forest, with its recreant knights and strange adventures, disrupt the celebration. A hart, a white hunting dog, and thirty black hounds, followed by a wailing maiden and a fully armed knight, burst into the hall. When the noisy maiden is abducted under his nose, Arthur rejoices; Merlin, however, insists that Arthur's "worship," and thus his power, depends on a successful response to the chaotic scenario that has just played out in front of his high table. Tor, Gawain, and Pellinore are dispatched to assert Arthur's authority, and in the adventures that follow, they defeat various knights, most with names, such as Bryan of the Foreste and Alardyne of the Oute Iles, associated with the kingdom's uncontrolled and threatening borders. These defeated knights are incorporated into the Arthurian order. However, as was the case in the tale of Balin, these adventures, in which Gawain accidentally beheads a fair maiden when he refuses to grant mercy to his enemy and in which Pellinore leaves his daughter to die in his single-minded pursuit of glory, also show that Arthur must find a way of controlling individual knights. Their various personal and familial agendas, along with their impulsive violence, undermine the unity and power of the Round Table. These adventures end with Arthur's attempts to bind his knights to him, not only by giving them land but also by introducing the chivalric oath:

never to do outrageousity nor murder, and always to flee treason; also, by no means to be cruel, but to give mercy unto him that asketh mercy, upon pain of forfeiture of their worship and lordship of King

Arthur for evermore; and always to do ladies, damosels, and gentle-women succour, upon pain of death. Also, that no man take no battles in a wrongful quarrel for no law, nor for no world's goods. Unto this were all knights sworn. . . . And every year were they sworn. (100–101)

This moment in Malory is often seen as the high point of the text, inau-gurating Arthur's political and social golden age. The language of the vow, however, with its emphasis on consequences and enforcement, coupled with the recognition that this vow constantly needs negotiation and reaffirma-tion, suggests that this utopia, while ideal, is not a reality. As Laurie Finke and Martin Schichtman point out, the oath merely "govern[s] the times and places at which violence can occur, the individuals who can participate, and the means by which violence may be applied" (119).

Book IV ratifies this suggestion. It begins as Merlin falls "in a dotage" (102) over a Damosel of the Lake "that hight [was called] Nimue" and "lay about the lady to have her maidenhood, and she was ever passing weary of him" (103). Finally, in self-defense, the text implies, she imprisons him under a great stone, and Merlin passes from the text, leaving Arthur and his precarious kingdom at the mercy of his own faults, his knights' inability to adhere to the oath they have sworn, the hostile inhabitants of the wild and enchanted forests of adventure, his sister Morgan's malice, and ambitious foreign kings.

The king's misadventures begin with the invasion of five kings and their vast hosts, who "burnt and slew clean afore them" (104). Arthur, lamenting that "had I never rest one month since I was crowned king of this land" (104), rides out to defend his rights. As soon as he has successfully defeated the invaders, Arthur finds himself embroiled in controversy. He offends Bagdemagus by advancing King Pellinore's illegitimate son, Tor, to the Round Table before him, and Bagdemagus gallops off in a huff. This brief incident exposes a danger in Arthur's new order: its hierarchy is based on a concept of honor violently gained and maintained at the expense of an-other's honor. In the next episode Arthur, trapped by Morgan's tricks, finds himself enmeshed in this ongoing competition for honor. Hunting in the forest, he, Uriens, and Accolon come across a beautiful ship and board it for the night; when the king awakens, he is in "a dark prison, hearing about him many complaints of woful knights" (111). The knights inform him that he is imprisoned by a wicked traitor who has despoiled his own brother of his property and that the traitor now needs a knight to fight to uphold his "rights" in this wrongful quarrel—something all of these prisoners, adhering to Arthur's oath, have refused to do. Arthur, however, is much more pragmatic, even if it necessitates violating his oath. Concluding, "had I liefer to fight with a knight than to die in prison," the king agrees to the terms (112).

Meanwhile Accolon, Morgan's lover, also awakens far from the ship. A dwarf appears, gives Accolon Excalibur and its magical scabbard that protects its wearer from harm, both of which have been stolen from the sleeping Arthur, and tells Accolon that Morgan desires him to fight a knight "without any mercy" (113) which would violate another Round Table oath. Accolon agrees and goes to battle, unknowingly, against his own king. In the ensuing combat, Accolon wounds Arthur; this wound alerts Arthur that the scabbard at his side is not his own magical scabbard. Furious that he has been betrayed, Arthur nevertheless adheres to his bargain with the evil knight, insisting that the battle continue as promised "while me lasteth the life. . . . I had liefer to die with honour than to live with shame . . . for though I lack weapon, I shall lack no worship, and if thou slay me weaponless, that shall be thy shame" (117). Arthur here holds to an economy that the chivalric oath he instituted has attempted to change. Before the oath, honor depended upon might and adherence to one's sworn word, even when one's might and oath are placed in the service of a wrongful quarrel. After the oath, honor theoretically depends on following the code of might-for-right. In the end Arthur's life, and with it his political order, is saved only by magical intervention. The Damosel of the Lake sees that Arthur has been betrayed, and she casts an enchantment that returns Excalibur to the hapless king. Accolon, realizing what he has almost done, confesses and affirms Arthur's preeminence as the "most man of prowess, of manhood, and of worship in the world" (119). Having proved his might, Arthur is now able to establish order. Interestingly enough, he does not dispossess the evil brother; he merely insists that the usurper restore to his sibling what was rightfully his and cease harassing errant knights. To the younger, more worthy brother, Arthur offers advancement, a place at court where he will in time earn the means "to live as worshipfully as your brother" (120).

After chronicling Morgan's further futile attempts to harm her brother, book IV turns to the adventures of Gawain, Ywain, and Marhaus, which begin when Arthur banishes Ywain on the suspicion that he may have somehow aided his mother, Morgan, in her last bit of treachery: sending Arthur a poisoned cloak. Gawain, sticking to family rather than national unity, indignantly joins his cousin. Soon they encounter Marhaus of Ireland, who faces a problem with twelve ladies. These women, while in the company of two knights, spit and throw mud on Marhaus's shield. Marhaus handily kills both of the knights in combat and turns to Ywain and Gawain. Ywain points out that, considering what they just witnessed, Gawain should not fight this man. Gawain disagrees, claiming that their honor demands it: "it were shame to us were he not assayed, were he never so good a knight" (129). Ywain agrees and asks to fight first, as he is the weaker, and Gawain can avenge him if he is killed. After Marhaus wounds Ywain, he fights Gawain, and after a fierce battle they decide that it would be a pity to kill each other and instead swear to be brothers. The three knights ride off together to "the country of strange adventures" (131) to affirm their chivalric worth.

Gawain, Ywain, and Marhaus soon meet three damsels by a fountain, each promising to lead a knight on a yearlong series of adventures. The knights agree and depart into the forest to test both their prowess and their ability to live up to Arthur's chivalric oath. Gawain does not fare well; he fails to come to the rescue of a knight beset by ten others, arguing that since the knight made no resistance, he needed no help. Disgusted, his damsel sneaks away with another knight. Gawain then swears to aid Pelleas in his quest for the love of Ettard, only to enjoy the lady himself, which initiates a series of events that not only brand Gawain as false and a traitor but also lead to Ettard's death. Marhaus and Ywain, on the other hand, behave as Arthurian knights should. Indeed, Marhaus finds himself cleaning up after Gawain, as he is forced to do battle with a man intent on avenging his seven sons whom Gawain has killed. Gawain has transformed the man into a sworn enemy of Arthur's, and so Marhaus defends himself without touching the man or his remaining sons in order to convert this enemy into an ally. He then defeats a giant and frees a series of prisoners. Similarly, Ywain takes the prize in a tournament and proceeds to defend a lady's rights against her brothers who have taken her lands; he kills one and commands the other to appear at the king's Pentecost court. Book IV ends as the three knights return to court for the Pentecost feast and recount their adventures, with Pelleas and Marhaus taking their place at the Round Table, replacing two knights slain in the last year. The tone is celebratory, but Malory never lets his readers rest securely in Arthurian plenitude. The end of this book reminds readers of Pelleas's hatred of Gawain, and looks forward to Marhaus's death at Tristram's hands and to Pelleas's achievement of the Grail. It also introduces Lancelot.

The *Morte* postpones the looming moment of Arthurian doom, return-ing in book V to the world of the chronicle by relating Arthur's victory against the emperor Lucius, a tale that follows the same plot we saw in Geof-frey, Wace, Layamon, and the *Alliterative Morte*. By divorcing this victory from Mordred's betrayal and the fall of the Round Table, Malory allows Arthur and his court to enjoy their successful military conquest of Rome and the Continent. This book ends with the text's one moment of unalloyed triumph: Arthur's military knights support his imperial ambitions, and in the end both national and class status are confirmed as the pope himself crowns Arthur emperor. The newly ratified emperor "established all his lands from Rome into France, and gave lands and realms unto his servants and knights, to everych after his desert, in such wise that none complained, rich nor poor" (173). In addition, Arthur "made dukes and earls, and made every man rich" (1734). This vision of the conquest of the Continent, resulting in an empire in which there are lands, riches, and social advancement for all, must have functioned therapeutically both for a populace still reeling from the loss of England's Continental territories and for an aristocratic class worried about its own possibilities for increased wealth and position. After consolidating power and enriching his knights, Arthur and his retinue return triumphantly home, with the stage seemingly set for the Arthurian utopia that has eluded the king in the earlier books.

Book VI begins with Arthur's knights returning to court for an elaborate celebration. The knights of the Round Table are now poised to embark on the adventures that should mark the high point of Arthur's chivalric golden age: the time between consolidation and dissolution. Instead these adventures emphasize the fragility of the Arthurian order. Time and time again, the court must meet external challenges, including renegade knights and strange enchantments, while also addressing internal strife. Book VI focuses on Lancelot, whom it immediately establishes as the epitome of Arthurian knighthood: "at no time he was never overcome but if it were by treason or enchantment; so Sir Launcelot increased so marvellously in worship and in honour" (175). For those who know the story, however, Malory's assertion of the bond between Arthur's best knight and his queen immediately undermines Lancelot's position: "for her," he asserts, "he did many deeds of arms, and saved her from the fire through his noble chivalry" (175). By looking ahead to the end of the *Morte*, to Guinevere's near-execution for treason and adultery and Lancelot's bloody rescue of her, Malory inflects these adventures, which celebrate the court at the height of its powers, with melancholy, figuring them as a prologue to the court's certain doom.

Furthermore, Lancelot's adventures take place in a world in which chaos is always only a knight away and in which order must be continually reinforced and reinstituted by violence. As he journeys through the forest, he must constantly rescue distressed maidens and unfortunate Arthurian knights from the clutches of hostile knights who resist Arthur's sovereignty: Sir Lionel, thrown to the ground, beaten with thorns, and carried away, naked, on his own horse; Sir Ector, whisked away as prisoner to Turquine (Tarquin); Sir Gaheris, also prisoner to Turquine; an assortment of knights and ladies imprisoned by evil bullies and giants; a lady about to be slain by her irate husband. And he must do so while avoiding the clutches of various evil and deceitful women such as the four queens, Morgan le Fay and the unnamed queens of Northgalis, Eastland, and the Out Isles, who kidnap him by enchantment and demand that he choose one of them, and the treacherous lady who lures him into a tree, ostensibly to fetch her falcon, but actually to make him vulnerable to her husband, who then attacks the unarmed knight. As he journeys through the forest, Lancelot imposes order by means of constant violence, but it is a never-ending struggle. As soon as he defeats one threat, another appears. At the end of book VI, when all of Lancelot's freed prisoners return to court—all of the knights whom he has "converted" to the Arthurian way of life yield to the king, and the Round Table hears his stories and celebrates his success, confirming his status as the greatest knight in the world—Malory's readers are also aware of just how provisional that status, and thus Arthur's court, is. It lasts only until the next challenge.

Book VII, which turns from the most proven of Arthur's knights to one who has yet to earn his reputation, begins by reinforcing this sense of fragility. It moves from Lancelot's Pentecost celebration to an explanation of the larger function of Arthur's Pentecost Court, which is the time of year when all the knights return to recount their adventures and reaffirm their oath. It is also the time of year when new knights are promoted to seats left vacant by slain knights. These celebrations of victory, however, are merely a stopping point, a brief rest before Arthur's knights must scatter again to prove their individual and collective worth. To this particular Pentecost feast comes a beautiful young man seeking a boon—meat and drink for a year, at the end of which he will ask for two more gifts of the king. Despite the young man's refusal to reveal his name, Arthur grants his boon and hands him over to Kay, who assumes, from the lad's pedestrian request for food instead of a horse and armor, that he is lowborn. Kay endows him with the mocking nickname Beaumains (Fair Hands) and sends him off to the kitchens. The story that follows belongs to the same genre as *Lybeaus Desconus* and bears a striking resemblance to that narrative. A year later, a damsel arrives at court and begs a champion to free her lady, who has been besieged and despoiled by the evil Red Knight of the Red Lands. Like Beaumains, she refuses to reveal her lady's name, but without this information the knights of the Round Table refuse to take up the quest. Beaumains chooses this moment to make his two additional requests: to set out on the lady's adventure and to receive knighthood at Arthur's hands. The maiden, incensed that she has been relegated to a kitchen knave, gallops off in a huff, with Beaumains in pursuit.

In the adventures that follow, Beaumains assumes the role of Lancelot in book VI, asserting Arthurian order and mores as he polices the borders, slays recreant knights and giants, restores besieged lands to their rightful owners, frees prisoners, and integrates salvageable enemies into the Arthurian court. Unlike Lancelot, he does so while enduring the constant scorn of the lady he pursues, who belittles him as a low-class knave, reinterprets all his victories as happy chances, and does her best to make his life miserable. Not until the middle of the book does she admit that Beaumains must be of noble blood and therefore worthy of her respect and attention. This admission does not allow for social mobility; the damsel and the various knights whom Beaumains defeats never entertain the possibility that one who is truly of low birth could behave as valiantly and courteously as he does. His acts prove his bloodline, and thus his status. He is actually Gareth, Gawain's brother and cousin to the king. Bloodline and status earn him knighthood, a castle, and a lady—not the damsel, Linet, who taunts him on his journey, but her sister, the Lady of Lionesse, whom he frees from the Red Knight. Gareth's adventures demonstrate that the Arthurian lineup includes numerous valiant knights, not just Lancelot, and a younger generation ready to take up their places at the Round Table. At the end of this book Malory returns his readers to a feast, multiple weddings, and a celebratory tournament in which, for a brief moment, time and status stand still.

Before book VII ends, this moment passes. Lamorak and Tristram depart, leaving King Arthur and his court "sore displeased" (277), and book VIII, the Book of Sir Tristram, begins. In these adventures, which unfold in books VIII–X, the *Morte*, through its French source, grafts an entirely different tradition, the Tristram (Tristan) and Isolde legend, onto the Arthurian story. In this version of the tale, however, the love between Tristram and his uncle's wife takes a backseat to these books' primary concerns: the violence inherent in, and absolutely necessary to, the chivalric system.

Malory's exploration of this violence in the Tristram narrative takes place on multiple planes. Chivalric prowess determines what realms owe "obeisance" and pay homage; martial success ensures the family honor; and a knight's victories in both individual combat and group contests establish individual reputation and worth. Thus, while books VIII–X lack even the minimal plot motivation provided by the quests in the earlier books, they cohere around an examination of the ways in which knights achieve and maintain chivalric reputation now that the kingdom is purportedly united and the forest, for the most part, tamed.

The events that begin Tristram's chivalric career focus on a knight's primary function in the economy of Arthur's realm: to enforce "the rights" of his lord. King Anguish of Ireland sends to King Mark of Cornwall, demanding that he pay tribute to Ireland. Mark replies, if "he will always have truage of us of Cornwall, bid him send a trusty knight . . . that will fight for his right, and we shall find another for to defend our right" (283). Anguish dispatches Sir Marhaus to take up the challenge, a choice that leaves Mark scrambling, as none of his Cornish knights "durst have ado" (284) with a man of Marhaus's strength and reputation. When his nephew, Tristram, hears of the Cornish king's predicament, he spies a perfect opportunity both to obtain knighthood and to win worship. He sets off to defeat Marhaus and confirm the rights of Cornwall. Tristram's success in the ensuing battle is only the first time that he will rescue Mark from invasion and enforced tribute; without Tristram, the narrative clearly shows, Cornwall is vulnerable to the military might of other kings.

King Mark, however, seems to be the only ruler who needs a knight to defend his property rights in this section of Malory's tale. Within Arthur's united kingdom, pitched battles over property rights have mostly been replaced by tournaments, grand and dangerous sporting events that last for several days, in which teams from various kingdoms compete against each other. The prize is not land, but chivalric honor and reputation for both individual knights and the "party" to which they belong. In these tournaments, as in the more serious combats over territory, a king's status depends upon his knights, and Arthur's ability to incorporate the best knights from all of the "many countries" into his Round Table confirms his place as "whole king." Books VIII–X explore this facet of the chivalric economy, centering on a series of tournaments in which Arthur's party battles those of his client kings. Many of these tournaments begin with Arthur missing his key knights: Lancelot, Tristram, Lamorak. Without them the outcome seems uncertain, but by the end of the tournament one or all of them appear (usually after fighting in disguise for another team) to win the day and confirm Arthur's preeminence.

These tournaments pit the various realms within the Arthurian order against each other, confirming each one's place in the chivalric pecking order. They also work both to establish the place of various groups or factions within these realms—Lancelot's kin, the Saracens, the Orkney brothers—and to determine individual worth. At the end of each day, the judges award a prize to the knight who has demonstrated the most military prowess on the field. Winning this prize launches a knight to the top of the chivalric pecking order.

However, there is always another day or another tournament, and a knight's reputation and position are permanently in flux, as becomes all too clear in Tristram's adventures in the forest, away from the organized world of the tournament. These encounters, a succession of contests and battles, illustrate that the very premise upon which knightly honor is based, prowess and noble deeds, necessitates a cycle of violence in which the best knights are doomed continually to establish their place in the hierarchy by fighting one another. Books VIII–X focus on Tristram, Palomides, Lancelot, and Lamorak as they make their way through the chivalric landscape, fighting both a series of random knights and each other in their quest to establish their "name." In some battles they win honor; in some they are shamed. Other knights constantly compare them to each other, measuring their respective worth.

Because these books lack a quest to unite them, focusing instead on what seems like random chivalric combat with little motivation beyond the proving of one's martial prowess, the violence in them feels more marked. Injuries and deaths, beatings and beheadings abound. However, as they hurtle from combat to combat, the three knights insist on a distinction between themselves and the knights, like Sir Bruce sans Pity and King Mark, whose misdeeds punctuate the text, and between proper violence (chivalric contests, vanquishing evil customs, and rescuing maidens) and improper violence (attacking without warning, imprisoning passing knights, and abducting women). Still, as Lancelot recognizes, all violence carries risk: "when men be hot in deeds of arms oft they hurt their friends as well as their foes" (416).

Indeed, the line between friend and foe is, as Tristram's adventures show, quite blurred. When Tristram shames Lamorak in battle, Lamorak sends a chastity horn to King Mark's court (similar to the one in *The Jeaste of King Arthur*) intended to reveal Isolde's adulterous relationship with Tristram. Tristram seeks revenge for this deed in single combat. And Tristram and Palomides, in spite of their repeated promises of friendship, are continually at odds, over both Palomides's unrequited love for Isolde and Tristram's constant besting of Palomides at tournaments. Add blood feuds, such as the

Orkney brothers' vendetta against Lamorak, which culminates in Gawain slaying his own mother while she lies in Lamorak's arms, and you have a world in which any unity among Arthur's knights-errant is temporary at best. Alliances may form in the course of these books, but they are quickly dissolved. In this, the summer of Arthur's golden age, as Felicity Riddy observes, "peace and friendship are temporarily achieved truces in a world of faction and feud" (84). Battles and combats, feuds and betrayals blend into one another in seemingly endless repetition. The Tristram books emphasize the ultimate futility of a chivalric economy based on acts of violence and aggression that must be constantly reenacted to secure and maintain masculine identity.

Book XI turns to Lancelot and the adventures that will lead inexorably to the Grail quest and the beginning of Arthur's doom, the prophecy of which has hung over the entire narrative. It begins with an unfilled seat, the Siege Perilous, at the Round Table. This seat remains empty because whoever tries to sit in it is immediately killed, a fact that puzzles Arthur. A hermit arrives at court and solves the mystery: the Siege Perilous can be occupied only by the knight destined to achieve the Grail. The empty seat signifies, throughout books XI and XII, that the king's utopia, for all his power and wealth, lacks true plenitude. Despite Lancelot's miraculous rescue of a beautiful maiden entrapped in a boiling bath early on, these books suggest that this lack can be filled only by a force outside Arthur's flawed and impotent secular world.

The narrative quickly descends into seduction, violence, and madness. The rescued maiden, Elaine, daughter of King Pelleas, aided by her maid and some strong wine, seduces Lancelot, who leaps into bed so eagerly that he fails to notice he is not embracing Guinevere. This night of passion leads, as Elaine knew it would, to the birth of Galahad, the knight destined for both the Siege Perilous and the Grail. Years pass and Elaine and Galahad come to court, where Elaine repeats her bed trick. Discovering Lancelot and Elaine in bed, a furious Guinevere calls him a traitor knight and exiles him from court; Lancelot leaps from the window and disappears into the forest, broken in mind and body. Lancelot's departure deprives Arthur's court of its best knight and threatens its authority. The blame is laid squarely on Guinevere's shoulders, as Bors angrily indicates: "now have ye lost the best knight of our blood, and he that was all our leader and our succour" (623).

While Lancelot runs mad in the forest, matters disintegrate at the Round Table. Arthur's knights embark on a quest for their absent champion, during which they fight one another more often than their enemies. As book XI ends, Perceval and Ector nearly kill each other unwittingly "for a simple matter" (631), seemingly the mere fact that the other one was there: "In a forest he met a knight with a broken shield and a broken helm; and as soon as either saw other readily they made them ready to joust" (630). They are saved from the consequences of their folly only by the appearance of the Grail. This miraculous intervention sets the tone for book XII, in which the Grail reappears to heal Lancelot, again suggesting a lack in the secular chivalric ethos. In fact, Lancelot's self-exile from the Arthurian economy on Joyous Isle leads to one of the longest stretches of peace and security in Malory's text, one that ends when Lancelot returns for a tournament and enters the fray. He reaffirms his identity, smiting down five hundred knights in five days, and makes his way to court where "the king and all the knights made great joy of him" (647). After Lancelot's return, book XII rejoins the Tristram plot, as Isolde's orders also pull Tristram back into the chivalric world of Arthur's court. On his way he encounters Sir Palomides and, after a series of battles, definitively defeats him, converting the pagan knight to both Christianity and the Round Table. The book concludes with the first celebratory court since Gareth's wedding, but as at Gareth's wedding, the festivities are disrupted; the coming of Galahad and the Grail soon has "dissevered all the knights of the Round Table" (654).

Malory's Grail quest is one of the rare English examples of this popular medieval narrative. There is a Welsh version of a later French Grail text, *Perlesvaus* (*Y Seint Graal*), and a Middle English adaptation of Robert de Boron's Grail history, but the Middle English version of Chrétien's *Perceval*, which introduced the Grail into the Continental tradition, eliminates the Grail and Perceval's quest to understand it. In part, the British Arthurian tradition's paucity of Grail narratives may stem from its explicit concern with originary history and the role that Arthur plays in the legitimization of aristocratic and monarchal ambitions. If both Arthurian romance and chronicle displace a problematic present with an ideal past to authorize those ambitions, the Grail narratives take the process one step further, reaching back before Arthurian history and into biblical history to endow their visions with the stamp of divine approval. Beginning with the thirteenth century and such key recontextualizations of Chrétien's text as Robert de Boron's *Histoire du Graal* and the *Queste del San Graal*, Arthur's court is presented as having a place in a typological history. In this view of history, early events are "types" that come to real fulfillment later on. Abraham's sacrifice of Isaac, for instance, is a type of God's sacrifice of his only son. Typological history stretches from Eden to Eternity; through it, God works out his plan for the salvation of the universe. In these versions of the legend, Galahad figures as the heir to the objects and privileges of a divine genealogy, grafted onto a family tree that branches from Adam to Abraham to Moses to Solomon to Joseph of Arimathea, who provided Christ's tomb and, as legend had it, fled to England with the Grail, to himself. Thus he displaces Arthur and his secular, political chivalry and institutes an order in which utopia can be achieved only by leaving that world behind.

The *Queste del San Graal*, which provides the basic narrative for Malory's account, stands apart from Arthur's earthly history and tragedy, valorizing this turn from the secular to the spiritual world and ending with its heroes' triumphant removal from history and into typology. In Malory's version of the tale, however, the Grail quest, firmly situated in history, offers the Arthurian world neither redemption nor a viable alternative to the endless cycle of chivalric violence. It merely signals, as King Arthur laments, the end of the Arthurian court and the change in the order of knighthood that is heralded by Lancelot's demotion. When Balin's sword floats down the river, declaring, in letters of gold, "Never shall man take me hence, but only he by whose side I ought to hang, and he shall be the best knight of the world" (658), Lancelot refuses even to try the adventure, recognizing that as the Grail quest begins, his time ends. Galahad displaces him; it is he who sits in the Siege Perilous and draws the sword. A maiden rides into court seeking Lancelot, not, as in times past, to ask the aid of Arthur's best knight, but to confirm his change in status: "ye were this day the best knight of the world, but who should say so now, he would be a liar, for there is now one better than ye, and well it is proved by the adventures of the sword whereto ye durst not set to your hand; and that is the change and leaving of your name" (662). While the maiden emphasizes that Lancelot has changed, he is still the same knight he was that morning, the same knight who has proved over and over again his worth in the martial economy of Arthur's order. It is the world that has changed, and the knights who fail to realize this seismic shift and cling to the military and chivalric values of the Arthurian court fail miserably on their quest.

Ironically, Gawain is one of the most hotheaded and least spiritual of Arthur's knights in Malory's version of Arthurian legend, but he sets the quest in motion. After the covered Grail passes through Arthur's hall during the Feast of Pentecost and serves each knight with "such meats and drinks as he best loved in this world," thus occupying the conventional narrative position of the challenge that sends the knight or knights from court to reaffirm the

Round Table's reputation and preeminence, Gawain vows never to return to court "till I have seen it more openly" (664). The other knights echo Gawain's sentiments, and Arthur recognizes that his fragile utopia has come to an end: "Ye have bereft me the fairest fellowship and the truest of knighthood that ever were seen together in any realm of the world; for when they depart from hence I am sure they all shall never meet again in this world, for they shall die many in the quest" (665).

Arthur's prediction of mass casualties does not come true. But while many knights return, it is to a court that has lost its authority and moral center. And the knights who do return, with the exception of Bors, are those whose chivalric values have caused them to misread the allegorical world of the Grail. This failure to read the Grail world on its own terms happens again and again during the quest. Melias, coming to a sign at a crossroads, chooses the left-hand path because it promises trials by which he can prove his prowess, which would be the correct choice in an economy that defines a knight's worth in terms of those he has defeated. Similarly, Lancelot sides with a group of outnumbered knights, armed in black, assuming that the most glory goes to the man who wins in spite of adverse circumstances. Both of these decisions prove wrong: in the spiritual Grail world, "left" and "black" signify sin and transgression, and a man's worth is calculated not in terms of prowess but in terms of Christian virtues, particularly purity achieved either by virginity or by clean confession. In fact, knights such as Gawain who refuse to recognize the spiritual nature of their quest and confess their sins return to court without having any adventures at all. Only Bors and Perceval, the knights who abandon their chivalric code and learn to read the world in terms of spiritual truths, join Galahad and achieve the Grail. In their adventures they rely on hermits to interpret the meaning of their adventures, recognize that fair maidens might be demons, and champion a lady who represents the "new law" of Christ instead of the lady who represents the "old law" (736).

When they achieve the Grail, it is removed, first from England to Sarras, and then from the earth itself. In Malory's text, the adventures of the Grail are merely brought to an end rather than fulfilled, and the court simply endures. At the end of the Grail quest, the Arthurian court has learned little, as indicated by Lancelot's return to Guinevere's bed. Also the Grail knights, Arthur's best, have removed themselves from the chivalric economy and can no longer aid their king. The court must continue, even though both the Grail world's shift in perspective and the court's collective failure on its quest have destabilized its identity and reputation. This destabilization becomes apparent in the final books of the *Morte* as the fissures that have run through Arthur's kingdom from the beginning—immoderate desire, the military ethos of blood feud, the cycle of violence perpetuated by the notion of chivalric honor—crack wide open. Lancelot's still-burning love for Guinevere leads him to fear slander. Her jealousy sends him from court, and the text slides into an adaptation of the *Stanzaic Morte*. Sir Pinel, who has a blood feud against Gawain, seeks to slay him with a poisoned apple, slipped in with others at a feast that Guinevere gives. When the wrong man eats the apple and falls dead, Guinevere is accused of the plot. The slain man's kin demand justice, and Guinevere finds herself sentenced to death, with no champion to defend her. Finally Bors, the lone returning Grail knight, agrees to step in if absolutely necessary. Lancelot appears to save his beloved and then immediately disappears.

These events, recounted at the beginning of book XVIII, set the pattern for the rest of the *Morte*. Lancelot's adulterous love for Guinevere keeps him from Arthur's court, depriving the king of the knight upon whom the unity and preeminence of his court depend. Books XVIII and XIX keep circling back to the forbidden love between Arthur's queen and his best knight, as well as to Arthur's impotence without Lancelot at his side. When Lancelot in disguise chooses to fight against Arthur's team at a tournament, they lose. When Meliagrance kidnaps the queen, only Lancelot can rescue her. When Sir Urre appears at court seeking a knight capable of healing his wounds, Arthur and many of his knights fail. Again, only Lancelot can reaffirm the court's reputation. In book XX, without Lancelot and beset by Mordred and other malcontents, Arthur loses the ability to control his knights, and the text reverts to the chaos of private vendettas, blood feuds, rival courts, and usurping kings found in the opening books of the *Morte*. Such chaos is abetted by the "mishap," a word that runs through the last books of Caxton's text, inflecting it with the melancholy hopelessness of the Balin and Balan story.

Book XX begins with the plot against Lancelot and moves to the ambush in Guinevere's chambers, from which Lancelot fights his way to freedom, leaving a trail of dead knights in his wake and, as Arthur recognizes, irrevocably breaking the fellowship of the Round Table. Many knights side with Lancelot against the king, and the situation worsens when Lancelot kills Gawain's brothers while rescuing Guinevere from the flames. In spite of a brief moment of reconciliation forced on them by the pope, the resulting blood feud with Gawain pushes the enmity between the two factions past the point of no return. Book XXI brings the readers to the end of Malory's *Morte*: Gawain's death, Arthur's battle with Mordred and the death of both, the casting of Excalibur into the lake, and Guinevere's and Lancelot's retreat into the religious life—at Guinevere's insistence—in an attempt to atone for their sins against God, king, and kingdom. After both Guinevere and Lancelot are dead and buried, Constantine takes the throne and Arthur's remaining knights leave England to live out their lives as holy men.

This melancholy ending should come as no surprise. From its beginning, the *Morte*'s vision of an Arthurian golden age has been portrayed as provisional—a moment of possibility, immediately undermined by both prophecy and the conditions under which it exists. As he concludes his book, all Malory can offer his readers is a potential return to this moment: "Yet some men say . . . that King Arthur is not dead but . . . that he shall come again . . . I will not say it shall be so, but rather I will say: here in this world he changed his life. But many men say that there is written upon his tomb this verse: HIC JACET ARTHURUS, REX QUONDAM REXQUE FUTURUS (926) [Here lies Arthur, king once and king to be]. Malory, however, is skeptical; all he can tell us for sure is that Arthur is dead.

It is ironic that, thanks to Caxton's edition, Malory's dark and disturbing text stands at the beginning of a modern tradition celebrating the Arthurian golden age. Caxton's Malory refocuses the original text, presenting the *Morte* as a chronicle of English nationalism. His Arthur, framed by the preface, is a decidedly English king who reigns from Winchester and whose attested historical feats place him among the Nine Worthies, the historical who's who of the medieval world. Caxton's tale of this, the greatest of English kings, ruler over a unified island and conqueror of Continental lands, was published three weeks before the Battle of Bosworth Field and played right into Henry VII's political rhetoric. This monarch fought under the Welsh Red Dragon as the *mab darogan* (son of prophecy), the long-awaited returning British king. During his reign, Henry continued to exploit the Tudors' supposed Arthurian connections. He permanently incorporated the Red Dragon into the Tudor arms; he saw to it that his heir, named Arthur, was born at Winchester; and he had the putative Round Table painted in Tudor colors to celebrate the occasion. Henry VIII, in his turn, as Carole Levin argues, used the chronicle of Arthur and Lucius to justify both his Continental ambitions and his independence from the pope, and Elizabeth I, following in the Tudor footsteps, figured the prosperity of her reign as a return to the days of King Arthur.

Conclusion

As this study has shown, Arthurian narrative played a central role in medieval Britain. From his first brief appearances as an extraordinary battle leader in early accounts of the Saxon invasions to his transformation into a fifteenth-century monarch desperately attempting to impose order on an unruly realm, Arthur and his history addressed the fears and desires of the authors' historical moments. The legend was never fixed; each tale remade Arthur: Welsh warrior king, Norman ruler, English hero. Thus there is no "one" medieval tale, no undisputed authority on the "real" legend or the "original" Arthur. This may explain why the legend of King Arthur and his Round Table, in spite of its medieval origins, remains a part of a living literary tradition. We study the tales of Chaucer, Gower, and Dante, but with very few exceptions (Paul Bettany's portrayal of Chaucer in Brian Helgeland's *A Knight's Tale* and the Dante video game, for instance) these tales remain in the classroom. New Arthurian narratives, on the other hand, appear on a regular basis: "historical" retellings, television shows, fantasy novels, comic books, role-playing games. This book has provided, in addition to a survey of their medieval origins, the tools to think about these contemporary Camelots critically. What visions of political utopia do they offer? What is the role of martial violence in these visions? How do they deal with class and race? What about questions of power and hierarchy? What is the role of women? How is masculinity constructed? What values are we being asked to embrace along with the fantasy of knights in shining armor, the ladies who love them, and Arthur's dream of Camelot?

Glossary

Agravain: Son of Morgan/Morgause and King Lot of Orkney, brother of Gawain, Gareth, Gaheris, and Mordred; often associated with the plot against Guinevere and Lancelot and the subsequent fall of Camelot.

Alliterative Revival: Late-fourteenth-century literary movement in the Northwest of England characterized by a return to the Anglo-Saxon alliterative poetic line. Products of this revival include *Sir Gawain and the Green Knight* and the *Alliterative Morte Arthure.*

Angevin Empire: Lands controlled by Henry II when he ascended the throne in 1154: England, Normandy, Anjou, and Aquitaine.

Avalon: Magical island to which Arthur is carried to be healed at the end of several of the tales; often associated with Glastonbury.

Balan and **Balin:** Two brothers fated to kill each other in book II of Malory. Balin's sword floating down the river inaugurates the Grail Quest.

Baldwin: Bishop and Arthurian knight; appears in *The Avowyng of Arthur* and *Sir Gawain and the Carle of Carlisle.*

Bede: British cleric and historian (ca. 673–735), author of *The Ecclesiastical History of the English People.*

Bedivere or **Bedwyr:** One of the last surviving knights. Arthur orders him to cast Excalibur back into the lake.

Beowulf: Old English tale chronicling the deeds of Beowulf, the ultimate Anglo-Saxon warrior, including his killing of the monster Grendel and his mortal battle with a dragon.

Bertilak: The Green Knight, sent by Morgan to challenge Arthur's court in *Sir Gawain and the Green Knight.*

Black Death: The bubonic plague that ravaged Europe and, in 1348–50, England.

Black Prince: Edward (1330–1376), son of Edward III; responsible for much of England's success in the Hundred Years War.

Bors: Arthurian knight, one of the few to achieve the Holy Grail.

Bosworth Field: Site of battle in 1485 where Henry Tudor defeated Richard III to take the throne as Henry VII.

Breton lai: A short romance, usually involving the marvelous; associated with the Celts in Brittany.

Brutus: Legendary founder of Britain who, guided by Diana, led a group of Trojan survivors to the island after the fall of Troy.

Caer Leon at Usk or **Caerleon** or **Caer Llion:** Site of a Roman amphitheater and barracks in Wales; identified as the location of Arthur's court in many of the Welsh tales.

Caliburn: See **Excalibur.**

Camelot: Arthur's chief court in later tradition, sometimes associated with South Cadbury Castle in Somerset.

Camlann: Site of Arthur's fatal battle against Mordred.

Carl: Churl, someone of low birth.

Caxton, William: London printer (ca. 1422–1491) who established the first English printing press; editor and publisher in 1485 of Caxton's Malory.

Celtic otherworld: A realm parallel to "our" world, often associated with forests and mounds, characterized by abundance, magic, and marvels; the literary ancestor of both the mysterious forests of Arthurian romance and Tolkien's Lothlorien.

Chanson de geste: Medieval genre focused on warfare, most famously exemplified by the eleventh-century French text *The Song of Roland.*

Chivalry: Originally a class of people, the *chevallerie* or chivalry of England, who were armed knights. The word increasingly came to designate virtuous character and the adherence to an elaborate code of conduct.

Chrétien de Troyes: Often called the Father of Arthurian Romance; author of a series of Arthurian tales for the French aristocracy in the late twelfth century that were later translated into most of the major European languages.

Chronicle: A historical account. Arthurian chronicles relate the rise and fall of Arthur's kingdom, usually in the context of the larger history of Britain.

Courtly love: Also called *fin amor*; a system in which a knight offers service to a lady in hopes of winning her favors; thought to ennoble the knight by inspiring him to high deeds of valor and virtue.

Cuckold: A man whose wife has been unfaithful.

Culhwch: Arthur's nephew and titular hero of the medieval Welsh Arthurian romance *Culhwch and Olwen.*

Doomsday Book: A census and record of land ownership in England, drawn up in 1086, the year before William the Conqueror's death.

Double-course romance: A romance that begins at court, sends its hero off on a series of adventures, concludes those adventures (usually with a marriage), and then sends its hero off on a second series of adventures before finally ending with another triumphant celebration.

Ector: Knight who, at Merlin's request, raises Arthur from infancy until Arthur pulls the sword from the stone.

Elaine, the Fair Maid of Astolat (or **Ascolot**): Maiden, daughter of King Pelleas and mother of Galahad, who dies from love for Lancelot. Her family sends her body floating downriver to the court, with a note explaining her death. The note's contents cause a rift between Lancelot and Guinevere that results in Lancelot's descent into madness.

Enide: Wife of Erec, ordered to be silent and subjected to a grueling series of adventures after she criticizes Erec for no longer participating in tournaments.

Erec or **Gereint:** Hero of Chrétien's *Erec and Enide* and its Welsh counterpart *Gereint.*

Excalibur or **Caliburn:** Arthur's sword. In many versions of the tale it is given to him by the Lady of the Lake and either it or its scabbard possesses magical qualities.

Excommunication: Exclusion of an individual from the religious community; imposed by medieval Catholic Church authorities as a punitive measure in hopes of inducing the excommunicated individual to mend his/her ways.

Fabliau: A bawdy tale usually involving trickery and sex.

Fall of kings: A series of tales that relates the demise of kings and lords, often at the hands of a capricious Fortune; Arthur's dream at the end of the *Alliterative Morte Arthure* is an example of this genre.

Feudal lord: The grantor of a fief (land) in return for service (usually military) from his vassals.

Fief: A grant of land given by a feudal lord to his vassal in return for service.

Fortune's Wheel: A Ferris-wheel-like tool of Lady Fortune, who places men on this wheel, allows them to rise to glory, riches, and fame, and then whimsically spins the wheel and casts them to the ground. See **Fall of kings**.

Gaheris: Arthurian knight, brother to Gawain, Gareth, Agravain, and Mordred; killed by Lancelot during Lancelot's rescue of Guinevere.

Galahad: Son of Lancelot by Elaine, who deceives Lancelot into her bed. Replacing his father as the best knight in the world at the beginning of the Grail quest, he is the finest and purest of the knights who achieve the Holy Grail.

Gareth: "Beaumains," brother of Gawain, Gaheris, Agravain, and Mordred. Coming to Arthur's court in disguise, he works in the kitchens before proving his chivalric worth in book VII of Malory. He is killed by Lancelot during Lancelot's rescue of Guinevere.

Gawain or **Gwalchmai:** Arthur's nephew; in the popular romances, the epitome of Arthurian chivalry and courtesy; in the French tradition, a somewhat troublesome hothead and ladies' man. Both Gawains figure in Malory.

Gereint: See **Erec.**

Giant of Mont-Saint-Michel: Cannibalistic enemy whom Arthur must defeat upon arriving in France on his way to conquer Rome.

Glastonbury: Town in Somerset, reputed site of both the legendary Avalon and the graves of Arthur and Guinevere, supposedly unearthed by monks in 1190–91.

Gododdin, Y: Eighth- or ninth-century Welsh text that contains an early reference to Arthur.

Gorlois: Duke of Cornwall and husband of Ygerne, mother of Arthur. He breaks his treaty with Uther after Uther propositions Ygerne, and is killed in battle while Uther sleeps with his wife.

Great Chain of Being: In medieval thought, the natural and social order in which all creation extended in a continuum from God to minerals and all social order in a continuum from king to serfs. To attempt to move out of one's established place on the Chain was to defy divine and natural order.

Guinevere: Wife of King Arthur, instrumental in the fall of his kingdom through her association with either Mordred (in earlier versions of the tale) or Lancelot.

Holy Grail: A mysterious and undefined object introduced in Chrétien's *Perceval* and later associated with the Cup that caught the blood of Christ in later tradition. The quest for the Holy Grail signals the beginning of the end for the Round Table.

Homage: Feudal ceremony in which a vassal submits to his lord, swearing to serve him, and the lord grants him land and the promise of protection.

Hubris: Excessive pride that leads to the proverbial fall; often identified as the tragic flaw in Greek tragedy.

Hundred Years War: Ongoing war between England and France (1337–1453) over territories on the Continent.

Hywel Dda: Legendary king of a united Wales; reputedly responsible for the codification of Welsh law.

Igraine or **Ygerne:** Mother of Arthur; originally the wife of Gorlois, Duke of Cornwall. Uther's lust for her starts a war between him and Gorlois. When Gorlois is killed in battle, Uther marries her.

Interdiction: The exclusion of persons or communities from receiving the sacraments, such as baptism, marriage, Communion, and last rites.

Isolde: Adulterous wife of King Mark of Cornwall, whose love for Tristan (usually blamed on a love potion) is often equated with Guinevere's adulterous love for Lancelot.

Joan of Arc: One of the patron saints of France; a peasant girl who claimed to be inspired by divine visions to rally the French led by the future Charles VII to resist the English during the Hundred Years War; burnt for heresy in 1431; canonized in 1921.

Joseph of Arimathea: Biblical figure who in medieval legend becomes the keeper of the Grail, bringing it from the Holy Land to England.

Kay or **Cei:** Relative of Arthur; in later versions his foster brother, son of Ector; in many tales the boorish bully who serves as a foil for Gawain's perfect courtesy.

Lady of the Lake: Mystical enchantress who bestows Excalibur on Arthur (and takes it back after his final battle).

Lancelot: Arthur's greatest knight; lover of Guinevere; father of Galahad.

Laudine: The Lady of the Fountain in *Yvain*, *Gereint*, and *Ywain and Gawain*. After Yvain kills her husband, she marries Yvain, only to repudiate him when he fails to return after a year on the tournament circuit. They later reunite.

Launfal or **Lanval:** Hero of Marie de France's lai and Thomas Chestre's adaptation of Marie. He is rescued twice by a fairy lover, first from poverty and then from Guinevere's malicious accusations; finally he flees court to live with his lover.

Leodegrance: Guinevere's father, rescued by Arthur from a siege by hostile barons.

Liturgical calendar: Division of the year based on biblical events and religious festivals, such as Lent, Advent, and Pentecost.

Loathly lady: A device in tales such as *The Wedding of Sir Gawaine and Dame Ragnelle* in which a knight is forced to marry an ugly hag who turns out to be other than she seems.

Lot: King of Orkney, husband of Arthur's malicious sister Morgan/Morgause, and father of Gawain, Agravain, Gareth, and Gaheris.

Lucius: Roman emperor whose demand for tribute from Arthur sends Arthur and his knights off on Continental conquest; defeated by Arthur.

Lunette or **Luned:** Laudine's woman-in-waiting who advises her to marry Yvain; later sentenced to death for this advice and rescued by Yvain.

Magna Carta: Document that the barons of England forced King John to sign in 1215, limiting royal power and guaranteeing the rights of "free men."

Marie de France: Late-twelfth-century poet, probably French-born but writing in Anglo-Norman French; author of a series of Breton lais, some of which, such as *Lanfal*, are set at the Arthurian court.

Medievalism: Postmedieval reconstructions of the Middle Ages, e.g., Las Vegas's Excalibur Hotel, the Medieval Times dinner theaters, and Arthurian films and novels.

Merlin: Magician and advisor to King Arthur, introduced into the legend by Geoffrey of Monmouth.

Mordred or **Medraut:** Son and/or nephew to King Arthur; in later versions the product of Arthur's incest with Morgan le Fey; responsible for the fall of Camelot.

Morgan or **Morgana** or **Morgause:** Half sister of Arthur, daughter of Ygerne, wife of King Lot of Orkney, mother of Gawain, Gaheris, Agravain, and Gareth. Also the mother of Arthur's son, Mordred. One of Arthur's most persistent enemies.

Mount Badon: Site of Arthur's successful battle against the invading Saxons.

Nine Worthies: The medieval pantheon of Great Men, divided into the three pagans (Hector, Alexander the Great, and Julius Caesar), three Jews (Joshua, David, and Judas Maccabeus), and three Christians (Arthur, Charlemagne, and Godfrey of Bouillon).

Partible inheritance: Division of estate and lands among all available male heirs; practiced in Wales until the time of Llewelyn ap Iowerth.

Peasants' Revolt: A popular uprising protesting a poll tax, led by Wat Tyler, Jack Straw, and John Ball, that succeeded in occupying London for three days in 1381.

Pelleas: Arthurian knight, father of Elaine, the mother of Galahad.

Pentangle or **pentagram:** Five-sided star, often used as a religious symbol.

Pentecost: The feast that celebrates the descent of the Holy Spirit, fifty days after the Resurrection; in Arthurian romance a major feast day on which, in Malory, the knights return to reaffirm their chivalric oath.

Perceval or **Peredur:** Hero of a series of romances in which his mother isolates him in the forest and he must learn how to function as a knight.

Chrétien's version of this tale introduces the Holy Grail, and in later romances he is one of the Grail knights.

Percy Folio: Seventeenth-century manuscript, discovered by Bishop Thomas Percy in the eighteenth century, compiling earlier English ballads and romances including many of the popular Arthurian tales.

Philology: The historical study of languages.

Porter: Important figure in the Welsh tales who guards the gate and regulates access to the lord's presence.

Primogeniture: System of inheritance in which the entire estate goes to the firstborn son; a Norman practice introduced into Wales by Llewelyn ap Iowerth as he sought to consolidate his power.

Prose Lancelot or Vulgate Lancelot: Thirteenth-century French compilation of Arthurian tales that served as one of Malory's major sources.

Romance: In the Middle Ages, a text written in the vernacular language rather than Latin. The genre came to be identified with three major subjects: the Matter of Rome (Troy and its survivors), the Matter of France (Charlemagne), and the Matter of Britain (Arthur). Medieval romances are tales of adventure and the marvelous, and often focus on the knight's acquisition of a bride or a lover.

Round Table: Arthur's legendary table, sometimes identified as a wedding present and sometimes as the suggestion of a clever carpenter so that Arthur's knights would not squabble over seating precedence.

Saracens: In medieval parlance, all those who practice Islam.

Sarras: Mythical island kingdom to which the successful Grail knights take the Holy Grail.

Serfs: Peasants, bound to the manor, who worked the lord's land and, in return for its use, paid various fees, rents, and duties.

Siege Perilous: Empty seat at the Round Table that awaits the best knight. Galahad claims it at the beginning of the Grail quest.

Statute of Wales: Decree issued by Edward I in 1284 annexing Wales to the crown of England and establishing a modified version of English common law in Wales.

Sumptuary laws: Laws governing consumption that limited the purchase of luxury products such as foods, textiles, and fur on the basis of class and income; these laws were particularly prevalent in the period following the Black Death.

Tarn Wathelene: Mysterious lake associated with the marvelous and the otherworld in popular Arthurian romances such as *The Adventures of Arthur* and *The Avowyng of Arthur*.

Three Christian Worthies: See **Nine Worthies.**

Three Estates: Medieval model of a society divided into "estates": those who fight (the aristocracy), those who pray (the clergy), and those who work (everyone else).

Tintagel: Castle where Gorlois sequesters Ygerne when he goes off to fight Uther and where Arthur is begotten by Uther disguised as Gorlois.

Treaty of Paris: Treaty of 1259 whereby Henry III ceded all French territories except Gascony, which he agreed to hold as a fief from the French king.

Tristan or **Tristram:** Nephew of King Mark of Cornwall, adulterous lover of Mark's wife, Isolde; one of the central figures of books IX and X of Caxton's edition of Malory.

Twrch Trwyth: Magical and malicious marauding boar which Arthur must fight and defeat in *Culhwch and Olwen*.

Typological history: A theory of history, usually associated with divine history, in which earlier events serve as types to be fulfilled in later events as God's plan unfolds. For instance, Abraham's sacrifice of Isaac is a type of God's sacrifice of Christ.

Uther Pendragon: Arthur's father, king of England, who magically disguises himself as Gorlois, Duke of Cornwall, to sleep with the duke's wife, Ygerne. In early chronicles he is the son of Constantine and the brother of Ambrosius Aurelius, both of whom are betrayed by an evil counselor, Vortigern, who is allied with the Saxons.

Vassal: The holder of a fief from a feudal lord.

Wager romance: A tale in which a husband wagers everything on his wife's fidelity, and the other party to the wager then tries to seduce the wife.

Wars of the Roses: Civil war in 1455–71 between the House of Lancaster (red rose), represented by Henry VI, and the House of York (white rose), represented first by Richard of York and then by his son Edward IV, for the crown of England.

Welsh Triads: A series of "threes," organized around themes, that recount names and places from Welsh folklore and history. For instance, "Three Generous Men of the Island of Britain: Nudd the Generous, Son of Senyllt, Mordaf the Generous, son of Serwan, Rhydderch the Generous, son of Tudwal Tudglyd. And Arthur himself was more generous than the three." Versions of the triads appear in all major medieval Welsh manuscripts.

Winchester Manuscript: A 1469 manuscript of Sir Thomas Malory's *Morte*

Darthur, which seems to indicate that Malory intended his tales to be read as a series of episodes rather than a whole history.

Ygerne: See **Igraine**.

Ysbaddaden: Chief Giant, father of Olwen. His series of demands occasions the Arthurian adventures in *Culhwch and Olwen*.

Yvain or **Ywain** or **Owein:** Hero of a series of romances revolving around his conquest of and marriage to Laudine, the Lady of the Fountain, later incorporated into the *Prose Lancelot* and Malory.

Suggested Reading

Arthurian Texts

Alliterative Morte Arthure. Edited by Larry D. Benson, revised by Edward E. Foster. 1994. www.lib.rochester.edu/camelot/teams/allitfrm.htm.

Arthurian Chronicles: Wace and Layamon. Translated by Eugene Mason. 1912. Toronto: University of Toronto Press, 1996.

The Avowyng of Arthur. Edited by Thomas Hahn. 1995. www.lib.rochester.edu/camelot/teams/avowfrm.htm.

The Awyntyrs off Arthur [The Adventures of Arthur]. Edited by Thomas Hahn. 1995. www.lib.rochester.edu/camelot/teams/awnfrm.htm.

The Carle of Carlisle. Edited by Thomas Hahn. 1995. www.lib.rochester.edu/camelot/teams/carintro.htm.

Chrétien de Troyes. *Arthurian Romances.* Translated by D.D.R. Owen. London: J. M. Dent, 1987.

Culhwch and Olwen. In *The Mabinogion,* 95–136.

Geoffrey of Monmouth. *The History of The Kings of Britain.* Translated by Lewis Thorpe. New York: Penguin, 1966.

Gereint Son of Erbin. In *The Mabinogion,* 229–73.

The Greene Knight. Edited by Thomas Hahn. 1995. www.lib.rochester.edu/camelot/teams/greenint.htm.

The Jeaste of Sir Gawain. Edited by Thomas Hahn. 1995. www.lib.rochester.edu/camelot/teams/jeastint.htm.

King Arthur and King Cornwall. Edited by Thomas Hahn. 1995. www.lib.rochester.edu/camelot/teams/cornfrm.htm.

The Knightly Tale of Gologras and Gawain. Edited by Thomas Hahn. 1995. www.lib.rochester.edu/camelot/teams/golfrm.htm.

Lancelot of the Laik. Edited by Alan Lupack. 1994. www.lib.rochester.edu/camelot/teams/lanceint.htm.

Layamon. *Brut.* In *Arthurian Chronicles,* 117–264.

Lybeaus Desconus. Edited by George Shuffelton. 2008. www.lib.rochester.edu/camelot/teams/sgas20int.htm.

The Mabinogi, and Other Medieval Welsh Tales. Translated by Patrick K. Ford. Berkeley: University of California Press, 1997.

The Mabinogion. Translated by Gwyn Jones and Thomas Jones. 1949. New York: Knopf, 2001.

Malory, Thomas. *Le Morte D'Arthur.* Caxton's edition. Introduction by Elizabeth J. Bryan. New York: Random House, 1999.

The Marriage of Sir Gawain. Edited by Thomas Hahn. 1995. www.lib.rochester.edu/camelot/teams/marintro.htm.

Of Arthour and of Merlin. Edited by O. D. Macrae-Gibson. 2 vols. EETS. London: Oxford University Press, 1973–79.

Owein [The Lady of the Fountain]. In *The Mabinogion,* 155–82.

Peredur Son of Efrawg. In *The Mabinogion,* 183–227.

Sir Corneus. Edited by George Shuffelton. 2008. www.lib.rochester.edu/camelot/teams/sgas21int.htm.

Sir Gawain and the Green Knight. Edited and translated by James Winny. Peterborough, Ont.: Broadview, 1992.

Sir Gawain and the Carle of Carlisle. Edited by Thomas Hahn. 1995. www.lib.rochester.edu/camelot/teams/gawcfrm.htm.

Sir Launfal. Edited by Anne Laskaya and Eve Salisbury. 1995. www.lib.rochester.edu/camelot/teams/launint.htm.

Sir Perceval of Galles. Edited by Mary Flowers Braswell. 1995. www.lib.rochester.edu/camelot/teams/percint.htm.

Stanzaic Morte Arthur. Edited by Larry D. Benson, revised by Edward E. Foster. 1994. www.lib.rochester.edu/camelot/teams/stanzfrm.htm.

Wace. *Roman de Brut.* In *Arthurian Chronicles,* 1–114.

The Wedding of Sir Gawain and Dame Ragnelle. Edited by Thomas Hahn. 1995. www.lib.rochester.edu/camelot/teams/ragintro.htm.

Ywain and Gawain. Edited by Mary Flowers Braswell. 1995. www.lib.rochester.edu/camelot/teams/ywnint.htm.

Critical and Supplementary Texts

Armstrong, Dorsey. *Gender and the Chivalric Community of Malory's "Morte d'Arthur."* Gainesville: University Press of Florida, 2003.

Ashe, Geoffrey. *The Discovery of King Arthur.* 1985. New York: Holt, 1987.

Batt, Catherine. *Malory's "Morte Darthur": Remaking Arthurian Tradition.* New York: Palgrave, 2002.

Boccaccio, Giovanni. *The Decameron.* Translated by Mark Musa and Peter Bondanella. 1982. New York: Signet, 2002.

Bromwich, Rachel, A.O.H. Jarman, and Brynley F. Roberts, eds. *The Arthur of the Welsh.* Cardiff: University of Wales Press, 1991.

Burns, E. Jane. *Arthurian Fictions: Rereading the Vulgate Cycle*. Columbus: Ohio State University Press, 1985.

The Camelot Project at the University of Rochester. www.lib.rochester.edu/camelot/cphome.stm.

Davies, R. R. *Domination and Conquest: The Experience of Ireland, Scotland, and Wales, 1100–1300*. Cambridge: Cambridge University Press, 1990.

———. *The First English Empire: Power and Identities in the British Isles, 1093–1343*. Oxford: Oxford University Press, 2000.

Dean, Christopher. *Arthur of England: English Attitudes to King Arthur and the Knights of the Round Table in the Middle Ages and the Renaissance*. Toronto: University of Toronto Press, 1987.

Eco, Umberto. "The Return of the Middle Ages." In *Travels in Hyperreality*, translated by William Weaver, 59–85. San Diego: Harcourt Brace Jovanovich, 1986.

Field, P.J.C. *Romance and Chronicle: A Study of Malory's Prose Style*. Bloomington: Indiana University Press, 1971.

Finke, Laurie A., and Martin B. Schichtman. *King Arthur and the Myth of History*. Gainesville: University Press of Florida, 2004.

———. "No Pain, No Gain: Violence as Symbolic Capital in Malory's *Morte d'Arthur*." *Arthuriana* 8.2 (1998): 115–34.

Green, David. *Edward the Black Prince: Power in Medieval Europe*. Harlow, Essex: Pearson, 2007.

Hahn, Thomas. Introduction to *Sir Gawain, Eleven Romances and Tales*. 1995. www.lib.rochester.edu/camelot/teams/genint.htm.

Heng, Geraldine. *Empire of Magic: Medieval Romance and the Politics of Cultural Fantasy*. New York: Columbia University Press, 2003.

Hodges, Kenneth. *Forging Chivalric Communities in Malory's "Le Morte Darthur."* New York: Palgrave. 2005.

Horrox, Rosemary, and W. Mark Ormrod, eds. *A Social History of England: 1200–1500*. Cambridge: Cambridge University Press, 2006.

Ingham, Patricia Clare. *Sovereign Fantasies: Arthurian Romance and the Making of Britain*. Philadelphia: University of Pennsylvania Press, 2001.

Lacy, Norris J., ed. *The Arthurian Encyclopedia*. New York: Garland, 1986.

Levin, Carole. "Most Christian King, Most British King: The Image of Arthur in Tudor Propaganda." *McNeese Review* 33 (1990–94): 80–90.

McDonald, Nicola, ed. *Pulp Fictions of Medieval England: Essays in Popular Romance*. Manchester: Manchester University Press, 2004.

Moll, Richard J. *Before Malory: Reading Arthur in Later Medieval England*. Toronto: University of Toronto Press, 2003.

Orme, Nicholas. *From Childhood to Chivalry: The Education of the English Kings and Aristocracy, 1066–1530*. London: Methuen, 1984.

Pachoda, Elizabeth T. *Arthurian Propaganda: "Le Morte Darthur" as an Historical Ideal of Life*. Chapel Hill: University of North Carolina Press, 1971.

Radulescu, Raluca L. *The Gentry Context for Malory's "Morte Darthur."* Woodbridge, Suffolk: D. S. Brewer, 2003.

Ramsey, Lee C. *Chivalric Romances: Popular Literature in Medieval England*. Bloomington: Indiana University Press, 1983.

Riddy, Felicity. *Sir Thomas Malory*. Leiden: Brill, 1987.

Rigby, S. H. *English Society in the Later Middle Ages: Class, Status, and Gender*. New York: St. Martin's Press, 1995.

Saul, Nigel, ed. *The Oxford Illustrated History of Medieval England*. Oxford: Oxford University Press, 1997.

Sklar, Elizabeth S. "Marketing Arthur: The Commodification of Arthurian Legend." In *King Arthur in Popular Culture*, edited by Elizabeth S. Sklar and Donald L. Hoffman, 9–23. Jefferson, N.C.: McFarland, 2002.

Warren, Michelle R. *History on the Edge: Excalibur and the Borders of Britain, 1100–1300*. Minneapolis: University of Minnesota Press, 2000.

Whetter, K. S. *Understanding Genre and Medieval Romance*. Aldershot, Surrey: Ashgate, 2008.

Index

Susan Aronstein is professor of English and associate director of Honors at the University of Wyoming. She is the author of *Hollywood Knights: Arthurian Cinema and the Politics of Nostalgia* and the co-editor with Tison Pugh of *Disney's Middle Ages: A Fairy Tale and Fantasy Past*. Her articles on medieval Arthurian romance, medieval film, medievalism and popular culture have appeared in numerous books and journals, including *Exemplaria, Prose Studies, Assays, Cinema Journal, Theatre Survey, Women's Studies,* and *Studies in Medievalism*.

New Perspectives on Medieval Literature: Authors and Traditions

EDITED BY R. BARTON PALMER AND TISON PUGH

This series offers compact, comprehensive, and up-to-date studies of important medieval authors and traditions written by leading scholars. These volumes will appeal to undergraduate and graduate students, academics, and general readers interested in the vibrant world of medieval literature. Our philosophy in New Perspectives on Medieval Literature is that good scholarship should excite both interest in and accessibility to a field of study, and this principle of combining the scholarship of teaching with student learning informs our editorial decisions.

An Introduction to Christine de Pizan, by Nadia Margolis (2011; first paperback edition, 2012)

An Introduction to the "Gawain" Poet, by John M. Bowers (2012; first paperback edition, 2013)

An Introduction to British Arthurian Narrative, by Susan Aronstein (2012; first paperback edition, 2014)

An Introduction to Geoffrey Chaucer, by Tison Pugh (2013)

An Introduction to the Chansons de Geste, by Catherine M. Jones (2014)

www.ingramcontent.com/pod-product-compliance
Lightning Source LLC
Chambersburg PA
CBHW021400090426
42742CB00009B/932